The Politics of Immigration

The Politics of Immigration

Contradictions of the Liberal State

JAMES HAMPSHIRE

polity

First published in 2013 by Polity Press

Polity Press
65 Bridge Street
Cambridge CB2 1UR, UK

Polity Press
350 Main Street
Malden, MA 02148, USA

ISBN-13: 978-0-7456-3898-0
ISBN-13: 978-0-7456-3899-7 (pb)

A catalogue record for this book is available from the British Library.

Typeset in 9.5 on 12 pt Swift Light
by Toppan Best-set Premedia Limited
Printed and bound in Great Britain by Clays Ltd, St Ives plc

For further information on Polity, visit our website: www.politybooks.com

Contents

Tables and Figures

Acknowledgements

The ideas in this book have evolved through discussions with many colleagues. I can't mention here all those whose work has shaped my thoughts on this subject, but I would like to thank a few people in particular. Randall Hansen has gone from being an excellent postdoctoral mentor to an even better colleague and friend. Few people combine iconoclasm with intellectual generosity in such equal measure. Others who have shaped my ideas through conversations and comments in formal or informal contexts, often both, include Erik Bleich, Christina Boswell, Michael Collyer, Terri Givens, Simon Green, Christian Joppke, Desmond King and Paul Statham. Thanks to them all. My friend and fellow researcher, Pontus Odmalm, has leavened our conversations about migration with a lot of good humour (as well as giving the wittiest best man's speech I've ever heard). I'd also like to thank my colleagues in the Department of Politics at Sussex and the Sussex Centre for Migration Research for providing a most collegial and stimulating working environment. And I'd like to thank my PhD students, in particular Erica Consterdine, who read most of the chapters of this book as they were drafted and provided very helpful comments.

An awful lot of things have happened while writing this book (which I like to think is why it took me so long). Above all, I have been fortunate to marry Pauline and to become the father of Clara and Otto. Pauline deserves a world of thanks for her tolerance and myriad kindnesses, not to mention her intellectual curiosity and originality. I'd like to thank Clara and Otto for sometimes sleeping through the night but more importantly for always being a source of joy and wonderment. This book is dedicated to all of them and to the memory of little Constantin, who came and went in 2009.

CHAPTER ONE

Immigration and the Liberal State

For anyone who pays the slightest attention to politics in the liberal democratic world it won't come as a surprise to hear that immigration is controversial. What was once viewed as a technocratic policy problem has morphed
into one of the most contested issues on the public agenda. In Europe, loud
and contradictory claims are made for and against immigration: according
to some, immigrants are rejuvenators of ageing populations, motors of economic growth, and saviours of the European welfare state; to others they are
to blame for native unemployment, wage depression and welfare costs, not
to mention social and cultural disintegration. The debate is barely less polar-
ized in North America and Oceania, despite their longer historical experience
of large-scale immigration and their self-identification as nations of immigrants. In the United States, the largest destination country in the world,
attempts to pass much needed immigration reform have foundered amid
heated congressional debates and public protests. And even such measures
as have been agreed, such as the construction of a 600-mile fence along the
southern border with Mexico, are deeply controversial. It is clear that, across
the rich liberal democracies, immigration is an issue freighted with a lot of
political baggage.

About the only thing that is not in dispute is that immigration is ever more
significant and complex. According to the International Organization for
Migration (IOM), there were approximately 214 million international
migrants in the world in 2010. This represented an increase of almost 40
million during the first decade of the twenty-first century and a doubling
since 1980. While the rate of migration flows slowed in 2007–8 as the economic crisis took hold, migrant stocks have not been significantly reduced,
and preliminary data for 2011 suggest a return to greater flows (OECD 2012a:
3). While international migration is now a global phenomenon, affecting
Southern as well as Northern regions, the majority of international migrants,
57 per cent, live in high-income countries. Europe is home to some 72.6
million migrants, North America (Canada and the USA) accounts for 50
million, while Oceania (Australia, New Zealand, plus several small islands of
Polynesia and Micronesia) accounts for 6 million (IOM 2010). As mentioned
above, the United States remains the top migrant destination in the world,
with a migrant stock of 42.8 million, and four European Union countries

1

(Germany, France, the United Kingdom and Spain) appear in the top ten, as does Canada.

These numbers tell only a fraction of the story, however, as international migration is not only increasing in scale but also becoming more variegated and complex. Today, people migrate to and from an ever wider range of countries, for diverse reasons, with diverse implications for both sending and receiving states. The catch-all term 'international migrant' encompasses *inter alia* high-flying executives transferring between the offices of multinational companies, students travelling abroad to study at universities and colleges, seasonal workers recruited to pick crops, husbands, wives and children joining overseas relatives, people fleeing persecution and seeking asylum, undocumented migrants looking for a better life, and so on. Migration patterns have also changed, becoming more fluid and circular compared with traditional patterns of long-term immigrant settlement. For receiving countries, the scale and complexity of international mobility means that immigration is one of the most difficult policy issues to address, as well as one of the most politically charged.

This book provides an analysis of the politics of immigration in the rich liberal democracies, primarily the countries of Europe, North America and Oceania (Australia and New Zealand). It is therefore necessarily wide-ranging and cannot do justice to the complexities of individual countries. But, by taking a panoramic view, it aims to provide a comparative introduction to this thorny topic and, at the same time, advance an argument about immigration and the liberal state. The point of departure for this argument is the claim that the state 'matters' when it comes to understanding immigration – indeed, that immigration cannot be understood without probing into the complexities and contradictions of modern liberal statehood. From this starting point, the book aims to show that the contested nature of immigration has its roots in the institutions of the liberal state, an understanding of which is essential to explain why effective and coherent immigration policies are so elusive. Contrary to claims often heard in popular debate, the intractable nature of immigration policy is not a failure of governance but rather a reflection of contradictory imperatives of the liberal state. This, at least, is the claim I seek to justify throughout the rest of the book.

The claim that the state matters for understanding immigration is on one level virtually tautological because the state system is constitutive of international migration, and therefore of immigration and emigration. On another level, states matter because they seek to intervene in and influence migration flows using a range of policy instruments. Although migration may be driven by economic, demographic and environmental factors, the actions of states affect migration in myriad ways, including the decision to migrate in the first place, where to migrate, how to migrate, what routes to follow and, later, the trajectories of integration. Hence this book heeds the now familiar (but still sometimes inadequately realized) injunction to 'bring the state back in' to migration research (Hollifield 2007). Bringing the state back in requires more than the insertion of an abstract and monolithic entity – 'the state' – into existing migration debates. Rather, we must unpack and deconstruct the actors and institutions that constitute the state. When we do so, we discover that different actors and institutions have conflicting agendas on migration and are, to varying degrees, able to mobilize support behind these agendas. Policies reflect these conflicts.

When contemporary liberal states meet the fact of immigration, four constitutive features of liberal statehood shape their response: representative democracy, constitutionalism, capitalism and nationhood. As will be seen, each of these features is an abstraction or shorthand that captures a distinct constellation of actors, institutions and ideas which combine to produce dynamics of openness and closure across immigration, citizenship and integration policymaking. While this approach implies certain commonalities in the politics of immigration across liberal states, it is important to stress that it does not preclude cross-national variation between them. On the contrary, it provides a way to make sense of similarities and differences in the patterns of political contestation that shape policy outcomes.

At the same time, the book does argue that there are common patterns of conflict arising from these generic features of liberal statehood. Representative democracy, constitutionalism, capitalism and nationhood each generate distinct imperatives for government action on immigration. And none of these imperatives can be ignored because each is rooted in the legitimation of the liberal state. To put it very simply, mobilization through majoritarian democratic institutions, often based on claims about the protection of national identity and values, generates pressure for more restrictive immigration and integration policies; whereas employer demand for migrant labour and appeals to universal rights both generate pressure for more open, inclusive policies. Thus the governments of liberal states are pulled in different directions because core activities that they are expected to undertake to secure their legitimacy generate contradictory imperatives for immigration policy.

International Migration and the Modern State

If migration is as old as human history, *international* migration is a product of the modern world order and its defining political institution, the nation-state. As Aristide Zolberg has written, 'it is the political organization of world space into mutually exclusive sovereignties that delineates the specificity of international migration' (Zolberg 1994). The modern state is at once a territorial and a membership unit. It is partly defined by its claim to sovereignty over a specific expanse of physical territory, within which it claims the exclusive right to make laws backed up with what Max Weber famously described as a 'monopoly of the legitimate use of physical force' (Weber 1991 [1919]:

78). One of the key aspects of sovereignty is the right to decide who is allowed to enter that territory. At the same time, states are also membership institutions, comprised of a *demos* or people who share a common identity as citizens (or, in earlier times, as subjects) and who enjoy certain rights and obligations as a result of this status. Today, citizenship is typically acquired at birth according to place or parentage or some combination of the two, and one of the core rights of citizenship is a right to reside in the state of which one is a member.

It is the combination of these two aspects of modern statehood – the carving up of physical space into sovereign jurisdictions combined with the ascription of politico-legal identities to persons depending on their place of birth and/or parentage – that structures the two sides of the international migration coin. Immigration consists of persons without membership of state *a* entering and residing within the territory of *a*; emigration occurs when a person with membership of state *a* leaves its territory to reside in the territory of state *b*, *c*, *d*, and so on.[1] Therefore, without the dual territorial and membership aspects of modern statehood neither immigration nor emigration would exist. To see the significance of this, imagine a world without defined state territories or membership statuses. In such a world, moving from the city of Lahore (Pakistan) to London (UK) would in principle be like moving from Leicester to London (both in the UK). The latter journey would be quicker and cheaper, but absent state boundaries neither would require a visa application, a valid passport, entry checks, and so on. And that is just the journey itself. In reality the status of being a legal immigrant, as opposed to a citizen, affects a person's access to rights (see chapter 6). But, in our fictional example, the impact on rights for the migrant from Lahore to London would have no more significance than today's migrant from Leicester to London. Moreover, in our fictional world there would be no such thing as an 'illegal' immigrant, just as today there is no such thing as illegal-citizens-of-Leicester-residing-in-London. That this world is so far-fetched only goes to show just how fundamental territoriality and citizenship are to the contemporary world order.

This simple thought experiment also points to the depth of the challenges that international migration poses to the modern state system. For many of the state's day-to-day operations, as well as its bases of legitimacy, rest on an assumption that most people will spend their lives in the territory of the state of which they are a citizen. Voting systems, tax regimes and welfare systems all have what might be called a sedentary bias, insofar as they are ill-suited to cope with mass migratory movements. Though the majority of humanity (approximately 97 per cent) *do* live within their country of origin, the 3 per cent who are international migrants have increasingly led states to adapt their practices to accommodate immigrants (and also emigrants, though this is beyond the scope of this book). Practically, immigration requires states to adapt to the presence of newcomers in their political systems, societies and economies. Normatively, immigration raises profound questions about how to legitimate state power, not least since in liberal democracies the coercive power of the state is legitimated principally through the election of governments, but in almost all such countries the right to vote in national elections is based on citizenship, not residence.

Four Facets of the Liberal State

Thus international migration is at once a product of the modern state and a challenge to many of its underlying assumptions. While true, this observation does not begin to explain the complex processes that shape immigration policies in the contemporary world. To do this, we must move beyond the assertion that 'the state matters' and seek to identify and unpack the constituent parts of liberal states that are most relevant for understanding immigration policy. While liberal states undoubtedly vary in terms of their histories, economies, cultures, and so on, they nevertheless share certain features which enable their common labelling and moreover create similar political and policymaking dynamics in the field of immigration. This book argues that four facets of contemporary liberal statehood are crucial to understanding the politics of immigration: representative democracy, constitutionalism, nationhood and capitalism. These facets combine to generate often conflicting demands for immigration policies. They are introduced briefly here before being considered in more detail in chapters 2 and 3.

The liberal state as a democratic state

One of the defining characteristics of contemporary liberal states is their democratic character. All of the immigrant receiving countries discussed in this book are representative democracies, which is to say that their citizens elect political representatives through multi-party elections. Numerous different electoral systems, party systems and forms of government (e.g., presidential or parliamentary) are compatible with this broad definition, all of which are relevant to understanding exactly how representative politics influences immigration policymaking in any specific case. But even at this level of generality it is possible to spell out some of the implications that the institutions of representative democracy have for understanding how immigration is governed in liberal states.

First, in representative democracies, public opinion matters. What the voters of a given country think about immigration influences the kinds of policies candidates for office will propose, as well as the tone of discourse and atmosphere in which immigration is debated. Though political parties do not simply ape public opinion – since they try to shape it to some extent as well – they certainly cannot ignore it. This is true of most issues but especially so of sensitive and salient ones, which immigration has certainly become in recent years. In less politicized or technocratic policy areas, public opinion is less important. But when an issue such as immigration rises on the public agenda, becoming a matter of regular media coverage and popular debate, the importance of public opinion increases. Elected politicians cannot afford to be seen as 'out of touch' with public opinion on these issues.

Yet publics rarely think with one mind, especially on issues as controversial as immigration. Therefore it matters which parts of the public are able to get their voices heard and organize themselves to influence government. In representative democracies the chief mechanism for linking the government and public is political parties. It is parties that compete for electoral support from voters, parties that form governments, and governments which make immigration policies. Thus the ideologies and policy platforms of political parties, and how these are shaped through electoral competition, require consideration. In addition to political parties, any plausible account of immigration politics in democratic countries must include the myriad interest groups, ranging from employers' organizations to human rights groups, who seek to influence individual policies as well as the wider political agenda.

Finally, any understanding of democratic politics today requires consideration of the role of political communication. The mass media – television, newspapers, radio and, increasingly, the internet – act as a forum in which the political agenda is set and policy issues are framed. The media do not form a neutral channel through which pre-formed opinions are communicated back and forth between politicians and voters. Even when not explicitly partisan, the media have their own values, styles and formats, which affect how and indeed what issues are presented. An important power of the mass media, if one that is hard to measure, lies in their ability to politicize certain issues while depoliticizing others, and to frame them in ways that make some positions appear more legitimate or feasible than others. This is especially relevant for debates about immigration, which are often characterized by uncertainty about the actual impacts of migration flows and are therefore particularly susceptible to claims and counter-claims that are not easily verified or refuted. Moreover, certain 'impacts' are on intangibles such as national identity and culture, where it is difficult to identify objective evidence to support or refute different positions.

In summary, it is through the cut and thrust of democratic politics that public perceptions of immigration are shaped, party strategies forged and government policies made. Thus immigration policies cannot plausibly be understood as functional outcomes of economic or demographic facts; they are rather the products of sometimes intense political conflict in which numerous interested parties attempt to shape the agenda and influence public perceptions. To say that 'politics matters' (Bale 2008) for immigration policymaking means that public attitudes towards immigration and immigrants matter, how those attitudes are or are not mobilized matters, and how immigration is depicted in and through the mass media matters.

The liberal state as a constitutional state

A constitutional state is a 'state of laws' or *Rechtsstaat*, in which the authority of government is derived from and limited by law. A constitutional state has at least three distinctive features (Rawls 2007: 85). First, a constitution defines the institutional architecture of the system of government. As the word suggests, this *constitutes* government by setting out the roles and powers of the executive, the legislature and the judiciary and defining the limits of those powers. These rules are usually written down in a single document or code, such as the United States Constitution or the Basic Law of the Federal Republic of Germany (*Grundgesetz*), and even in a country such as the United Kingdom, which famously lacks a codified constitution, there is still a body of statutes, court rulings and customs which can be referred to as its constitution. Second, a constitution typically spells out the basic rights of citizens, including rights to due process, habeas corpus, and freedoms of speech, religion and assembly. Third, since constitutions require interpretation and application to specific cases (to adjudicate whether a given law or government action violates a constitutional rule or right), some form of judicial review is central to constitutional states. This implies a system of courts empowered to strike down laws or actions that are incompatible with the constitution.

These three features – a codified constitution, rights and judicial review – limit the powers of government and ground government legitimacy in the observation of those limits. As John Rawls, the leading liberal philosopher of the twentieth century, put it, in a constitutional state 'political power is legitimate only when it is exercised in accordance with a constitution' (Rawls 2001: 41). It is important to recognize that this constitutional foundation of the liberal state can, and often does, come into conflict with majoritarian decision-making. Indeed, one of the main points of constitutionalism is to limit the permissible outcomes of majoritarian processes. As Rawls puts it, a 'constitution should put certain fundamental rights and liberties beyond the reach of the legislative majorities of ordinary . . . politics' (Rawls 2007: 4–5). Constitutions are not beyond the reach of democratic politics – since they can typically be amended through special procedures involving referendums, super-majorities or consensus across the various branches and levels of government – but they set the parameters of everyday politics.

These constitutional protections are founded upon core liberal principles, including individual freedom, equal treatment and human rights. These are *universalistic* principles in that they are intended to apply to all persons, not just to persons belonging to this or that group. This is most clear in the case of human rights, which by definition are rights universally held by humans *qua* humans. Likewise, a liberal state should uphold the principles of individual freedom and equal treatment of all persons within its jurisdiction – certainly of all citizens and, crucially for the subject of this book, also in most respects of immigrants and legal aliens. A state cannot be considered liberal if it systematically discriminates between persons on the basis of sex, ethnicity or sexuality; nor is it a liberal state if it seeks to prevent the practice of some religions or belief systems (what liberal philosophers call 'conceptions of the good'). These norms are the essence of liberalism and they act as a kind of moral baseline: equal treatment is the default setting, and divergence requires special justification, otherwise a state loses its liberal credentials.

Universalistic discourses of human rights and the legal process are sources of expansion and inclusion in liberal states' immigration policies: expansionary in the sense that government attempts to restrict so-called unwanted migration flows have been constrained through legal advocacy in the courts; inclusionary in the sense that the rights of immigrants have been promoted through appeal to universalistic principles of equality and non-discrimination (Guiraudon 2000; Gurowitz 1999; Joppke 1998). As one of the leading proponents of this view, Christian Joppke, puts it, liberal state sovereignty is 'self-limited' (Joppke 1998: 271–2), and these limits become especially visible when the state attempts to deploy its coercive powers, as is often the case in immigration control. This is not to say that coercion is absent from liberal states – far from it – but rather that the institutions and ideals of liberal constitutionalism provide a resource with which coercive practices can be contested and sometimes delimited.

The liberal state as a nation-state

The third facet of contemporary liberal statehood that is fundamental to understanding immigration is the idea of nationhood. According to the political theorist David Miller, nationhood has five key aspects:

1 nations are constituted by belief, which is to say they exist when members recognize one another and believe that they share the relevant characteristics;
2 national identity embodies historical continuity with its origins often 'conveniently lost in the mists of time';
3 national identity is an active identity, in that nations are communities that do things together;
4 national identity connects a group of people to a particular place or territory;
5 national identity requires that people have a set of characteristics in common, often a shared language, cultural traditions, or historical memory (Miller 1997: 21–6).

Nations are, to use Benedict Anderson's (1991) famous phrase, 'imagined communities' – groups of people who recognize one another and believe that they share a common history, culture and territory. In a nation-state, this imagined community is the foundation of the apparatus of government: the state is seen as a political expression of the nation, which confers authority upon it. As Miller puts it, nations are regarded as 'active political agents, the bearers of the ultimate powers of sovereignty', and the state's 'institutions and policies could be seen as somehow expressing a popular or national will' (Miller 1997: 31).

A profound tension exists between the liberal universalism discussed in the previous section and the nationalist commitment to the construction and maintenance of a particular national identity. Nations cannot be distinguished from one another by universal principles, as by definition these principles refuse distinctions based on culture, ethnicity, and so on. Yet the construction and maintenance of national identity require that distinctions are made between human beings on the basis of particular attributes, such as place of birth, ancestry, language, and so on. Thus liberal nation-states are committed to universalism and at the same time dependent upon particularistic ideas of community and belonging. Moreover, the governments of liberal states are not – indeed, they arguably cannot be – impartial bystanders in the emergence and maintenance of national identity. As the political philosopher Will Kymlicka has argued, in liberal and non-liberal nation-states alike, 'government decisions on languages, internal boundaries, public holidays, and state symbols unavoidably involve recognizing, accommodating, and supporting the needs and identities of particular ethnic and national groups. The state unavoidably promotes certain cultural identities, and thereby disadvantages others' (Kymlicka 1995: 46).

This has a number of implications for the politics of immigration. Historically, throughout the nineteenth and twentieth centuries, immigration was central to nation-building in many of the states that are today regarded as liberal, such as the settler states of North America and Oceania. During the first half of the twentieth century in particular, these states used immigration policy as a tool to populate their nations by selecting newcomers on the basis of national or ethnic origin. In 1924, for example, the United States established the National Origins Quota system, which restricted 'undesirable' immigration from Southern and Eastern Europe and prohibited Asian immigrants altogether (King 2000; Zolberg 2006: 243–92); while from 1901 to 1973 the Australian government privileged white European settlement through its White Australia policy (Jupp 2007: 6–13). Over the course of the twentieth century the ability of states to 'select by origin' (Joppke 2005) came under increasing pressure, and since the 1960s the selection of immigrants on the basis of ascriptive criteria such as nationality or ethnicity has given way to selection according to other criteria, especially human capital. Nevertheless, several liberal states continue with 'ethnic migration policies' in one form or another, and, for those that do not, the history of nation-building through ethnically selective immigration policies still shapes the cultural and ethnic make-up of their societies today.

Moreover, it would be a serious mistake to think that the importance of nationhood for immigration is consigned to the past. Current debates about the impact of immigration on the societies and cultures of receiving countries, as well as the appropriate policy responses to these impacts, are profoundly shaped by ideas about national identity. This is especially true in the case of immigrant cultural integration, an issue that unavoidably invokes ideas about national culture – what it is that immigrants are supposed to integrate into. In Europe, this can be seen in controversies surrounding multiculturalism, debates about cultural integration tests, the prohibition of the Muslim veil (in France), bans on the construction of minarets (in Switzerland), and debates about free speech in multicultural societies (most famously, the Danish cartoon controversy) – all issues where national identity lies just beneath the surface, and sometimes becomes quite explicit, as for example when integration tests are designed to assess knowledge of national culture or values.

In the self-defined 'nations of immigrants', similar heated debates have occurred, especially since the reforms of the 1960s and 1970s diversified the national, ethnic and cultural background of immigrants. In the United States, conservatives have alleged that Latino immigration is dividing the American nation into two cultures, creating a 'crisis of national identity' (Huntington 2004: 3), while in Australia nationalist opposition to Asian immigration and multiculturalism developed during the 1980s and 1990s. These and other examples of the nativist backlash are not new, as throughout history immigration has been depicted by opponents as a threat to the national culture. What contemporary nativism does show is that claims about how the nation-state is in supposed decline in the face of post- or transnational identities are at best premature. From the 'banal nationalism' (Billig 1995) of flag-waving and support for national sports teams to the mobilization of national symbols for explicitly xenophobic ends, the power of national identity remains potent. Nationality is an important part of many citizens' identity, and one that bears directly on their attitudes towards immigration.

The liberal state as a capitalist state

Contemporary liberal states are capitalist states, and they are part of regional and global capitalist formations.[2] Liberal states are all mixed economies, in which private ownership and market exchange co-exist with government regulation and the public provision of some infrastructure and services. There is of course considerable variation in the institutions of capitalism in different countries, as analysed in the literature on 'varieties of capitalism' (see, e.g., Hall and Soskice 2001). For example, while the United States and Germany are both capitalist economies, there is substantial variation between them in terms of their institutions and regulatory regimes; the former is a typical 'liberal market economy', the latter a typical 'coordinated market economy' (see ibid.: 19–20). The different varieties of capitalism found across liberal states are highly consequential for the kinds of immigration regimes they adopt. As we will see, variation in immigration policies can partly be explained by differences in systems of political economy, especially industrial relations and labour market structures, and the different constellations of interests that are associated with these systems. Certainly, cross-national variation in the role of business and organized labour, and the interaction of these actors with state institutions, is crucial to understanding variation in immigration policies. This notwithstanding, across all liberal states the importance of a capitalist political economy for immigration policies is clear.

Indeed, immigration has become integral to advanced capitalist economies. Over thirty years ago, Gary Freeman observed that migrant labour was 'not merely a temporary convenience or necessity, but a structural requirement of advanced capitalism' (Freeman 1979: 3). At this time, interest in labour migrants was concentrated mainly in unskilled Fordist manufacturing positions and some primary sectors. Today, Freeman's claim is even truer than it was thirty years ago, but with the major difference that today's migrant workers fill skills gaps and address labour shortages across the labour market. At the top end of the labour market, there is growing competition between liberal states to attract highly skilled mobile labour in sectors such as IT and financial services, while, in lower-wage sectors, migrant workers often fill jobs that the relatively affluent and educated indigenous populations are reluctant to do, the so-called 3D jobs that are dirty, dangerous or degrading. According to the dual labour market hypothesis (Piore 1979: 35–43), the organization of capitalist economies creates a permanent low-skill, low-pay secondary tier that requires migrant labour.

Given that this demand for migrant labour is endemic to advanced capitalist economies, it is not surprising that 'migration management' has become an increasingly explicit part of liberal states' accumulation strategies. As Georg Menz describes it, 'an economistic fixation with migration as a constituent factor in ensuring continued patterns in accumulation and surplus extraction has spawned an obsession with managing migration' (Menz 2009: 30). This obsession is to a large extent acceptance of an unavoidable reality. Governments have little choice but to accept greater flows of people across their borders on account of the way in which the regional and global integration of markets for goods, services and capital often go hand in hand with increased flows of people (Hollifield 2004). To give just one example, foreign direct investment in the form of large multinational firms siting offices and factories in a given country inevitably generates flows of intra-corporate transferees. Thus, if states want to promote trade and investment, they must accept more migration. Advanced capitalist states cannot afford – literally as well as metaphorically – not to solicit immigrants. The problem here, hinted at above and explored more fully in chapter 2, is that, while it may be una-voidable for advanced capitalist economies, immigration is not popular with voters. This creates a dilemma for governments. On the one hand, they must respond to the demands of employers for migrant labour; on the other, they must address popular scepticism towards immigration, mobilized in some countries by anti-immigrant parties. This is just one of the cross-cutting pres-sures that lead governments to welcome some immigrants with open arms while shunning others.

Liberal Paradoxes

The different imperatives associated with representative democracy, consti-tutionalism, nationhood and capitalist accumulation are all essential to understanding how immigration is governed in contemporary liberal states. The existing literature tends to focus on how one of these aspects impacts on immigration policy, often on a particular sub-field, without considering their interactions across the wider field. Thus political economists have made important contributions to our understanding of labour migration (e.g., Caviedes 2010; Cerna 2009; Freeman 1995, 2006; Hollifield 1992; Menz 2009); institutionalist scholars have shown how liberal norms, courts and judiciar-ies facilitate asylum and family migration in the face of executive opposition (e.g., Guiraudon 2000; Guiraudon and Joppke 2001; Guiraudon and Lahav 2000; Joppke 1998) and how norms are mobilized to constrain coercive poli-cies (e.g., Ellermann 2005, 2009; Gibney and Hansen 2003); party politics scholars have analysed how both mainstream and extreme parties mobilize on the immigration issue (e.g., Bale 2003, 2008; Bale et al. 2010; Carter 2005; Mudde 2007; Norris 2005; Schain 2006; Van der Brug et al. 2005); public opinion researchers have examined the drivers of anti-immigrant sentiment (e.g., Citrin et al. 1997; Ivarsflaten 2005; McLaren and Johnson 2007; Sides and Citrin 2007); and researchers of national identity have explored the interaction of immigration and nation-building (e.g., Fitzgerald 1996; King 2000; Zolberg 2006). Yet few studies have sought to examine how these factors interact to produce conflicting policy outputs.

The interaction of the four facets of liberal statehood will be explored further in the chapters to come, but for now it is already possible to observe that they pull in different directions. Two of them (representative politics and nationhood) tend towards a restrictive dynamic, whereas the other two (con-stitutionalism and capitalism) are associated with openness towards immi-gration. This gives an initial view of why there are both inclusionary *and* exclusionary aspects to immigration policies in liberal states. The fact that liberal states are neither entirely open nor entirely closed to immigration reflects these contrasting pressures and the conflicting interests – electoral, rights-based, economic and cultural – that influence who is admitted and who is excluded, and on what terms.

It is these conflicting dynamics that lie behind the 'liberal paradox' of immigration (Hollifield 1992: 3ff). For, while some defining institutions and ideas of liberal states generate demands for restrictions on immigration, leading to practices that may even be deemed illiberal, others generate pressures to admit and recruit immigrants. Thus the liberal state's Janus face towards immigration is not something that can be wished away, as both anti-immigrant populists and pro-immigrant campaigners are wont to do. Liberal states are unavoidably characterized by degrees of openness towards some kinds of immigration and degrees of closure towards others. The question then becomes one of explaining the dynamics that shape these apparently paradoxical tendencies.

It is important to note that the fourfold framework outlined above is intended neither as a definition of the liberal state nor as a fully fledged theory of immigration politics. A definition of the liberal state is beyond the scope of this book. The four facets are proposed not as an exhaustive definition but rather as empirically observable commonalities of the major immigrant destination states that are widely labelled as liberal. The fourfold framework also does not provide a theory that could predict outcomes in specific cases. By setting out four facets of the liberal state, the aim is rather to provide a framework for analysis, which can be used to examine both similarities and differences between liberal states. Yet while these facets cannot explain outcomes in particular cases, insofar as they are common to liberal states the dynamics that they generate should be present to some degree in most cases. The significance of each facet for immigration policy will depend both on the type of immigration in question and on the particular form of a given state's representative institutions, its constitution, conception of national identity and economic structures.

It is also important to distinguish between different types of immigration – some of which are 'wanted', others 'unwanted'. Labour, family, humanitarian and irregular immigration are all associated with distinct patterns of policymaking in which different political dynamics are at play. For example, lobbying by business plays a more important role in labour migration policy than asylum policy. This can be further refined according to policy sub-type – for example, the politics of immigration policy vis-à-vis the highly skilled can be distinguished from that concerning temporary low-skilled workers. On the other hand, it is necessary to examine the specificity of each facet in a given country (for example, the type of government or the content of national identity) and the interrelations between these various elements (for example, to what extent the executive is subject to constitutional constraints). Thus the framework outlined in this chapter is entirely consistent with in-country variation between different immigration policy domains, as well as cross-national variation between liberal states; indeed, it is intended to help understand that variation.

Plan of the Book

The next two chapters of the book elaborate on the ideas sketched above to demonstrate how the four facets of the liberal state generate conflicting dynamics of openness and closure. Chapter 2 focuses on dynamics of closure. A consideration of public opinion, party politics and political discourse about immigration in the major destination countries of Europe, North America and Oceania shows that, with few exceptions, representative politics creates demands for restrictive policies. The restrictionist tenor of representative politics leaves us with a puzzle to be explained. Why does restrictionist public opinion and political rhetoric not translate into equally restrictionist policies? Why is there an apparent gap between what the public want and politicians promise, on the one hand, and what governments actually do, on the other?

Chapter 3 picks up this question by exploring how dynamics of openness are embedded in liberal states. It first considers arguments that seek to explain the gap in terms of a loss of state control over migration flows. These arguments are shown to be overstated. Rather, it is argued that dynamics internal to liberal states help to explain why restrictive policy inputs do not (always) translate into restrictive policy outputs. Two key sources of openness are examined: capitalist political economy and constitutionalism. A third factor, historical path dependence, is also shown to play a role. Again, these arguments are illustrated with reference to the major immigrant-receiving countries of Europe, North America and Oceania.

The rest of the chapters trace the implications of these conflicting dynamics of openness and closure for immigration, citizenship and integration policies. Chapter 4 outlines how contemporary states seek to manage migration – what policies and instruments they develop and why. The chapter maps out the main immigration sub-fields – labour migration, asylum, family migration and irregular migration – and compares policies in these areas across liberal states. While there is a generalized political demand for governments to adopt more restrictive approaches towards immigration, the chapter shows how this is more readily translated into policy in some areas than others.

Chapter 5 considers the international governance of migration. It reviews the range of institutions and processes that have been established on a bilateral, regional and international scale. While there is a growing amount of international cooperation on migration, there is a dearth of multilateral initiatives in comparison with other global issues such as trade or finance. States jealously guard their prerogative to set the number and type of immigrants that they admit to their territories. Compounding this, conflicts of interest between Northern and Southern countries make formal global agreements all but impossible. Instead the chapter shows how states have sought to develop a limited number of formal agreements on a largely bilateral basis, but have mostly pursued informal modes of cooperation on a regional basis. Even in the European Union, which has by far the most developed supranational migration policy regime, nation-states retain considerable powers to regulate immigration.

Chapters 6 and 7 consider citizenship and integration policies respectively. Chapter 6 shows that immigration to liberal states has created pressures to liberalize citizenship laws, while at the same time leading to a 'revaluation' of citizenship and naturalization procedures. Contra post-nationalists, the acquisition of national citizenship continues to matter, and citizenship policy has become increasingly contested in recent years. While liberal norms undoubtedly generate an inclusionary logic, when citizenship is politicized the effect is often to retard or even roll back liberalization. Similar dynamics can be identified in political debates about immigrant integration. Chapter 7 first considers the inherent complexity of integration in a liberal context, in terms of both the differentiated and self-limited nature of liberal societies and the diversity and multidimensionality of immigrant integration processes. The literature on immigrant integration has seldom paid sufficient attention to this complexity, while the political debate has increasingly fixated on cultural integration to the detriment of other arguably more important dimensions, especially economic integration. The chapter argues that anxieties about national identity in an era of globalization, compounded by concerns about Muslims since 9/11, underlie the focus on culture. In response, especially in Europe, governments have denounced multiculturalism and promoted new civic integration policies based on what the British prime minister called 'muscular liberalism'. The chapter argues that these policies are latter-day nation-building instruments, albeit nation-building in a liberal register.

Chapter 8 revisits the four facets outlined above and, in light of the intervening chapters, considers why the conflicting imperatives they generate are difficult or even impossible for governments to reconcile. Immigration, it is argued, reveals deep contradictions at the heart of the liberal state.

CHAPTER TWO

The Politics of Closure

The politics of immigration in liberal states is characterized by both exclusionary and inclusionary dynamics. Governments must attempt to reconcile demands to control the number and rights of immigrants entering their territory, as well as demands for more open, inclusive policies. The following two chapters consider each side of this equation, starting with the politics of closure. Where do demands to restrict immigration come from? This chapter argues that democratic politics is the main source of these demands. It shows how popular (and populist) attitudes and party competition generate substantial pressure for governments to talk and act tough on immigration. These elements of representative democracy are intertwined with the nationhood of states because collective mobilization on immigration often appeals to national identity and presents immigration as a threat to that identity.

Race, Nation and the Immigrant Threat

The idea that immigration poses some kind of threat to the nation has a long history (Lucassen 2006). Indeed, contemporary opposition to immigration based on ethnic or cultural protectionism is not a quirk of our time, but rather the most recent manifestation of a recurring and widespread phenomenon. This section provides a short historical sketch of responses to immigration in some of today's liberal democracies from the late nineteenth to the late twentieth century as background context for the discussion of contemporary developments below.

Take the archetypal nation of immigrants, the United States, where the huddled masses who crossed the Atlantic were often met with suspicion and hostility by earlier settlers. According to John Higham's classic work *Strangers in the Land* (1955), during the latter part of the nineteenth century the United States moved from openness to closure as a result of nativist pressure. As immigration flows diversified, American 'natives', who were in many cases second-generation immigrants themselves, mobilized to oppose the growing numbers of Southern and Eastern European and Chinese immigrants. According to Higham, this popular opposition pressured the federal government to establish what one contemporary commentator described as a 'racial ring fence' with the aim of 'keeping America American' (Warner Parker, cited in Joppke 2005: 40). The 1924 Reed–Johnson Immigration Act excluded Asian immigrants and established a quota system privileging Northwestern over Southern and Eastern Europeans that lasted until 1965, when it was finally abolished for its openly discriminatory nature.

This neat story of nativist hostility driving the federal government to restrict immigration is, however, partial at best. Without denying the presence of atavistic sentiments among native citizens, recent scholarship has shown that the national origins system was part of a wider project of nation-building, in which government and political elites played an active role (Zolberg 2006). This was not a case of an illiberal public pushing an enlightened elite into a restrictive policy, as voices for racial selection could be found among intellectual and political elites as well. As Desmond King (2000: 166–95) has shown, scientific racism, in the form of the eugenics movement, played a key role in the development of the national origins policy. Eugenicists argued that immigrants of 'inferior stock' (including Asians, Africans, Jews, and Southern and Eastern Europeans) threatened to dilute the American 'race' and induce racial degeneracy. Eugenics had a broad political appeal, and eugenicists such as Dr Harry H. Laughlin influenced policymakers in the 1920s. Laughlin advised Congress on the 'biological aspects of immigration' and formed a close relationship with Congressman Albert Johnson, one of the architects of the 1924 legislation. As King (2000: 195) writes, the 'alleged scientific authenticity' of eugenics converged with 'populist racist stereotypes', and perceptions of immigration as a threat could be found in both popular and elite attitudes.

A similar story of racially exclusive nation-building through immigration policy unfolded in Australia between 1901 and 1972. During the latter decades of the nineteenth century, popular journals aligned with radical factions in the labour movement to lobby for restrictions on Asian immigrants (Jupp 1998: 74). When the six Australian colonies were federated into the Commonwealth of Australia, one of the first actions of the newly constituted state was to pass the Commonwealth Immigration Restriction Act of 1901. This established what became known as the White Australia policy: an ethnic selection policy that privileged white European, especially British, immigrants and excluded Asians and other non-Europeans. The 1901 Act did not itself refer to 'races' or 'nations' but achieved its exclusionary effect by granting immigration officers a discretionary power to require immigrants to pass a dictation test in a 'European language' of their choice. The practice was evidently successful, as the Chinese population in Australia shrank from 29,907 to 9,144 between 1901 and 1947 (Palfreeman 1967: 145).

The White Australia policy was essential to national self-definition; indeed, it was the cornerstone of a racialized understanding of Australian nationhood in which non-Europeans had no place. As Alfred Deakin, the leading politician of the day, put it in the parliamentary debate on the Act: 'we should

be one people, and remain one people without the admixture of other races
. . . The unity of Australia is nothing if it does not imply a united race' (cited
in Joppke 2005: 43). The centrality of the White Australia policy to national
self-definition helps to explain why it persisted for so long. It was only in 1972
that it was finally abolished, mainly because it conflicted with Australia's
foreign policy objectives in the region. In that year, the Whitlam government
announced that race, colour or creed would no longer be the basis for immigration control (Jupp 2007: 11).

In Europe, the historical narrative is very different to that of the classic
settler countries, as European nations became major destination countries
only following the Second World War, long after the major phases of nation-
building had been consolidated. This is not to say that opposition to immigration, or the idea that immigration represented a threat to national identity,
was absent from popular or elite discourse. On the contrary, it figured promi-
nently in several countries. But, whereas immigration policy in settler states
was shaped by an active attempt to populate their nations for the long term,
in Europe immigration policy was not tied to nation-building. Rather, in the
postwar years European immigration policy had two main syndromes: first,
largely reactive measures to control unsolicited immigration from colonial
and postcolonial territories; and, second, labour migrant recruitment on a
temporary basis, the so-called *Gastarbeiter* or guestworkers.

Both colonial and guestworker migration developed in the context of
strong economic growth, the *trentes glorieuses* or thirty years of economic
prosperity from 1945 to 1975. A core difference, however, was that guestworker immigration was state-initiated, whereas colonial immigration mostly
was not. As imperial subjects, colonial immigrants typically had the right to
settle in European countries (Hansen 2000; Hampshire 2005), which meant
that their movement was difficult to control, particularly at a time of politically sensitive negotiations about decolonization. Although there were some
state-sponsored schemes to recruit workers from colonial territories, the vast
majority of colonial immigrants came on their own initiative. For most, it
was a case of seeking work and a better life in the European motherlands that
imperial propaganda had eulogized for decades.

In Britain, colonial immigration caused immediate concern within government circles, and increasingly so as its scale and permanence became apparent. Among the political elite, 'coloured immigration' was approached as a
problem almost immediately (see Hampshire 2005: 20–1). Initially, the British
government tried to use administrative measures to restrict immigrants
(Spencer 1997: 46–8), but when this failed to reduce numbers it passed successive pieces of primary legislation in 1962, in 1968, and again in 1971. The
most well-known, indeed infamous, political intervention of this period was
made by Enoch Powell, a prominent Conservative politician, who claimed in
a 1968 speech that, if non-white immigration continued, the streets of Britain
would flow with 'rivers of blood'. Powell was sacked from the shadow cabinet

for his inflammatory rhetoric, but he became an enormously popular figure, achieving higher approval scores between 1968 and 1974 than any other politician in the history of UK polling. Liverpool dockworkers – usually core Labour supporters – famously marched 'for Enoch'. According to one analysis, Powell's interventions on race and immigration were decisive in securing the Conservatives victory in the 1970 election (McLean 2001: 145–52).

In wider society, colonial immigrants often faced xenophobia and racism. Sometimes this was quite explicit, such as overt discrimination in the labour or housing market, captured by the infamous 1950s boarding-house sign that read 'no coloureds, no Irish, no dogs'. At other times the influence of racism was more insidious, percolating through public debates about the effects of immigration on British society. Thus popular newspapers made lurid allegations about welfare scrounging, criminality and immorality among 'coloured' immigrants, while state actors ranging from senior police officers to government ministers worried about the social effects of Britain becoming a multi-racial society (see Hampshire 2005). There were of course individuals and groups who spoke in favour of immigration (the Treasury considered it economically beneficial) and against discrimination (the Labour government passed race relations legislation in the 1960s), but the overall tenor of debate was characterized by anxiety about the effects of increasing ethnic diversity.

The story of guestworker migration to Europe was rather different. As the name suggests, guestworkers or *Gastarbeiter* were temporary labour migrants, recruited overseas by European labour ministries acting on behalf of employers. West Germany had the most extensive guestworker programme, but several countries, among them France, Belgium and Switzerland, also recruited migrant workers through such schemes. At first, guestworkers came mostly from the Southern and Southeastern peripheries of Europe, notably Italy, Greece, Portugal and Yugoslavia, but these schemes were later expanded to include countries such as Turkey, Morocco, Algeria and Tunisia.

Guestworker migration represents an exception to the cases discussed so far in that it generated little populist opposition based on ethnic or cultural change. There were specific reasons for this, however. First, the economic expediency of recruiting overseas workers during a time of high growth and full employment generated a robust political consensus in which the mainstream political parties avoided competition on the issue. Indeed, by today's politicized standards, it is remarkable how guestworker recruitment was viewed as an essentially technocratic administrative issue. In West Germany, for example, which issued an estimated total of 14 million guestworker permits between 1955 and 1973 (Bade, cited in Green 2004: 33), all of the main political parties supported the scheme. This consensus was made possible by a second factor, a myth of return, which largely explains why guestworkers were not perceived as a threat. As Simon Green argues, 'guestworkers were considered by all concerned to be a purely temporary measure to alleviate labour market shortages' (ibid.). Since 'their entire existence was seen solely from this perspective', they were not perceived as having the potential to change German society on a permanent basis. Over time, both employers and unions pushed for permanent contracts, and when the German government wound up guestworker recruitment after the oil shock of 1973, many workers did not return 'home' and instead began to bring their families. This transformed a temporary labour force into a permanent immigrant minority, 'the guests who stayed' (Castles 1985). A third, related factor that explains why guestworkers were not perceived as a threat was their exclusion – physical, legal and social – from German society. Most were housed in company-run hostels, with little interaction with German citizens and few possibilities to integrate into wider society. Nor could they hope to acquire German citizenship without meeting highly stringent requirements. Indeed, until the citizenship reforms of 1999 introduced the principle of *jus soli* into German nationality law, even the children of immigrants, despite being born and raised in Germany, were not German nationals unless they naturalized as 'young foreigners'. These three factors – an elite consensus, a myth of return, and both *de jure* and *de facto* exclusion from society – makes the history of guestworkers stand out as an example of a mass immigration that did not encounter significant popular opposition or political controversy. While this shows that immigration need not always be perceived as a threat by native citizens, it equally suggests that very specific conditions need to be met if this outcome is to be avoided.

Overall, the history of immigration to Western countries since the late nineteenth century provides many more examples of anxious opposition than relaxed welcome among both public and elites alike. The cases briefly discussed are of course just a few selected examples, but they serve to illustrate that, well before international migration flows burgeoned in the 1990s, immigration to Western countries was often perceived as a threat to national identity. In the case of settler societies, nation-building motivated the construction of ethnically selective immigration regimes; in the case of European postcolonial countries, it led to restrictions on non-white immigration; only in the case of the guestworker countries was the perception of threat minimized, but this was due largely to a misplaced belief that migrant workers could be recruited without long-term implications for the countries that recruited them.

Public Opinion and its Causes

The perception that immigration poses a threat to national cultural identity persists today. Public opinion data show that opposition to immigration is a persistent feature of public attitudes across liberal democracies. Although there is variation across countries and over time, the core findings of public opinion polls are remarkably consistent: substantial segments of the citizens of liberal states express negative attitudes towards immigration; many people believe that there are too many immigrants in their country of residence (though this is often based on an overestimation of the actual numbers); many people want more restrictive policies to be implemented; and few people trust their governments on immigration or think that they manage it very well (see Simon and Lynch 1999). These are of course generalizations, masking variation at the individual level (anti-immigrant opinion varies according to the age, class, education, ethnicity, gender and political ideology of the respondent) and between countries, but it is safe to say that the citizens of liberal democratic states are not, by and large, enthusiastic supporters of immigration. The overall picture that emerges is one of public scepticism and, for some parts of the population, outright hostility.

In an analysis of Eurobarometer public opinion surveys from the 1990s, Alan Kessler and Gary Freeman found that the proportion of Europeans who thought there were 'too many' non-EU foreign nationals living in their country ranged from 37.4 per cent in 1988 to 51.6 per cent in 1993 (Kessler and Freeman 2005: 831). Behind these EU15 averages there was significant cross-national variation: for example, in 2000, some 58.3 per cent of Greek citizens, compared with just 17.3 per cent of Finns, thought there were too many foreigners in their country. Overall, negative responses peaked around 1993, at a time when there were large numbers of asylum-seekers arriving from former communist states. Notably, when asked whether there should be restrictions on people coming to work within the EU (i.e., labour migrants) the negative attitudes softened considerably (ibid.: 832). These important nuances notwithstanding, the overall European picture during the 1990s could be described as moderately anti-immigrant, with at least a third and sometimes just over a half of Europeans saying that they thought there were too many foreign nationals in their country. More recent Eurobarometer polls (albeit based on different questions) are broadly consistent with the finding that the European public is sceptical of immigration. A poll conducted in 2009 in the midst of the economic crisis found that 62.8 per cent of Europeans thought that the presence of people from 'other ethnic groups increases unemployment in our community', and 48 per cent thought that other ethnic groups are a 'cause of insecurity' (Eurobarometer 2012).

Given their long histories of settlement and the centrality of immigration to their national stories, it might be expected that citizens of countries in North America and Oceania would be more sympathetic towards immigrants. In fact, public opinion data from North America and Australia reveal similar, and in some cases higher, levels of anti-immigrant sentiment compared with Europe. In the United States, a 2006 survey found that 40 per cent of Americans thought legal immigration should be decreased. Moreover, 20 per cent of the population were more than just mildly concerned by immigration, agreeing that it presented a 'very big' community problem (Pew Research Center 2006). Canadians, who are generally more open to immigration, nevertheless also express concerns about the levels: from the mid-1970s to the mid-1990s, between 32 and 53 per cent of Canadians wanted a decrease in the number of immigrants (Simon and Lynch 1999: 459). Over the same period, Australians were more sceptical: during the 1980s and much of the 1990s clear majorities claimed that there were too many immigrants (Betts 2000: 61), though Australians appeared to become more 'relaxed and comfortable' about immigration in the late 1990s, with a roughly even split between those reporting that the level was about right or too low and those who thought it was too high (Goot 2000).

The most recent systematic comparison of North American and European public opinion on immigration asked respondents whether they thought immigration presented more of a problem or an opportunity for their country (Transatlantic Trends 2010). Majorities in the United States (52 per cent), the UK (65 per cent) and Spain (53 per cent) saw immigration as more of a problem, while Italian, German, French and Dutch respondents were divided (45, 44, 42 and 39 per cent respectively saying it was more of a problem). Of the eight countries surveyed, only Canadians clearly saw immigration as an opportunity. The survey also asked for respondents' views about how well governments managed immigration. Majorities in the United States (73 per cent), the UK (70 per cent), Spain (61 per cent), France (58 per cent) and the Netherlands (54 per cent) believed that the government was doing a poor job. The only country to evince a remotely positive view of the government's migration management was Canada, with 48 per cent offering positive views and 43 per cent responding negatively.

These surveys give an indication of public attitudes towards immigration, but they don't explain the origins or drivers of anti-immigrant sentiment. Who, among the citizens of liberal states, opposes immigration? And what causes them to do so? There is now a sizeable body of research on these questions (Burns and Gimpel 2000; Citrin et al. 1997; Hainmueller and Hiscox 2010; Ivarsflaten 2005; McLaren and Johnson 2007; Sides and Citrin 2007; Sniderman et al. 2004) from which several conclusions can be drawn. Research on which parts of the citizenry of liberal states oppose immigration reveals that individual-level factors, including age, education, political ideology and prejudice, have important effects on attitudes. Older people, those who are ideological conservatives or support right-wing parties, and those who report prejudicial attitudes towards minorities are more likely to oppose immigration than the average respondent (Kessler and Freeman 2005: 840). Conversely, education is negatively correlated with anti-immigrant sentiment: the more educated a person is, the less likely they are to hold negative attitudes towards immigration (ibid.). A person's position in the labour market plays a role, but it is not as strong as the previous factors.

Explanations of attitudes towards immigration tend to fall into two camps. Interest-based theories hypothesize that opposition to immigration is shaped principally by economic self-interest on the part of citizens. According to these theories, individuals who compete directly with immigrants for jobs and wages will hold stronger anti-immigrant attitudes than those who do not. In other words, attitudes to immigration are essentially instrumental; immigration is opposed because of the (real or perceived) effect it has on a person's economic well-being. In contrast, identity-based theories hypothesize that opposition to immigration is driven less by calculations of individual self-interest and more by deep-seated affective and cognitive predispositions. These predispositions are based on in-group favouritism and out-group hostility, and are typically manifested as a desire to maintain both cultural and ethnic identity and prejudice towards outsiders. On this account, immigration is opposed because of the ethnic and cultural changes it brings to receiving societies.

Statistical analyses of these hypotheses using both European and North American data converge on two core findings: first, that identity is more important than economics as a determinant of anti-immigrant attitudes; and, second, to the extent that economic factors are important, it is sociotropic concerns about the overall economy rather than egocentric concerns about an individual's own economic standing that influence attitudes (Sides and Citrin 2007; Hainmueller and Hiscox 2010). That is to say, most people who want to see fewer immigrants do so not on self-interested economic grounds (i.e., because they perceive immigrants as a direct threat to their economic well-being) but because they view immigration as a threat to culture and identity and, to a lesser degree, because they believe immigration has a negative impact on the economy as a whole (Citrin et al. 1997; McLaren and Johnson 2007; Sides and Citrin 2007; though compare Aalberg et al. 2012). As one analyst of European attitudes puts it, people support restrictive asylum and immigration policies because they are 'threatened by diversity' (Ivarsflaten 2005).

These findings suggest that attitudes towards immigration have less to do with rational assessments of economic impacts and more to do with atavistic tendencies to protect 'our' way of life and an associated fear of cultural difference. If correct, this suggests continuities with the fears of an immigrant threat discussed in the previous section. If opposition was once more likely to be expressed in openly racist or xenophobic terms, ethnic and cultural anxieties about immigration do not appear to have diminished. Could it be that out-group hostility, which was once readily articulated in racist terms, has morphed into a cultural idiom as explicit racism has been delegitimized? This is not to imply that all identity-based opposition to immigration is racism in disguise; rather, that a tendency to protect existing national and cultural identities in the face of change brought about by immigration finds different expression in different historical periods. This is something to which we will return below.

The implications of identity-based explanations for anti-immigrant sentiments are particularly problematic for policymakers. If cultural identity matters more than economic interests, then arguments and evidence about the net socio-economic benefits of immigration are unlikely to make significant inroads into anti-immigrant opinion. Instead, as two US scholars put it, 'creating more favourable attitudes towards immigration may require reimagining national identities in many countries' (Sides and Citrin 2007: 478). The problem is that reimagining national identities to be more hospitable to cultural diversity is a tremendously tall order – certainly harder than presenting evidence that immigration brings economic benefits. Narratives of national identity are not created overnight. To the extent that liberal states are nation-states, drawing upon deep reservoirs of feeling and emotion to underpin their authority, identity-based opposition towards immigration poses real challenges to governments.

The Party Politics of Immigration

The evidence of public scepticism towards immigration does not mean that governments will necessarily seek to restrict immigration, however. Public opinion on immigration, as with any other policy issue, needs to be mobilized if it is to influence government policies. The main mechanism for the mobilization of public opinion in representative democracies is political parties. There are other channels through which publics can influence governments, notably interest groups and social movements (more of which in chapter 3), but only political parties represent broad-based constituencies and seek to form governments for the purpose of making policies. Therefore, to understand the significance of the attitudes discussed in the previous section, it is necessary to consider the extent to which they have been mobilized through party politics.

Immigration is difficult for mainstream parties to handle because it is does not align with the classic left–right cleavage based on material interests, and therefore it has the potential to divide the core constituencies of both centre-left and centre-right. For centre-right parties, immigration exposes tensions between market liberalism (which mandates an expansive approach to immigration) and value conservatism (which is associated with the maintenance of cultural traditions and the nation-state, and thus a more restrictive approach to immigration). In terms of the centre-right's core support, this generates divisions between the demands of business and the demands of cultural conservatives and nationalists (Bale 2008). Immigration is also divisive for centre-left parties. Liberal elements within these parties typically support pro-immigrant policies, often for human rights reasons, while welfare state and labour market protectionists support restrictions on immigration to protect lower-skilled workers against competition from migrant labour and also to address identity-based concerns among core voters. Furthermore, the maintenance of social solidarity as a foundation of the welfare state may generate calls from within the left for restrictions on immigration (e.g., Goodhart 2004).

Because of the divisive nature of immigration, mainstream parties have often sought either to fudge the issue or to depoliticize it. The fudging strategy requires different messages to different audiences: typically a tough stance in public and a more accommodating stance to pro-immigration lobbyists. The problem with this strategy is that it is open to a charge of hypocrisy or elite conspiracy, and thus counter-mobilization by populist anti-immigrant actors. The depoliticization strategy may work under certain conditions – for example, if there is genuine consensus on policy among parties (as was the case in postwar Germany) or if all main parties struggle to such an extent that they see a common advantage in avoiding it (as was the case for periods in postwar Britain (Messina 1989)). The problem with this strategy is that it is at best unstable, because if one or another party espies an electoral advantage in breaking ranks and 'speaking out' on immigration then it is likely to do so, and it is just as susceptible to populist anti-immigrant mobilization as fudging.

Populist anti-immigrant mobilization is exactly what has occurred in several liberal democracies in recent years. In Europe especially, the rise of far-right parties has been one of the most notable political trends of the last twenty years (see Betz 1994; Carter 2005; Givens 2005; Ignazi 2003; Kitschelt and McGann 1995; Mudde 2007; Norris 2005; Rydgren 2005; Schain et al. 2002). Some of the far right's early breakthroughs, such as the defeat of the Socialist prime minister Lionel Jospin by the Front National's Jean-Marie Le Pen in the first round of the 2002 French presidential elections, sent shockwaves through the European political elite. Since then the far right has become a more routine, if controversial, feature of the European political scene, with parties joining or supporting coalition governments at various points in Austria, Denmark, Italy, the Netherlands and Switzerland. Table 2.1 summarizes the main far-right parties and their levels of support in European countries.

It is important to recognize that European far-right parties are ideologically diverse. Some, such as the former National Alliance in Italy or the British National Party, have their origins in neo-fascist movements, but many others do not. Some, such as the former List Pim Fortuyn, are libertarian, whereas others, such as the Front National in France, are authoritarian. Some have agendas that are particular to the context in which they operate: for example, secessionist agendas (e.g., the Lega Nord in Italy or the Vlaams Belang, formerly Vlaams Blok, in Belgium), or anti-tax, anti-state policies in the Scandinavian social democracies (e.g., the Danish and Norwegian Progress

TABLE 2.1 Far-right parties in selected European countries

Country	Far-right parties	Highest % vote in national elections	% vote at most recent election	Parliamentary seats at most recent election	Period in government
Austria	Freedom Party of Austria (FPÖ); Alliance for the Future of Austria (BZÖ)	26.9 (1999) 10.7 (2008)	17.5 (2008) 10.7 (2008)	34/183 17/183	Coalition with ÖVP, 2000–5, then 2005–6 as BZÖ.
Belgium	Vlaams Belang [Flemish Interest] (VB)	12.0 (2007)	7.8 (2010)	12/150	No
Czech Republic	Workers Party of Social Justice	1.1 (2010)	1.1 (2010)	0	No
Denmark	Danish People's Party (DF)	13.9 (2007)	12.3 (2011)	22/179	Supported Liberal-Conservative government, 2001–11; no cabinet posts but policy influence
Finland	Perus [True Finns]	19.0 (2011)	19.0 (2011)	39/200	No
France	Front National (FN)	15.3 (1997)	4.3 (2007)	0	No
Germany	National Democratic Party of Germany (NPD)	1.6 (2005)	1.5 (2009)	0	No
Greece	Golden Dawn	7.0 (2012)	7.0 (2012)	18/300	No
Hungary	Jobbik, the Movement for a Better Hungary	16.7 (2010)	16.7 (2010)	47/386	No
Ireland	None	–	–	–	–

		LN: 10.1 (1996); AN: 15.7 (1996)	LN: 8.3 (2008)	LN: 59/630	LN: coalition 1994–6, 2001–6, 2008–11
Italy	Northern League (LN); National Alliance (AN) (merged into People of Freedom 2008)				
Luxembourg	None	–	–	–	–
Netherlands	Party for Freedom (PVV); List Pim Fortuyn (LPF) (disbanded 1 Jan 2008)	PVV: 15.5 (2010); LPF 17.0 (2002)	PVV: 15.5 (2010)	PVV: 24/150	Supports minority conservative coalition government, 2010–present
Norway	Progress Party (FRP)	22.9 (2009)	22.9 (2009)	41/169	No
Poland	League of Polish Families (LPR)	8.0 (2005)	1.3 (2007)	0	Ministerial post in coalition 2006–7
Portugal	National Renovator Party (PNR)	0.3 (2011)	0.3 (2011)	0	No
Slovak Republic	Slovak National Party (SNS)	13.9 (1990)	4.6 (2012)	0/150	No
Slovenia	Slovene National Party	10.0 (1992)	1.8 (2011)	0/90	No
Spain	Some small fringe groups	–	–	–	–
Sweden	Sweden Democrats (SD)	5.7 (2010)	5.7 (2010)	20/349	No
Switzerland	Swiss People's Party (SVP)	28.9 (2007)	26.6 (2011)	54/200	1/7 members Federal Council, 2003–8, 2008–present
United Kingdom	British National Party (BNP)	1.9 (2010)	1.9 (2010)	0	No

Source: compiled from data at the European Election Database www.nsd.uib.no/european_election_database/ and various other sources.

Parties). Several have relied on charismatic or flamboyant individuals, such as Jörg Haider (FPÖ) or Pim Fortuyn, but again this is not always the case. Thus, in terms of history, political style and policy platforms, the far right is a motley crew.

One thing that all of these parties do share is an opposition to immigration. Indeed, the centrality of immigration to far-right ideology leads several scholars to label these parties as 'anti-immigrant parties' (Gibson 2002; Givens 2005: 20; Van der Brug et al. 2005), though others argue that they cannot be considered single-issue parties, nor can support for them be explained purely in terms of their anti-immigration positions (Mudde 1999). Even though issues as diverse as Euroscepticism, regional secession or tax reform have contributed to the success of these parties in different countries, across Europe far-right electoral gains have been strongly driven by their ability to capture popular anxieties about immigration and present political elites as out of touch on this issue. The cultural protectionism that they promote certainly resonates with significant parts of the electorate in European countries, and analysis of social attitudes surveys confirms that individuals who vote for the far right tend to express strong anti-immigrant attitudes (Ellinas 2010: 23–5; Norris 2005: 181–5).

Although the far right has achieved most success in Europe, anti-immigrant parties are not a uniquely European phenomenon. The centrality of immigration to the national cultures of countries in North America and Oceania arguably limits the popular appeal of explicitly anti-immigrant parties, but there have nevertheless been sporadic attempts to mobilize sections of the electorate around this issue. In Australia, Pauline Hanson's One Nation party experienced a brief surge of support in the late 1990s (Leach et al. 2000), while New Zealand's electoral reforms in 1993 opened the door to Winston Peter's New Zealand First, which received 13.4 per cent of the vote in the 1996 general election and formed a short-lived coalition with the centre-right National Party. More recently, New Zealand First's vote dropped to 4.1 per cent of the popular vote, and it held no parliamentary seats in 2008, but this increased to 6.6 per cent in the 2011 election, when the party took eight seats.

In North America, there are presently no significant far-right political parties. In Canada, the Canadian Reform Party achieved some success in the 1990s (Laycock 2001) before merging with the Progressive Conservative Party of Canada in 2003 to form the Conservative Party of Canada. The Canadian Action party calls for a reduction of immigration, but it receives well below 1 per cent of the vote in those seats it contests and has no representation in Parliament. While immigration and multiculturalism are increasingly debated, few public voices challenge the country's progressive approach to these issues. Matters are rather different to the south of the border, where debates about immigration are nothing if not heated and divisive. Yet, despite this, the United States does not have any anti-immigrant parties of note. This is largely explained by the two-party system, in which the Democrats and

Republicans are so dominant that it is difficult for third parties of whatever political persuasion to gain a foothold. The main United States parties are sufficiently heterogeneous and loosely organized to provide opportunities for anti-immigrant mobilization within the existing party system; the right wing of the Republican Party, in particular, provides such an outlet. The nativist and 'paleoconservative' Pat Buchanan did run on the Reform Party ticket in the 2000 presidential election, but he received just 0.4 per cent of the popular vote. Today, the most important anti-immigration organization at the federal level is the House Immigration Reform Caucus, which boasts 91 members, most of them Republicans. It opposes illegal immigration but avoids an openly nativist discourse (Mudde 2012: 8). Otherwise there are a few single-issue groups that run media campaigns and lobby politicians, the most significant being Numbers USA and the Federation for American Immigration Reform (FAIR).

There is clearly a distinction, then, between the more recent countries of immigration in Europe, where the far right has achieved some notable successes, and the classic countries of immigration, where, despite some flourishes, anti-immigrant parties have not become established. Even in Europe it is possible to overestimate their importance, something that the voluminous literature on the subject possibly encourages (Norris 2005: 78–80). In most countries, the far right's share of the vote, while significant, is not large (see table 2.1 above) and mainstream parties have often operated a cordon sanitaire, refusing to enter into coalition negotiations with far-right parties, thus limiting the latter's experience of government even where they have scored electoral victories.

Against this it should be said that, in Austria, Denmark, Italy, the Netherlands and Switzerland, far-right parties *have* either entered government or formed agreements with governing parties and have been able to exert direct influence over policymaking. In Denmark, for example, the Danish People's Party played a key role in drafting restrictive immigration and citizenship legislation as a condition of its support for the centre-right coalition, and in 2011 it forced the minority government to reintroduce border controls as a condition for approving its economic plan (since revoked). In 2009 in Switzerland, politicians from the Swiss People's Party initiated a federal referendum to prohibit the construction of minarets, a deeply illiberal measure that passed by the necessary double majority. Beyond these few countries, the far right has exerted more of an indirect influence on immigration and integration by influencing mainstream parties' policy positions and by shaping public debate (Schain 2006). Norris describes this phenomenon as a 'contagion of the right':

> if radical right parties are perceived as expanding their electoral popularity due to public demand for cultural protectionism, then . . . other parties within the same country will not simply stay static; instead they will seek to emulate their success

by adopting their rhetoric and taking a more right-wing position on their signature issues of immigration, anticrime, and cultural protectionism in subsequent elections. (Norris 2005: 29)

In other words, where the far right has scored electoral successes, or threatens to do so, centre-right and centre-left parties may shift rightwards on immigration in an attempt to avoid haemorrhaging votes to upstart parties (see Bale 2003, 2008; Bale et al. 2010).

There are certainly cases where a surge in support for the far right has been followed by a rightward shift in the position of other parties. The rise of the Austrian FPÖ from the mid-1980s to the mid-1990s and the success of the Norwegian FRP in the late 1980s were both followed by centrist parties moving to the right on immigration and other issues. Nor does the contagion require large electoral victories on the national stage. In 1970s Britain, small gains by the National Front in local and parliamentary by-elections led the Conservatives to tack to the right. And in Australia, after Pauline Hanson's One Nation won 23 per cent in the 1998 Queensland state election, the Howard government responded by introducing a controversial policy of interdicting boats of asylum seekers before they could land on Australian shores (Norris 2005: 68). As one scholar puts it, 'even a modest electoral breakthrough triggers a political dynamic that influences immigration policy' (Schain 2006: 286). There are, of course, contrary cases. Norris cites the success of the French Front National in the 1980s, which was not met with a rightward shift by the other parties at the time (Norris 2005: 269). A recent systematic study of election manifestos in five Western European countries found no evidence that mainstream parties had changed their programmes when confronted with electoral losses or successful populist parties (Rooduijn et al. 2012). Yet, beyond the realm of election manifestos, there are cases where a populist contagion has undoubtedly influenced centrist parties' discourse. In France, for example, Nicolas Sarkozy's hardline statements on immigration in the 2007 French presidential election, and in his unsuccessful 2011 campaign, represented a clear attempt to recoup votes from the Front National.

It is nevertheless important to recognize that far-right parties are not the only driver of restrictive immigration rhetoric and policy proposals. This should be clear enough, given that restrictive policies are not the preserve of those countries with significant far-right parties. In countries where the far right has not achieved a breakthrough, 'normal' dynamics of party competition in a context of sceptical public opinion can lead mainstream parties to adopt tough rhetoric and policy positions. Both centre-left and centre-right parties have their own reasons for doing this: the centre-left worries about losing votes from blue-collar workers who oppose immigration, while the centre-right risks losing votes from cultural conservatives. Moreover, the centre-right may seek to wrest votes from core constituencies of the left by adopting a harder line on immigration (as happened in Britain after Enoch

Powell's anti-immigration speeches in the late 1960s caused working-class voters to switch to the Conservatives); this in turn may incentivise the centre-left to adopt more restrictive policy positions in an attempt to try and claw back lost votes. As Jeannette Money (1999) has shown, restrictive immigration legislation in Britain and France pre-dated the rise of the far right and can be explained by electoral politics and competition between centrist parties. Further supporting this line of reasoning, a recent study found that the immigration and integration policies of governments including far-right parties do not differ much from those of centre-right governments without far-right involvement (Akkerman 2012).

Thus mainstream parties are not simply pushed into adopting restrictive immigration programmes by the far right, and not all attempts to politicize immigration are a response to the threat of the far right. In the absence of a significant far-right electoral presence, mainstream parties have few electoral incentives to adopt pro-immigration positions and will seek either to avoid the issue altogether or to compete on a restrictive platform. Once the far right enters the scene, any inter-party consensus to avoid politicizing immigration is likely to be broken (Schain 2006: 286–7), and mainstream parties are more likely to adopt elements of their discourse, even if in a muted tone, than to reject them out of hand.

Finally, it is important to note the limited extent of pro-immigrant political mobilization in national elections. For the reasons discussed above, few elected politicians are willing to speak unequivocally in favour of immigration. Those who do promote its benefits tend to hedge their comments by endorsing the need for 'tough' measures on border control and illegal immigration. There are no major political parties in the liberal democracies that are dedicated to representing immigrants' interests or organized around a pro-immigrant stance in the way that the far right is organized around an anti-immigration stance. Immigrants themselves tend to be insufficiently numerous to form dedicated parties and moreover often face obstacles to political participation – the most obvious one being a lack of citizenship – which generally excludes them from voting and standing for office in national elections (though not local or municipal elections), as well as socio-economic and linguistic barriers faced by many newcomers. This is not to say that there has been no pro-immigrant political mobilization. Within mainstream parties, particularly in settler states, lobby groups such as the US Congressional Hispanic Caucus or the Congressional Hispanic Conference represent the interests of groups of immigrants and ethnic minorities. And, beyond party politics, interest groups exert an important expansionary influence on policymaking (as discussed in the next chapter). There have also been occasions where social movements or mass protests have successfully mobilized in support of immigrants. Nevertheless, the extent of pro-immigrant mobilization is rarely sufficient to offset the restrictionist demands that are generated through electoral competition.

The Immigrant Threat Revisited

As we saw earlier in the chapter, the idea that immigration presents a threat to receiving societies is not new. However, with the growing politicization of immigration from the 1990s, and especially since the terrorist attacks of 9/11, anti-immigrant actors have articulated new discourses that depict immigration as a threat to liberal states. These discourses inform citizens' perceptions and provide resources for the mobilization of anti-immigrant sentiment. As Statham and Geddes argue:

> collective mobilisation is not a direct outcome of the distributed costs and benefits of immigration policies, but of the extent and way immigration is politicised and publicly mediated, and how certain positions are made to appear more feasible, reasonable, and legitimate, compared to alternative definitions of political reality. (Statham and Geddes 2006: 251)

Discourses about immigration, like all political discourses, do not exist 'out there' floating freely, but are constructed and manipulated by actors. The politics of immigration is to some extent a 'battle over discourse' in which actors seek to define issues and shape perceptions in ways that are conducive to their interests (Hansen and Koehler 2005). But discourse is not purely instrumental, something that is constructed with pre-given preferences in mind. It is partly constitutive of preferences and interests, because the terms in which actors think about an issue construct their preferences towards it.

The discursive construction of immigration as a threat to national identity is one of the most powerful weapons in anti-immigrant actors' armoury because it taps into deep-seated affective attachments and in-group favouritism. If anti-immigrant actors can successfully depict immigrants as threatening national identity, they are well placed to foment and mobilize anti-immigrant opinion. Evidence from the World Values Survey suggests a growing attachment to the national in-group in European countries from the 1980s to the present, which is conducive to (and may also be a consequence of) this kind of anti-immigrant mobilization (Ellinas 2010: 22–5). Once a discourse of immigration as a threat to national identity is established, it is likely to prove tenacious because of its self-reinforcing nature. Given the imagined nature of national communities (Anderson 1991), if people imagine that immigration is a threat to the nation, then, in a sense, it becomes a threat. This perception is difficult to contest because, unlike, say, a belief that immigration depresses wages, a belief that immigration threatens national identity is not easily disproven.

Cas Mudde (2012: 9–12) has identified five anti-immigrant 'frames' articulated by the European far right – cultural, religious, security, economic and political – of which the cultural frame, in which immigration is seen as a threat to the traditions and homogeneity of the nation, is the most important. Since the 9/11 attacks, this is increasingly conjoined to a religious frame, in which Muslim immigrants in particular, on account of the supposedly illiberal and anti-democratic nature of Islam, are depicted as a threat to liberal democratic values. A third frame depicts immigrants as a security threat. This includes allegations that immigrants are more likely to commit criminal acts than the host population, as well as claims that immigrants pose a terrorist threat. Since 9/11 this has been fused with the cultural-religious framing to produce a discourse in which Muslim immigrants are not only or even principally a threat through individual acts of terrorism, but due to a supposed project to transform European identity and allegiances; in the most paranoiac version, Muslims are depicted as a 'fifth column' bent on transforming Europe into 'Eurabia', an anti-American and anti-Zionist Euro-Arab axis (see Bawer 2006; Ye'Or 2005). A fourth framing depicts immigrants as an economic burden on the destination country, taking jobs from natives, depressing wages and draining social benefits. A fifth, political framing represents immigrants as tools of an international elite, which conspires to undermine the average citizen. This framing most obviously links anti-immigration claims with the populist rhetoric of far-right parties.

These five framings can be found at different times in different countries, but the most important are the cultural-religious and security framings. These have come to dominate anti-immigration rhetoric, especially in Europe, and are both a consequence and a cause of the importance of identity as a driver of anti-immigrant attitudes. It is striking how many similarities there are between these ideas that contemporary immigration poses a threat to the cultural, religious and ethnic homogeneity of the nation and the nineteenth- and early twentieth-century debates discussed earlier in this chapter. The main difference is that these neo-nativist discourses tend to refer to culture rather than race, so as to avoid violating anti-racist norms that are now established across liberal democracies. Even post-fascist parties such as the French Front National or the British National Party generally avoid explicit reference to race. The focus is nevertheless on immigrants who are ethnically or culturally different, depending on the specific national or regional context: Muslims in Europe, Latinos in the United States and Asian immigrants in Australia.

The European far right has had most success in articulating a cultural-religious anti-immigrant frame in which immigrants, especially Muslim immigrants, import alien customs and beliefs that debase national cultures and European values. One of the most virulent proponents of this kind of frame – Geert Wilders, the leader of the far-right Dutch Party for Freedom (PVV) – told the Dutch Parliament:

> If we do not stop Islamification now, Eurabia and Netherabia will just be a matter of time. . . . We are heading for the end of European and Dutch civilisation as we know it. . . . Dutch citizens . . . have had enough of burkas, headscarves, the ritual slaughter of animals, so-called honour revenge, blaring minarets, female

circumcision, hymen restoration operations, abuse of homosexuals, Turkish and Arabic on the buses and trains as well as on town hall leaflets.[3]

Depending on the national context, other far-right parties focus on other immigrants and ethnic minorities, including in some cases European Jews and the Roma. The common thread running through these discourses is a contention that migration and cultural diversity undermine the nation. As a spokesman for Jobbik, the Hungarian ethno-nationalist party, put it: 'we do not believe in the division between left and right. The true division is between those who want globalisation and those who do not' (quoted in Phillips 2010).

Mainstream politicians rarely articulate an explicit cultural threat discourse. Nevertheless, both centre-left and centre-right politicians sometimes signal to voters that they recognize the anxieties on which these parties feed and make nationalist moves of their own. Centre-right parties in the Netherlands and France have certainly done this, as has the British Conservative Party, despite the absence of a serious far-right challenge from the British National Party. In particular, the mainstream European debate has come to focus on the compatibility of Islam with liberal values and the alleged failure of multiculturalism to tackle extremism. David Cameron's (2011) speech denouncing 'state multiculturalism' and calling for a more 'muscular liberalism', delivered at a counter-terrorism conference, epitomized this linkage. The joining of a cultural-religious and security threat framing has tremendous potency because it both taps into deep-seated anxieties about identity and belonging in an era of globalization and connects these anxieties to one of the core functions of the state, the provision of collective security.

In the settler societies of North America and Oceania, countries where immigration is central to narratives of national identity (albeit narratives which obscure the history of racial exclusion), representing immigrants as a cultural threat is a more difficult discursive project. Canada conspicuously lacks a nativist tradition or significant white supremacist parties. Immigration Watch Canada, the most prominent group lobbying for restrictions on immigration, is moderate by both European and American standards (Mudde 2012: 9). In the United States, any number of American conservatives and right-wing radio hosts offer up invectives about immigration, but, compared to the European far right, they tend to focus on illegality and border security rather than on a cultural-religious threat. The leading neo-nativist is probably Patrick Buchanan, whose many books warn of the threat posed by Mexican immigration, including a supposed plot to recapture parts of the American Southwest (Buchanan 2006). A more academically respectable neo-nativist argument was developed by Samuel P. Huntington, whose book *Who Are We? The Challenges to America's National Identity* depicts Latino immigration as a threat to America's Anglo-Protestant culture (Huntington 2004). But these voices are outside the mainstream, and though there are immigration sceptics among Democrats and especially Republicans, in a country where many citizens' recent forbears were immigrants and where both parties look to court Latino votes, the representation of immigrants as a cultural threat faces serious obstacles.

Conclusion

This chapter has argued that representative democracy in liberal states creates powerful demands for the restriction of immigration. Contemporary public opinion is at best sceptical towards immigration, at worst hostile. A sizeable minority and sometimes a majority of citizens express opposition towards immigration. In several European countries, far-right parties have mobilized anti-immigrant sentiment and depicted immigrants and minorities, especially Muslims, as a threat to the culture and security of the nation-state. While there are currently no significant far-right parties in Australia, Canada or the United States, single-issue groups, factions within existing parties and media pundits have articulated similar themes. The impact of European far-right parties on immigration policy varies from country to country: in the few countries where they have entered government they have had a direct effect on immigration and integration policies; in countries where they have not entered government the evidence is mixed, but they have sometimes had an indirect effect on policy by shifting public discourse and the position of other parties. Faced with the option of ignoring the far right, opposing its ideology or ceding ground, mainstream parties have often hardened their own discourse and shifted towards more restrictionist policy positions.

This presents us with a puzzle, as opposition to immigration and anti-immigrant political mobilization have evidently not translated into a whole-sale restriction of immigration. On the contrary, in most countries immigration has increased as anti-immigrant politics has intensified. Why then do the governments of liberal states not appear to reduce numbers when there is significant political pressure for them to do so? How, in other words, can we explain mass immigration in a context of restrictionist politics? The next chapter seeks to provide some answers to these questions by considering the role of political economy and constitutionalism in shaping immigration policies.

CHAPTER THREE

The Politics of Openness

In the previous chapter we saw how representative democracy generates demands for restrictive immigration policies. Yet we have also seen that liberal states do not close their doors to all migrants: immigration to liberal democracies has increased in recent years; certain immigrants are actively solicited by receiving countries; and, despite political rhetoric about 'the fight against illegal immigration', many unauthorized migrants enter or do not leave. This is all the more puzzling because the numbers of immigrants have increased at the same time as has opposition to immigration – in terms of public attitudes, salience and political mobilization. This raises an obvious question: given the pressures to restrict immigration discussed in the previous chapter, why don't liberal states appear to do so?

To answer this question it is necessary to look beyond the restrictive logics of representative democracy and nationhood and consider potential sources of more expansionist policies. This chapter argues that the capitalist economies and constitutional orders of liberal states are the principal sources of openness towards immigration. The nature of advanced capitalism generates substantial demand for immigrants, while the normative and institutional foundations of a constitutional state impose limits on governments' ability to restrict immigration. Since capitalist accumulation and adherence to liberal norms are no less important than democratic mandates, this creates countervailing pressures on governments to those seen in the previous chapter.

Losing Control?

One possible explanation of why the restrictionist pressures discussed in the previous chapter do not result in more restrictive *outcomes* is that states are unable to deliver effective controls. This argument is associated with claims about the diminution of state sovereignty in the context of globalization. One of the chief exponents of this view, the corporate strategist Kenichi Ohmae, argued in the 1990s that a 'borderless world' was emerging in which transnational corporations and imperatives of the global marketplace would render the nation-state irrelevant. For Ohmae, this will lead to 'the free flow of information, money, goods and services, as well as the free migration of people and corporations' (Ohmae 1991: xii). More recently, the economist Jagdish Bhagwati (2006: 553) claimed that 'borders are beyond control and little can be done to really cut down on immigration', while the sociologist Saskia Sassen (1996: 104) has argued that economic globalization and the international human rights regime 'reduce the autonomy of the state in immigration policy making'. To put it simply, states are 'losing control'.

There is an element of truth to these claims, especially in the more nuanced version articulated by Sassen. The flow of people across national boundaries has indeed increased as a result of regional and global market integration, and international agreements do constrain state action, particularly regarding forced migrants (chapter 5). Even if they wanted to do so, therefore, states are unable to seal their borders. But this is a long way short of saying that states are 'losing control' or that borders are 'beyond control', much less that we are moving inexorably towards a 'borderless world'. Arguments along these lines overstate the role of exogenous constraints while underplaying the capacity of states to influence migration flows. Take irregular migration. Even if states may be unable to 'control' unauthorized entry and residence, their actions – ranging from border patrols to workplace raids – undoubtedly influence migrants' behaviour. While it is true that the fundamental drivers of migration are beyond the control of individual states, governments' policies act as an important intervening variable. As two economists of migration argue, 'immigration policies . . . serve as a filter between the desire to migrate and the actual moves that take place. Economic and demographic variables strongly influence world migration, but that fact does not diminish the importance of policy' (Hatton and Williamson 2002: 29). The idea that states are *losing* control also logically presupposes an era in which they enjoyed more control than they do today. This is questionable, to say the least. The advent of immigration controls is historically quite recent (dating from the early twentieth century) and it is arguable that states exercise *more* influence over migration flows today than in the previous century.

Most importantly for the argument of this book, the claim that forces of globalization have undermined the state's capacity to 'control' migration rests on a false dichotomy between supposedly exogenous factors and endogenous imperatives of the liberal state. The fact that economic globalization and human rights regimes influence migration means neither that liberal states are powerless nor that they are subject to global forces 'out there'. States are themselves actors in international and supranational regimes such as the EU, and moreover they have their own internal reasons for accepting migration flows on economic and humanitarian grounds. As this chapter will show, the imperatives both to maximize economic growth and productivity and to observe self-imposed constraints associated with liberal norms and human rights standards are endogenous to liberal states.

Demand for Labour Migration

Immigration has long been considered important to the performance of advanced capitalist economies. In his 1967 study, the economist and Marshall Plan architect Charles P. Kindleberger argued that Europe's economic recovery in the decades following the Second World War was due in large part to immigrants: immigration fed economic growth by boosting the labour supply while holding down wage inflation. Immigrants formed a flexible workforce that could fill labour shortages for low wages, acting as a counter-inflationary force during a period of sustained economic growth. Just over a decade later, the pioneering political economist of migration Gary Freeman argued that migrant labour had become a 'structural requirement of advanced capitalism' (Freeman 1979: 3).

Since the postwar years the advanced economies have of course undergone fundamental transformations. The various processes of economic globalization – including the integration of national economies into regional and global markets, the deregulation of transnational capital flows, the liberalization of international trade, increases in foreign direct investment, and the rise of multinational corporations – have changed the nature of capitalism and the role of governments in managing capitalist accumulation. These transformations have meant that international migration has become more economically important than ever. A side effect of the global integration of markets for goods, services and capital has been greater flows of people between and within those markets. The scale and velocity of cross-border flows of people may lag behind the flows of capital and goods, but the effect of increased economic interconnectedness has clearly been to stimulate migration. Rising demand for migrant workers, both high- and low-skilled, in the rich economies is more than matched by the potential supply of labour from low- and middle-income countries, while cheaper transportation has reduced the transaction costs of migrating for work. For the rich liberal democracies, this has meant increasing levels of labour immigration, as their economies draw in workers from a diverse range of origin countries.

As discussed above, it is quite misleading to view governments as being compelled to accept economic migrants. Rather, governments actively engage in the management of migration – soliciting some types and restricting others – as part of wider economic growth strategies. Such is the importance of economic migration to the accumulation strategies of OECD countries that James Hollifield (2004) argues a new type of state, the 'migration state', has emerged since the late twentieth century, for which the regulation of international migration is essential to the pursuit of competitive advantage. The numbers of labour migrants in rich economies certainly lends prima facie support to this view. According to the OECD (2010: 350), by 2008, foreign-born workers accounted for 26.5 per cent of the labour force in Australia and 16.5 per cent in the United States. In the larger European economies, foreign workers were also significant, amounting to 12.6 per cent of the labour force in the UK and 11.8 per cent in France. Most dramatically of all, in some European countries that have become major destinations only since the 1990s, the figures were higher still: 20.3 per cent in Ireland and 18.2 per cent in Spain. The scale of migrant labour flows has reduced since 2008, as the economic crisis has led to a reduction of inflows and caused some migrants to return home, especially free movement migrants in the European Union. But the downturn has been relatively modest: inflows of labour migrants to OECD countries totalled around 880,000 in 2007 and 780,000 in 2010 – not a massive reduction in the midst of the worst economic crisis for a century (OECD 2012a: 17).

To understand how labour migration is governed requires some disaggregation since low-skilled and temporary labour migration is associated with different patterns of demand and different regulatory frameworks than highly skilled migration. Some scholars have argued that demand for low-skilled migrant workers is structurally embedded in the advanced economies. In an influential analysis, Michael J. Piore contended that the labour markets of advanced industrial economies are split into two sectors: a primary sector largely reserved for natives and a secondary sector for migrants. Migrants provide a flexible, low-wage workforce to fill jobs at the bottom of the labour hierarchy that native workers are unmotivated to perform as much because of the low social status attached to them as the low remuneration. Migrants, who 'come from outside and remain apart from the social structure in which the jobs are located' (Piore 1979: 34), are more willing to work in these low-status occupations because they will focus on the income (which will be higher than in their country of origin) and will be affected less by the status since they are not so embedded in the social structure that frames the job hierarchy. In addition, temporary labour migrants provide a workforce that can respond to the 'flux and uncertainty' (ibid.: 36) of economic activity, such as variability in seasonal demand. Rather than being a permanent workforce that is inactive during periods of low demand or that requires costly layoffs, migrants provide a labour force for the 'variable portion of demand' (ibid.: 40) because they can be hired and fired according to short-term production needs.

Though aspects of the dual labour market hypothesis have not aged well – notably the idea that the primary sector excludes migrants – the argument that migrants fill low-status and low-wage jobs has been confirmed by developments since the late 1970s. The so-called 3D (dirty, dangerous or demeaning) jobs are increasingly undertaken by migrant workers, as are jobs that have high variability of demand such as seasonal work. A clear example of the latter are the agricultural sectors of many OECD countries, which are heavily reliant on migrant workers, often recruited on temporary programmes. Though there is cross-national variation depending on the specific labour market structures in particular countries, in general the main sectors in which low-skilled labour migrants work are agriculture, health care, social care, construction and tourism. As we shall see in chapter 4, in an attempt to tap into this pool of cheap labour, both employers and governments have developed a renewed interest in temporary labour migration programmes. It is also important to note that in many countries low-skill labour demand is met by irregular migrants, something which governments are often less than honest about, as 'illegal migration' is universally deplored in official discourse, even when tolerated in practice.

At the other end of the labour market, the advanced economies increasingly seek to attract highly skilled migrants. This is a more recent phenomenon than the structural demand for low-skilled labour, and is associated with the transition to post-Fordist production patterns and the rise of so-called knowledge economies. Skills shortages among native workforces have generated demand for highly qualified migrants in a number of sectors, including IT, engineering, medicine and scientific research. Most OECD countries are now net recipients of highly skilled migrants, particularly the United States, Canada and Australia, which have received significant inflows of tertiary-educated migrants (OECD 2009). Between 2000 and 2010, the proportion of migrants to OECD countries with a university degree rose five percentage points, to 31 per cent, while among the native-born population it rose four percentage points, to 29 per cent. By 2010, over 50 per cent of all immigrants to Canada and 47 per cent of immigrants to Britain had completed tertiary education, the highest levels among rich countries. Other countries had much lower levels. In Italy and Greece the proportion of university-educated migrants was 11 and 13 per cent respectively (OECD 2012b).

These figures show the considerable variation between countries, but the overall trend across the OECD has clearly been towards increased levels of highly skilled immigrants. In what is sometimes described as a 'competition for talent' or 'battle for brains' (Economist 2009), the governments of OECD countries have, to varying degrees, tried to solicit highly skilled migrants with favourable entry conditions, including statuses that lead to permanent settlement and come with generous rights for accompanying family members. While the classic immigration countries have led the field, a few European countries such as the UK have also entered into this competition, and the European Union has tried to encourage the recruitment of highly skilled migrants to member states with its Blue Card Directive (see chapter 5). A related though smaller-scale phenomenon has been the creation of special migration routes for foreign entrepreneurs and investors, who are offered advantageous visa packages in return for commitment to invest in destination countries. Compared to low-skilled migrants, who are discussed warily if at all by politicians, highly skilled and 'high-value' migrants are celebrated in official discourse. The need to attract the 'best and brightest' has become a mantra in many countries, with highly skilled migrants championed as essential to innovation, competitiveness and growth.

A third important type of labour migration is intra-corporate transferees (ICTs). One of the most noted developments in the globalized economy in recent years has been the rise of multinational corporations (MNCs), which by definition are based in more than one country. MNCs often seek to transfer employees between offices situated in different locations. In order to attract inward investment by these companies, many governments have adopted policies to facilitate such movements. As with migration policies aimed at the highly skilled, visa regimes for ICTs vary between countries, but the overall trend has been one of liberalization. In the UK, for example, 22,000 intra-corporate transferees entered the country in 2009, which represented 60 per cent of all non-EU skilled workers that year.

Another migration flow that is of growing economic importance for many of the advanced economies is international students. The number of students enrolled outside their country of citizenship has grown particularly sharply since the mid-1990s (OECD 2009: 3) and has continued to rise during the economic crisis (OECD 2012a: 36). Most international students enrol in OECD countries and most come from non-OECD countries. China and India are the largest source countries, while the main destination countries are the United States (660,600 international students enrolled in 2009), the United Kingdom (369,000), Australia (257,600) and France (249,100). In total, OECD countries received about 2.6 million students from around the world in 2009 (OECD 2012a: 36). The international education market has become big business, with universities and colleges competing to attract overseas students, who generally pay higher fees than domestic students. With this comes pressure from organized lobbies for governments to facilitate student inflows and offer incentives such as post-study work opportunities.

Mobilizing Labour Demand

If economic demand for migrant labour is structurally embedded in the advanced capitalist economies, it remains to be seen how this is translated into political demands for liberalized migration policies. In two influential papers, Gary P. Freeman (1995, 2006) has argued that immigration policymaking in liberal states is shaped by organized interest groups which are able to demand expansionist policies contrary to the broadly restrictionist wishes of the wider public. The influence of these pro-immigrant groups – or clients – helps to explain why there is what he calls an 'expansionary bias' (1995: 883) in the politics of immigration in liberal states and therefore a persistent 'gap' between public opinion and official policies.

Freeman's model inverts the usual idea that politics shapes policy, and instead proposes that the type of political mobilization around a given policy depends upon how its costs and benefits are distributed. The benefits (B) and costs (C) of a policy can be either concentrated (c) or diffuse (d), depending on whether they are borne by a relatively large or small number of actors. This yields four logical combinations and four possible modes of politics: client (cB, dC), interest group (cB, cC), majoritarian (dB, dC) and entrepreneurial (dB, cC). Freeman's central contention is that the economic benefits of labour migration are concentrated on relatively few actors, while the costs are diffused over a larger group. This distribution of concentrated benefits and diffuse costs means that pro-immigration 'clients' who stand to receive substantial benefits from immigration have greater incentives to organize than persons who bear its costs. The main clients who stand to gain are employers (who benefit from the cheap labour and skills that immigrants supply), as well as immigrant lobby groups (who advance the interests of families and ethnic groups of those who make up immigration streams). Those who stand to lose are those workers with whom immigrants compete in the labour markets, as well as, to some extent, the wider public, who bear adaptation costs associated with immigrant integration. Freeman's model predicts that highly organized employer and ethnic lobby groups who are supportive of larger intakes of immigrants will exercise greater influence over policy than the 'unorganized public' who want more restrictive policies.

There has been considerable debate about Freeman's contention that governments respond to pro-immigration organized groups while 'ignoring the widespread but poorly articulated opposition of the general public' (1995: 885) (see Boswell 2007a; Brubaker 1995; Joppke 1999; Statham and Geddes 2006). In the United States and the other traditional countries of immigrant settlement, employers' organizations and well-organized immigrant lobby groups do indeed exercise significant influence over immigration policymaking (Tichenor 2002). For example, recent attempts to control immigration across the US–Mexican border and to clamp down on irregular migrant workers in the agricultural sector have met with opposition from agribusiness in the Southern states. Moreover, in the classic countries of immigration, the description of public opposition as unorganized has some plausibility, given the relative absence of anti-immigrant party political mobilization, as discussed in the previous chapter. The model arguably works less well for European countries, however, where pro-immigrant lobbies are far less entrenched and public opposition to immigration has become increasingly organized through anti-immigrant parties (Joppke 1999).

Nevertheless, if we relax some of the assumptions of Freeman's model, its central insight that immigration policy is strongly influenced by organized interests can be applied in Europe as well. Indeed, precisely because of the levels of anti-immigrant sentiment and political mobilization in many European countries, the role of employers' organizations is essential to explain why many of those countries remain relatively open to labour migration. Two recent, and otherwise contrasting, studies of the political economy of migration both concur on this. Alexander Caviedes (2010) shows how labour migration policy is driven by firms whose demand for immigration is shaped by their sector-specific 'flexibility needs', leading to different labour migration policies within countries and similar policies in the same industries across countries. Drawing on the varieties of capitalism literature, Georg Menz's (2009) study argues that the lobbying of 'labour market interest associations' – in other words, employers' associations and trade unions – is influenced by nationally variable production systems. Despite their differences, both studies provide empirical support for the fundamental importance of employer demands in shaping economic immigration policies in Europe. And, as Menz argues, the decisive influence of business in pushing for more open economic immigration policies can be seen when this policy field is compared to asylum, where the relative lack of influence of migrants' rights NGOs creates less of a counter-weight to the populist demands that emanate from electoral and party politics.

This last observation points to an important limitation of the client politics framework, namely that it addresses only economic forms of immigration. Other immigration policy fields – for example, asylum or family migration – are populated by different actors and exhibit very different logics. On Freeman's own terms, the distribution of the costs and benefits of these types of immigration is very different from that of economic types. Given this, there is no reason to expect that all forms of immigration policy will be shaped by a client politics mode. In more recent work, Freeman has acknowledged this, and has developed his interest-based approach to consider other areas of immigration policymaking by disaggregating immigration policy into analytically distinct components. For example, while he maintains that labour immigration policymaking is characterized by client politics,[4] the different cost–benefit matrix of asylum claims means that this sub-field is characterized by 'entrepreneurial politics' (Freeman 2006: 238–40).

A more fundamental challenge to Freeman's model has to do with its implicit theory of the state. Freeman's account assumes that policy is determined by the relative strength of organized interests, with those interests that are able to mobilize most effectively exercising greater influence on government. Missing entirely are the state actors who actually make policy – legislators, civil servants, government advisors, etc. The state appears merely as a conduit or broker between conflicting interests – a passive mechanism for turning the 'inputs' of organized civil society into policy 'outputs'. As Boswell (2007a) argues, this is a questionable view of the state, as it fails to account for the interests of government actors themselves and the ways in which government strategies will influence which non-governmental actors are granted access and listened to. Particularly when faced with challenges from anti-immigrant parties, why would governments respond to the demands of employers for open immigration policies over populist appeals for restriction?

This question requires a reintroduction of the state perspective on immigration. One of the core imperatives of liberal states is to secure the conditions of capital accumulation, including a favourable investment climate for transnational capital. Since firms' investment decisions are informed at least partly by their ability to recruit migrant labour, and in the case of multinational corporations to transfer workers between offices, governments seeking to attract foreign direct investment and to promote domestic growth have powerful incentives to enable immigration flows. Immigration policy becomes part of a much wider competitiveness agenda. Exactly how much and what kind of immigration will depend upon the labour market conditions and sectoral composition of a given national economy, but some level of demand for migrant labour is inevitable under advanced capitalism. It is therefore misleading to depict governments as being pushed into adopting 'liberal' immigration policies by pro-immigrant interests, as if those interests were entirely exogenous to the project of governing. Rather, since governments have their own interests in promoting economic growth, to the extent that they perceive relatively free flows of migrant workers as essential to growth, they will concur with the need for economic migration. Another way of putting this is that, in advanced capitalism, the interests of state actors are closely aligned with the interests of capital, so that the 'demands' of the latter are also the 'needs' of the former.

Liberal Norms and the Limits of Control

A second source of openness in the politics of immigration is liberal norms. This section considers the core liberal norms and how these norms are embedded in state institutions. While all of the facets considered so far are important aspects of contemporary liberal states, the ideas and institutions discussed here represent the essence of liberal statehood.

In its very etymology, liberalism reveals a commitment to liberty. Although the implications of this commitment vary, all liberals share an understanding of freedom as a property of individual human beings and all support the limitation of constraints upon that freedom. One of the earliest liberals, John Locke, famously argued that human beings enjoy a natural right of self-ownership from which there follows a series of rights held against other human beings and, crucially, against the government (Locke 2003 [1689]). A later, equally influential architect of liberalism, John Stuart Mill, argued for maximal freedom of speech and expression and poured scorn on both political tyranny and the pressures for social conformity that he believed undermined human flourishing. The 'one very simple principle' that he proposed in *On Liberty* states that 'the sole end for which mankind are warranted, individually or collectively, in interfering with the liberty of action of any of their number is self-protection. That the only purpose for which power can rightfully be exercised over any member of a civilized community, against his will, is to prevent harm to others' (Mill 1974 [1859]: 68). More recently, the foremost liberal thinker of the twentieth century, John Rawls, began his argument for 'justice as fairness' with an assumption that individuals are 'free and equal persons' with an innate capacity to develop a sense of justice and a conception of the good (Rawls 2001: 18–19).

The primacy of freedom in liberalism has several implications for the organization of the state. A liberal political system is one that respects individual freedoms and treats persons as equals. Thus the state should not interfere in the private lives of individuals – telling them which religion to follow or what views can be expressed – nor should it discriminate against persons on the basis of their religion, their way of life, or ascriptive characteristics such as sex or skin colour. Citizens of liberal states are equal before the law and enjoy civil and political (and some liberals would also say social) rights, which must be respected by other citizens but also by the state itself. As Brian Barry puts it, 'the basic idea of liberalism is to create a set of rights under which people are treated equally in certain respects, and then to leave them to deploy these rights (alone or in association with others) in pursuit of their own ends' (Barry 1996: 538). If a person's rights are violated, a liberal state provides mechanisms for their redress. Of course, all of this is an ideal type, and many liberal states fail to live up to these descriptions in practice. But the point is that there is an identifiable core of liberal norms which gives rise to a distinct model of political organization that we call the liberal state.

Liberal norms are embedded in both public discourse and the political institutions of liberal states. At the discursive level, expressions that clearly violate principles of freedom and equality – for example, openly racist statements or misogynistic attitudes – are marginalized and in some cases even criminalized (see Bleich 2011 for a discussion of the tensions between upholding liberal freedoms and combating racism). And, in a liberal order, politicians and other public figures will often appeal to liberal norms to justify their policies and generate support for their actions. Indeed, such is the shared commitment to freedom in liberal states that virtually all profess to support it. Liberal values are also institutionalized through the constitutional order. In liberal states, political power is grounded in a constitution, which sets out the structure and functions of government and specifies the rights of citizens. Since constitutions need to be interpreted and laws evaluated in light of constitutional principles, liberal states have court systems and judiciaries whose role it is to uphold the constitution and protect the rights of citizens. One of the central principles behind constitutionalism is the idea that certain rights should be beyond the reach of democratic politics, so that, even if they enjoy majority support, actions that violate basic rights or freedoms are impermissible. This is central to liberals' historic concern about the 'tyranny of the majority' and the potential for abuse of individual and minority rights in democratic systems.

Liberal norms are an important source of expansionary dynamics in immigration policymaking. If the interests of capital generate demand for 'wanted' economic immigrants, liberal norms place limits on what governments can legitimately do in their attempts to restrict 'unwanted' immigration – irregular migrants, asylum-seekers and family migrants. According to an influential strand of the migration literature, liberal states accept 'unwanted' immigration and extend rights to immigrants because of the influence of liberal norms and the ability of pro-immigrant actors to oppose and constrain restrictive government policies that conflict with these norms (Guiraudon 2000; Hollifield 1992; Joppke 1998). In the words of two leading proponents of this view:

> constitutionally guaranteed fundamental freedoms have been successfully invoked by independent courts to protect migrants against vindictive state executives. This is a case of 'self-limited' sovereignty, in which liberal norms circumscribe the ability of democratic governments to control the entry and stay of people on their national territory. (Guiraudon and Joppke 2001: 12)

Contrary to the 'postnationalist' argument that states have lost sovereignty because of a global human rights discourse founded on 'universal personhood' (Soysal 1994; Jacobson 1996), these norms are not external constraints imposed upon liberal states by the international regime. They are, rather, constitutive of what it is to be a liberal state, and, to the extent that they limit the state's capacity to control migration, the limits are self-imposed – hence 'self-limited sovereignty'. As with Freeman's client politics, this thesis identifies conflicts between pro- and anti-immigrant actors primarily in domestic institutions, but, unlike client politics, which pits employers against publics, here the chief restrictionist actors are governments and the main expansionist actors are pro-immigrant interest groups and judges. Constitutional courts are venues in which migrant NGOs and migrants themselves can seek judicial rulings that limit the executive's capacity to exclude and remove them.

This line of argument offers a more promising way of explaining openness towards immigration in areas such as asylum and family reunion, where governments have little economic interest in promoting immigration, but where liberal norms commit them, formally at least, to respecting individuals' rights to refuge and a family life. It also helps explain the persistence of irregular immigration, since the kind of policy instruments that states have at their disposal to restrict unauthorized entry and overstay are highly intrusive and often in conflict with liberal norms. Immigration control is an example of what Antje Ellermann calls 'coercive social regulation': 'measures that control individual behaviour in highly intrusive ways, impose severe personal costs on the regulated, and often rely on the routine use of physical force for their enforcement' (Ellermann 2009: 12).

Many aspects of statehood rest ultimately upon the threat of violence, as Max Weber's reference to a 'monopoly of the legitimate use of physical force' (Weber 1991 [1919]) reminds us. Immigration control often requires the actual use of physical force to exclude, capture, detain and remove 'unwanted' immigrants. Moreover, it requires the use of force on people who are sometimes vulnerable and often guilty of nothing more than seeking a better life. Thus, for all the tough rhetoric in public debate, when it comes to the gritty business of excluding and removing unauthorized immigrants, the liberal state encounters its moral conscience and its constitutional limits. This is not to say that illiberal measures are absent from the immigration control practices of liberal states (Guild, Groenendijk and Carrera 2009; King 1999); rather that they are less readily deployed than is the case in non-liberal states, and that, when they are deployed, such measures are often challenged by civil society actors who use both normative appeals and legal avenues to mobilize against them.

Mobilizing Liberal Norms

There are many dimensions to the 'self-limited sovereignty' of the liberal state, and many ways in which liberal norms and institutions generate expansionary dynamics in immigration policy. This section considers how liberal norms limit the state's capacity to control immigration in four distinct ways: first, through normative constraints on selection criteria, which limit the state's ability to discriminate between immigrants on the basis of ascriptive characteristics such as ethnicity and race; second, family rights in national and international law, which limit the state's ability to control family migration, including marriage and family reunion; third, rights to humanitarian protection, again in both national and international law, which restrict the state's ability to exclude asylum-seekers; and, finally, normative constraints on the identification and removal of irregular immigrants.

One way in which liberalism delimits the state's room for manoeuvre consists of the normative constraints it imposes on the selection of immigrants. As we saw in chapter 2, during the early to mid-twentieth century, both Australia and the United States used immigration policy as a tool of nation-building. The White Australia policy and the US National Origins Quota were both designed to discriminate on the basis of race and ethnicity, so that, for certain ethnic and racial groups, it was virtually impossible to immigrate to those countries. As the century unfolded, the practice of 'selecting by origin' (Joppke 2005) in the classic settler countries as well as European postcolonial countries came under increasing pressure on account of its violation of principles of universalism and non-discrimination. Today, immigration policies in liberal states are largely 'de-ethnicized', which is to say that explicit selection on the basis of race or ethnicity is widely seen as illegitimate. It is true that there are many exceptions and special cases in various countries' immigration law for the nationals of particular countries, but these are invariably justified on grounds of national identity rather than ethnicity per se (even if ethno-cultural similarity is sometimes in the background). This notwithstanding, the universalistic thrust of liberal rights has significantly narrowed the parameters for selection of immigrants, making it all but impossible for governments to reproduce a particular ethnic understanding of nationhood through immigration controls. The main selection mechanisms avoid 'ascriptive' criteria and concentrate on economic criteria such as education and skills or income and wealth. As Joppke puts it: 'the state may consider the individual only for what she *does*, not for what she *is*' (ibid.: 2). An important implication of this is that immigration now invariably brings about ethnic and cultural diversification. Given the persistent importance of nationhood as a foundation of the liberal state, this has led to protracted debates about whether and how to maintain unity in a context of cultural pluralism (see chapter 7).

A further way in which states' admission policies are constrained by liberal norms relates to the moral and legal constraints on their ability to control two of the most important migration flows of recent years: family migration and asylum-seekers. The admission of family migrants has become increasingly important since the 1960s and 1970s, when the United States reformed its immigration system and many European countries wound up their guest-worker recruitment programmes. A secondary flow of family migrants developed from this time, and family migration now accounts for the single largest immigration category in many countries, including the United States, France, Austria and the Netherlands (see chapter 4). States accept family migration through a complex mix of self-interest and normative and legal constraints. It was once assumed that families are more likely than lone (mostly male) individuals to integrate into receiving societies, thus family reunification was condoned. However, with the problematization of family migration in many countries, especially in Europe, where the 'migrant family' is often depicted as an obstacle to integration (Kraler and Kofman 2009), it is increasingly clear that family migration has become an 'unwanted' flow, and that normative and legal constraints play a crucial role in explaining why liberal states remain open towards family migrants.

The term 'family migration' encompasses at least three distinct flows, each with different moral and legal implications: whole family migration, in which several family members migrate together; family reunification, when family members have previously been separated by migration; and family formation, when a person migrates to form a family, often through marriage (Kraler and Kofman 2009: 2). All three are protected to varying degrees through rights to family life enshrined in national law and international conventions. Article 8 of the European Convention on Human Rights, to which 47 European countries are party, provides a right to respect for a person's 'private and family life', and has significantly affected the immigration decisions taken by the public authorities of signatory countries. At the national level, constitutional provisions based upon the right to a family life have also required governments to revise their immigration policies. In a classic article on the issue, Christian Joppke showed how the German constitutional court made a series of decisions that delimited the federal government's attempts to restrict immigration, first by upholding residence rights and then by establishing that family rights constrained immigration policy on family reunification. Although he noted variation between states – showing that Britain in the 1970s and 1980s was altogether more effective at restricting family immigration because of its lack of a codified constitution and constitutional court to constrain parliamentary sovereignty – Joppke concluded that 'accepting unwanted immigration is inherent in the liberalness of liberal states' (Joppke 1998: 292).

Asylum-seekers form a second category of 'unwanted' immigration that is circumscribed by liberal norms. All of the liberal states discussed in this book are signatories to the 1951 UN Convention Relating to the Status of Refugees and its 1967 Protocol, which removed geographical and temporal restrictions from the Convention. These treaties, which are the basis for international refugee law, define what a refugee is, outline the rights of refugees, and create legal obligations for states in their treatment of refugees. In particular, Article 33 of the Convention establishes the principle of *non-refoulement*, which requires states not to 'expel or return a refugee in any manner whatsoever to the frontiers of territories where her life or freedom would be threatened'. Thus a person who arrives at the territory of a signatory state and claims asylum cannot be returned if he or she faces a well-founded fear of persecution because of his or her race, religion, nationality, membership of a social group, or political opinion.

Despite the politicization of asylum and the advent of ever more draconian asylum policies since the 1990s (see chapter 4), liberal states remain constrained by their commitment to the principle of asylum. Once a person has lodged an asylum claim, a legal process is set in train to establish whether that person does indeed have a 'well-founded fear of persecution'. The asylum determination process can be highly complex and is often fraught with legal, administrative and empirical complications. It can take a considerable period of time to decide a case, and there are usually various stages of appeal. At the end of the process, some claimants will be granted full refugee status, some a subsidiary status, and others will be refused. But, even for those who are refused protection, removal does not always automatically follow, as there are often problems with return if third countries do not accept a person as their national. In short, notwithstanding the considerable efforts that states make to prevent the entry of potential asylum-seekers, the asylum system creates an important route for entry and provides a further example of how liberal principles limit states' room for manoeuvre.

One flow that liberal states might be expected to face fewer legal and normative constraints in controlling is 'illegal' or irregular migration. It is central to both liberal self-understanding and international law that states are entitled to make decisions about whom they admit and to refuse entry to those without authorization. However, many irregular migrants actually *enter* with authorization – for example, on short-stay tourist or family visit visas – and become irregular by overstaying or violating the terms of their visa. Therefore, control of irregular immigration is as much, if not more, about identifying and removing undocumented persons who are already present on a state's territory as it is about policing territorial borders. The instruments used to identify and remove irregular immigrants are not only costly and logistically difficult but also highly coercive and therefore in potential conflict with liberal norms.

The 'cruel power' (Gibney 2008) of deportation is a case in point. Attempts to deport irregular migrants are generally challenged through the courts on a number of different grounds. This can significantly retard and sometimes block the state's ability to exclude unauthorized residents. Forced removal can also generate resistance from civil society actors. In a comparative study of deportation in Germany and the United States, Antje Ellermann (2005, 2006, 2009) shows that the coercive capacity of these states is strongly influenced by the ability of immigration officials to resist local opposition to removal efforts. Ellermann first challenges the idea that non-implementation is a result of immigration bureaucrats shirking their responsibilities. In fact, deportation officers demonstrate a 'strong commitment to fulfilment of their legislative mandates', but they operate in environments in which they regularly face opposition from local actors – including local politicians, migrants' rights groups, churches, members of the public, and immigrants themselves – who mobilize to resist the deportation efforts of the state (Ellermann 2005: 1240). Faced with the harsh human costs of deportation, Ellermann found that the organized public abandons its restrictionist preferences and campaigns for immigrants' interests (2006: 306). Even politicians who supported deportation policies at the legislative stage of the policy cycle will sometimes campaign against specific removal efforts if people in their constituencies are affected.

A similar dynamic of civil society resistance to government attempts to exclude irregular immigrants was identified in a study of 'human service workers' in the Netherlands. The context for the study was the Dutch Linking Act of 1998, which charged social service providers with the task of excluding undocumented immigrants from public services. According to Joanne van der Leun, the goals of this legislation were often 'vague and conflicting', and the service providers enjoyed a degree of autonomy and discretion in implementing it (2006: 315). She argues that the norms and values of these professionals sometimes led them to resist the official, exclusionary policy objectives. In sectors with a high level of professionalism, such as health care and primary education, service providers often bent the rules and effectively undermined the exclusionary intent of the policy. In sectors with a lower level of professionalism, such as social assistance, there was stricter adherence to the legislation.

Conclusion

We can now take stock of the argument so far. This and the previous chapter have unpacked the claim made in chapter 1 that immigration politics is shaped by four facets of the liberal state: representative democracy, constitutionalism, nationhood and capitalism. In chapter 2 we saw how public opinion and party politics generate pressures for the restriction and control of immigration. Popular debate about immigration is founded upon, and also shapes, beliefs about nationhood – about who 'we' are and what effect newcomers have upon the national community. Very often, both today and in the past, immigration is depicted as a threat to the identity and security of that community. Given these powerful pressures for closure, the question arises as to why liberal states admit as many immigrants as they do. The present chapter has sought to answer this question by identifying two primary sources of openness: first, by showing how immigration has become essential to the accumulation strategies of advanced capitalist economies that operate in increasingly integrated regional and global markets; second, by showing how liberal norms and values are embedded in the constitutional orders and civil societies of liberal states, which constrains governments' ability to control immigration. Despite populist demands for restriction, both demand for 'wanted' immigrants and limits on the control of 'unwanted' immigrants are inherent to the liberal state.

None of the conflicting imperatives for immigration policy that come from democratic politics, nationalism, liberal rights or capitalist accumulation can be ignored. Governments of liberal states are expected to seek democratic mandates for their policies and be responsive to the demands of citizens; they are expected to respect the rule of law and uphold human rights; they are expected to prioritize the interests of nationals and ensure the security of the national community; and they are expected to promote economic growth by securing the conditions for capital accumulation. Immigration exposes some deep, and potentially irreconcilable, tensions between these tasks. Is it possible to pursue an immigration policy that simultaneously promotes economic growth, upholds human rights and commands popular support? If not, how can governments manage the inevitable contradictions? As will be discussed in chapter 8, the short answer is that governments muddle through, sometimes appealing to populist and nationalist sentiment, yet often accommodating employer demands and accepting rights-based constraints. Yet, as immigration is increasingly politicized and demands for restriction grow louder in many countries, reconciliation with the structural demand for labour migration and the rights-based unavoidability of other kinds of migration becomes increasingly difficult to achieve.

At this point, some caveats should be made. It is quite clear that not all liberal states are alike when it comes to immigration. The settler states of North America have very different historical experiences of migration compared to the 'reluctant' European countries, such as Britain, France or Germany, not to mention the more recent countries of immigration such as Italy and Spain. It is equally clear that these historical differences influence patterns of political contestation as well as policy outcomes. The United States, for example, has an elaborate and highly entrenched policy regime that has evolved over many years, whereas a country such as Italy, which has experienced net inflows only since the 1980s (Calavita 2004), has an altogether less institutionalized pattern of immigration politics and a more nascent repertoire of policies. These cross-national differences are obviously important, and it is virtually a truism to observe that the specific experiences of different countries shape the wider political, social and cultural context in which immigration policies are made.

Furthermore, the four facets discussed in this and the previous chapter also vary cross-nationally, and this variation will influence policies. While we have seen that the generic influence of representative democracy on immigration policy is broadly restrictive, the extent to which this is the case will vary according to the precise nature of representative democracy in a particular country – for example, the type of electoral and party system, public attitudes and media culture. The presence of a far-right party or charismatic anti-immigrant politician can also be expected to affect the degree to which representative politics generates anti-immigrant policy 'inputs'. Similarly, the role of liberal norms will vary according to the constitutional structure of a country, such as the content of its bill of rights and the degree of judicial activism, as well as the strength and size of the NGO sector and civil society organizations at the local level. The influence of nationhood will depend upon how the national community is imagined, and in particular on the extent to which immigration is part of national narratives and myths. Although these are often deep-seated self-images, they evolve and change as political elites articulate different 'stories of peoplehood' (Smith 2003) for their own purposes, sometimes to celebrate, sometimes to denigrate the effect of immigration on a nation's way of life. And, lastly, while the influence of economic imperatives is broadly expansive, the nature of demand for migrant labour will vary according to a given country's labour market conditions, sectoral composition and industrial relations, together with the influence of business lobby groups. These points are summarized in table 3.1.

The fourfold analysis of the liberal state presented in this and the previous chapter provides a framework for considering the politics of immigration across different countries (as well as across policy sub-types). In some coun-

TABLE 3.1 Comparing the four facets across liberal states

	Actors and factors	Cross-national variation	Expected policy effects
Representative democracy	Political parties, public opinion, media	Electoral system, party system, size of far right, media culture and ownership	Restrictive, depending on politicization, success of anti-immigrant parties, and public opinion
Constitutionalism	Courts, judiciaries, NGOs	Constitutional structure, judicial review, number and size of migrants' rights NGOs	Expansive, depending on court system, constitutional rights, and strength of NGOs
Nationhood	Political elites, public opinion, national symbols and narratives	History of immigration, role of immigration in national stories of peoplehood	Restrictive, depending on role of immigration in national narratives
Capitalism	Businesses, unions	Variety of capitalism (e.g., liberal versus coordinated), labour market institutions, industrial relations	Expansive, depending on labour market conditions, influence of employers

tries, the effect of factors driving towards closure will be stronger than in others, and vice versa for factors that drive states towards openness. In countries where a far-right party participates in government and depicts immigration as a threat to national identity or security, we would expect immigration policies to become more restrictive relative to other countries. Equally, in a country where there is embedded demand for migrant labour and significant lobbying from influential business groups, and an absence of a significant far-right party, we would expect policies to be relatively expansive. The most open immigration policies are likely to be found in countries where immigration is relatively depoliticized, public opinion is moderate, constitutional protections are strong, narratives of national identity include immigration, and businesses demand labour migrants. Though no country fits this ideal type exactly, Canada is arguably the closest approximation. At the other end of the spectrum, the most restrictive liberal state would be expected to encounter negative public opinion, have a significant far-right party, maintain less robust constitutional protections, deny immigration as part of its national story, and lack significant pressure from employers for labour migrants. It is even harder to find individual countries that fit this ideal type, as a country that ticked all of these boxes would stretch the definition of a liberal state, but some European countries come close. In practice, most countries exhibit a complex assemblage of factors, some of which create pressures for openness, others for restriction.

Thus cross-national variation is entirely consistent with the analysis presented in this book. The argument that constitutive features of liberal states generate contradictory imperatives for immigration policy does not rule out differences between states. Policy variations between countries can be explained by unpacking the 'content' of each of the four facets and the way in which they interact in specific contexts. What *is* claimed is that, in any state that is commonly defined as liberal, the demands generated by representative democracy, constitutionalism, nationhood and capitalism will all influence immigration policies. And, however contradictory these demands may be, none can be entirely subsumed under the others. Even the presence of anti-immigrant populists in government will not result in the wholesale exclusion of immigrants so long as that government wants to oversee a functioning economy and retain constitutional legitimacy.

CHAPTER FOUR

The Sisyphean Task of Migration Governance

All liberal states seek to encourage the admission of some immigrants while preventing or deterring others. As we saw in chapters 2 and 3, the economic and normative foundations of liberal states generate demands for governments to admit immigrants, while political demands, often associated with cultural protectionism, drive restrictive policymaking. These competing dynamics of openness and closure give rise to complex assemblages of immigration policies. Indeed, in some ways it is a misnomer to speak of immigration policy in the singular, as the regulation of international migration flows involves multiple policy types and instruments.

This chapter turns from the political dynamics that shape immigration policymaking to the shape of immigration policies themselves. In other words, having in the previous chapters considered policymaking 'inputs', in this chapter we consider the 'outputs' of the policy process. We also further examine the role of representative politics, constitutionalism, capitalism and nationhood by contrasting their respective influence across different immigration policy sub-fields. Once immigration policy is disaggregated into its constituent parts, the contrasting dynamics surrounding different types of movement are brought more clearly into view.

Governing Immigration

Governments today make a more intensive effort to regulate immigration than at any previous point in history, spending considerable and growing amounts of money in their attempt to select those they deem to be wanted and to exclude those considered to be unwanted. Of course, they do not always – or even often – succeed in these efforts. Politicians may make promises about tougher controls and the budgets and personnel of immigration agencies may increase; but no state that is liberal will ever fully control immigration. Yet, if the task of governing immigration is endless and often unavailing, this does not mean that states' interventions are ineffectual or irrelevant. As argued in chapter 3, policy matters because states' interventions partly shape migration flows.

The complexity and diversity of migration flows, as well as the cross-national variation between immigrant-receiving countries, mean that it is impossible to discuss all relevant policies in this chapter. Nevertheless, some trends can be identified across liberal states. The overall policy trend since the early 1990s has been increased openness towards a few selective types of immigration combined with substantial efforts to control and limit other types. Policy development has therefore been *both* expansionist and restrictionist. Generally speaking, liberal states have become more interested in recruiting migrant workers to fill skills shortages in their economies, while at the same time strengthening their border controls to exclude undocumented migrants and creating measures that deter asylum-seekers. These contrasting objectives mean that liberal states cannot be straightforwardly characterized as either open or closed to immigration. Towards some kinds of immigrant, the liberal state shows an open inclusive face; towards many others, it reveals an exclusionary and sometimes illiberal profile.

This chapter maps out patterns and trends in four immigration policy sub-fields: economic migration, measures designed to exclude unauthorized migrants, asylum policies and family migration policies. Although these domains are not entirely separable in practice (because there is overlap as well as interaction effects between the different types of migration), they are sufficiently distinct policy fields to warrant separate analysis. As will be seen, government strategies, policy instruments and technologies vary across the domains, as do the constellations of interests and patterns of political mobilization that shape policy outputs.

The Rise of Managed Labour Migration

As discussed in chapter 3, demand for migrant labour is embedded in the economies of advanced capitalist states: at the top end of the labour market, firms compete to attract skilled workers while, at the lower end, in sectors such as agriculture and construction, many employers have come to depend upon a supply of low-paid economic immigrants. Unsurprisingly, then, employers lobby hard for liberalization of economic immigration channels. The governments of advanced industrial countries have increasingly responded to employer demand for migrant labour and at the same time sought a more active role in the selection and regulation of labour migration flows. Migration management has at least two distinct components: the selective recruitment of highly skilled workers and the temporary recruitment of low-skilled workers. As the labour economist Philip Martin puts it, the guiding aim of managed migration is to 'welcome the skilled and rotate the unskilled' (Martin 2006). 'Welcoming' highly skilled foreign workers involves offering them incentives such as permanent settlement and the right to bring family members, while 'rotating' low-skilled foreign workers involves temporary and often sector-specific visa programmes that do not come either with the right to settle or to bring accompanying family members.

Governments, of course, recruited migrant workers well before migration management became the term of choice around the turn of the millennium. Several European countries recruited guestworkers to fill labour shortages during the 1960s and 1970s, and those which had been or still were imperial powers received substantial numbers of colonial immigrants into their labour markets. In the settlement countries, where immigration was bound up with racialized nation-building for much of the twentieth century, governments began to select permanent immigrants according to human capital rather than ethnicity only from the 1970s onwards (Joppke 2005). Yet in these countries there was large-scale recruitment of temporary and seasonal workers – for example, the US Bracero programme, which recruited hundreds of thousands of Mexican contract labourers to work on American farms between 1942 and 1964. Thus today's labour migration policies are far from an unprecedented phenomenon (indeed, as discussed below, some view the current vogue for temporary labour migration programmes as a rebirth of guest-worker schemes).

What is new about contemporary migration management is the extent to which governments seek to regulate the size and composition of labour migration flows through selective and highly differentiated policies and programmes. This began during the 1990s, as economic growth and labour shortages led governments across OECD countries to relax existing channels for economic immigration and in some cases to create new programmes. By the turn of the millennium, the resumption of economic immigration was well established, and during the year 2000–1 most OECD countries relaxed their criteria for recruiting skilled foreign labour in order to meet labour market needs, especially in the hi-tech and health-care sectors. The rebirth of labour migration was temporarily interrupted by the collapse of the dot-com bubble and the fallout from 9/11, but the contraction of foreign labour recruitment was short-lived, and by 2003 numbers were rising again (OECD 2007). The EU enlargement of 2004, which saw ten new member states join the Union (eight countries in Eastern Europe, plus Malta and Cyprus), led to a substantial increase in free movement flows between member states. Under transitional arrangements, most pre-2004 member states opted to impose temporary labour market restrictions on citizens of the new member states, but in the UK and Ireland, which did open their labour markets at this time, there were substantial inflows. Most of the 304,000 A8 migrants (i.e., from the eight Eastern European countries) who entered the UK labour market between 2004 and 2009 filled vacancies in agriculture, construction, and hotel and catering services (Vargas-Silva 2011: 3).

The financial crisis of 2008 and the subsequent global recession have slowed migration flows to OECD countries, and most countries have tightened up their labour recruitment programmes. Total migration inflows to OECD countries fell by about 5 per cent in 2008 and by a further 7 per cent in 2009, with EU free movement migration and temporary labour migration falling the most: in 2009, by 22 and 16 per cent respectively (OECD 2011: 34). Yet, despite the ongoing economic crisis, levels of international migration remain higher than in any year before 2007, with a total of 4.3 million movements in 2009. And preliminary data show that, in 2011, immigration started to rise again in most OECD countries, bringing a three-year decline to an end (OECD 2012a). With the crisis far from resolved, the prognosis is unclear. However, given that the falls during the most serious economic crisis since the 1930s were relatively modest and may already be recovering, it seems unlikely that migration flows will fall significantly in the near future. Indeed, the structural factors behind international migration – massive differentials in income and living standards between the global North and South, demand-side factors including skills and labour shortages and ageing populations in several OECD countries (as discussed below), and an abundant supply of would-be migrants – persist despite the crisis.

This brief sketch of labour migration to OECD countries raises the question of *why* governments began to liberalize migration management policies around the turn of the century, as well as *how* they have done so. The political economist Georg Menz argues that the revaluation of labour migration since the late 1990s is 'due to the new economic prerogatives of the European competition state, which perceives of migration . . . as a valuable opportunity to avail oneself of attractive human resources with desirable skill portfolios' (Menz 2009: 29–30). Though Menz focuses his analysis on Europe, the idea of the 'competition state', and of economic competitiveness more generally, is of global significance. Across the OECD, governments increasingly perceive the need to ensure that their economies are competitive in regional and globalized markets. The neo-liberal paradigm of competitiveness has influenced thinking about migration, as governments see themselves competing with other countries to attract the skilled workers they need for their 'knowledge economies' and, at the same time, to ensure a steady flow of cheap labour into low-skill sectors. At the top of the labour market, immigrants are prized as a source of skills, innovation, investment and entrepreneurialism while, at the bottom end, those willing to accept low wages are valued for their counter-inflationary effects (i.e., they keep wages down) that help ensure price competitiveness in international markets. Whether or not these beliefs are well founded – the actual economic effects of immigration on competitiveness as well as much else are debated – the perception that migration is associated with competitiveness has certainly shaped the managed migration agenda. Indeed, the linkage of migration and competitiveness has become something of a mantra in official discourse, well captured by the European Commission's claim in its 2008 proposal for a common European immigration policy that 'appropriate management of economic immigration is an essential element of EU competitiveness' (European Commission 2008).

The new interest in managing migration has also been influenced by demographic trends in the rich industrial countries. Fertility levels in many of these countries have been relatively low since the 1970s, but they have declined in some to the point that the fertility rate (the number of children born per woman) is well below 2.1, which is the level required to ensure the replacement of generations in developed countries. By the 2000s, none of the developed countries had total fertility rates above 2.1 children per woman and only a few, among them Iceland, New Zealand and the United States, had levels above 2.0 (UNPD 2011: xi). In 2009 the EU fertility rate was just 1.6. Some member states, including populous countries such as Germany, Italy, Poland and Spain, have fertility rates well below replacement level (in 2009, approximately 1.4 for the countries mentioned). Others, such as France, Sweden and the UK, have higher levels (just under 2 for these countries). However, the only country in the EU27 with a replacement fertility rate is Ireland, where the rate is 2.07 (European Commission 2011: 28). Without immigration, the European population would be declining. A Eurostat forecast of future demographic trends, EUROPOP 2008, projected that the EU27 population will increase from 495 million in 2008 to 521 million in 2035, and then decline gradually. From 2015 onwards, deaths will outnumber births, hence population increase due to natural growth will cease. For two decades from 2015 to 2035, positive net migration will be the only population growth factor. However, from 2035, positive net migration will no longer offset negative natural change, and the total population of the EU27 is projected to fall back to 506 million by 2060 (just a little more than the population of the EU27 today) (Eurostat 2008).

Not only are the populations of many advanced industrial countries facing absolute shrinkage, they are also getting older. This is problematic for welfare states because rapid ageing raises the dependency ratio (the ratio of dependants – persons aged below 15 or above 64 – to the working-age population – those aged between 15 and 64). If this ratio becomes too high, welfare states become unsustainable, since there are too few persons active in the labour market and paying taxes relative to those who are economically inactive and dependent on state pensions and social security. This problem is especially acute in Europe. The old-age dependency ratio of the EU27 is projected to increase from 25 per cent in 2008 to 53 per cent in 2060. In other words, while there are four persons of working age to every person aged 65 and over today, by 2060 there will be only two persons of working age to every person aged 65 and over (Eurostat 2008). Ageing is also projected to affect the relatively buoyant population of the United States in the coming decades.

These demographic trends are a cause of serious concern for governments. A recent United Nations survey found that, whereas in 1976 just 21 per cent of developed country governments viewed their fertility levels as too low, by 2009 this figure had risen to 61 per cent (UNPD 2011: xii). Faced with declining or ageing populations, governments can pursue policies designed to increase the total fertility rate of the indigenous population or seek to import population from overseas through immigration. The latter option is increasingly seen as at least a part of the solution. As well as adding to the size of a population, immigrants rejuvenate it, since they tend to be younger than average and, if selected carefully, net contributors to the tax base.

Using immigration as a demographic strategy is not without its problems, however. With demographic trends as they are, the scale of immigration that would be needed to offset population ageing and maintain dependency ratios is so large as to be politically unviable. As a United Nations Population Division (UNPD) report pointed out, for the EU to keep its dependency ratio constant would require 674 million immigrants between 2000 and 2050 (13 million per year). As the report acknowledges, these numbers are 'extraordinarily large' and 'vastly more immigration than has occurred in the past' (UNPD 2001). Immigration is not therefore a panacea for the demographic problems in the advanced industrial countries.

Nevertheless, demographic trends have undoubtedly contributed towards pushing migration up the policy agenda. As the OECD (2011: 104) puts it, 'migration is increasingly seen or at least considered, in conjunction with other policies, as a means to tackle demographic challenges.' It may be that the approach of the Canadian government, where immigration policy has long been viewed in the context of wider population strategy (Reitz 2004: 101), will become more common. Australia, for example, appointed its first ever population minister in April 2010, charged with developing a sustainable population strategy that includes long-term migration planning. In contrast, and despite their deeper demographic deficits, European countries are generally more reticent to adopt an explicit migration strategy, but even here there are signs of change in some countries (OECD 2011: 104).

In short, a belief that immigration contributes towards international competitiveness and at least partially alleviates demographic ageing or decline helps to explain why the governments of liberal states have become increasingly committed to the selective encouragement of economic immigration. This leads to the second question: *how* have governments liberalized their migration policies? As mentioned above, the overall trend has been towards 'welcoming' highly skilled workers through permanent residency programmes combined with the 'rotation' of low-skilled workers on temporary worker schemes. Skilled and highly skilled worker programmes became more common across OECD countries during the early 2000s. Across the EU, countries as diverse as France, Germany, Ireland and the Netherlands developed programmes to recruit skilled migrants (OECD 2008: 103), while the UK emerged as a major receiving country on account of the liberalization of its existing work visa scheme and the creation of new schemes such as the Highly Skilled Migrant Programme (HSMP). By 2007, interest in skilled migration policy was also spreading eastwards, with former communist countries such as the Czech Republic and Lithuania introducing policy changes to make it easier for highly qualified workers to access their labour markets. In

2008, before the implications of the global economic crisis were fully apparent, the OECD reported that the recruitment of highly qualified workers had become a 'principal objective' of immigration policy in the context of a 'global competition for skills' (ibid.: 103).

One of the most notable policy developments during the 2000s was the spread of points-based systems (PBSs) to select skilled immigrants. These systems work by allocating points to would-be migrants on the basis of criteria such as the applicant's education, work experience, age and language proficiency. An applicant who reaches the pass mark, which can be achieved through various combinations of allocated points, is issued with a work-related visa. Most PBSs also incorporate shortage occupation lists and allocate additional points to applicants who have job offers for occupations on the list or relevant skills and experience. PBSs have often been introduced to rationalize existing work-related schemes, offering the advantage of administrative efficiency and simplicity for both immigration bureaucracies and employers. Governments also like PBSs because of their flexibility: the number of points allocated for different criteria, as well as the number and type of jobs on shortage occupation lists, can be quickly amended in response to changing economic conditions.

PBSs originated in the settlement countries of Australia, Canada and New Zealand, which have selected skilled migrants in this way for many years. The Australian General Skilled Migration Programme and the Canadian Federal Skilled Worker Programme, for example, select skilled workers for permanent residency visas against a published set of criteria. Until recently, this approach was wholly alien to European immigration policies, yet since 2008 Denmark, the Netherlands and the UK have all adopted PBSs, and Austria is in the process of doing so. The endorsement of human capital-based selection procedures should not be overstated, since they are far from universal (neither the United States nor most European countries have adopted them). Yet the trend towards PBSs is likely to continue. The introduction of these systems in Europe has coincided with the most serious economic crisis for several generations, yet the new PBSs have survived partly because they have afforded governments the option quickly to increase selectivity in the context of the downturn.

The management of low-skilled migrant workers has followed a different trajectory. Governments have generally tried to tap low-skilled migrant labour through temporary and seasonal schemes, without extending the range of rights that are offered to the highly skilled. Temporary labour migration programmes aim to add workers to the labour force without adding permanent residents to the population (Martin 2006). Since the 1990s, most industrial countries have developed such programmes of one sort or another. While there are similarities between these programmes and the European guestworker recruitment of the 1950s and 1960s, or the Mexico–US Bracero programme of the 1940s and 1950s, the new wave of temporary labour migrant programmes differ in some important ways. According to one influential labour economist, whereas the earlier 'macro'-programmes recruited millions of migrant workers in a 'shotgun-fashion' across multiple sectors, the new 'micro'-programmes aim to fill jobs in particular industries or occupations in 'rifle fashion' (ibid.: 5–7). This involves a more tightly regulated and targeted approach, including sector-specific schemes. Another important difference between pre- and post-1990s temporary labour migrant schemes is that, while the former were driven almost entirely by labour shortages and employer lobbying, the latter have increasingly been shaped by wider migration strategies (such as cooperation with sending countries in preventing unauthorized migration), and in some cases by a recognition of the need for cross-border commuting in 'natural' labour markets divided by national borders (ibid.: 11–12).

There were approximately 1.9 million temporary labour migrants across all OECD countries in 2009, a decrease on the 2007 peak of 2.4 million (OECD 2011: 45). Demand for temporary and low-skilled labour migration has been especially affected by the economic crisis. The tightening of labour market conditions across the OECD has prompted governments that operate a cap on temporary work visas generally to reduce their quotas or otherwise tighten the conditions – for example, by reducing the duration of work permits. Nevertheless, it is worth remembering that, even with the downturn, temporary labour migrants remain more numerous than permanent labour migrants (who numbered 1.5 million across all OECD countries in 2009).

Most temporary migrant programmes are oriented towards low-skilled work. The largest single category is seasonal workers, most of whom work in the agricultural sector. In 2009, Germany accounted for over half of all seasonal workers, the overwhelming majority of them Poles, who have since acquired access to the German labour market under EU free movement rules. But most countries operate seasonal worker schemes, including the H-2A programme in the US, the Canadian Agricultural Seasonal Workers Program (ASWP) and, since 2007, a Recognized Seasonal Employer Policy in New Zealand for horticulture and viticulture (OECD 2008: 107). The UK and France have also operated large-scale seasonal farm worker programmes.

The renewed interest in temporary labour migration reflects the competing demands from employers for a supply of low-wage labour, on the one hand, and the scepticism of electorates towards immigration, on the other. In a context in which immigration has become increasingly politicized, temporary and seasonal migration policies are intended to secure the benefits of migrant labour to capital, while avoiding both the political risks of permanent immigration and the social costs of integrating long-term immigrants. As the earlier experiences of guestworker programmes suggest, however, these schemes can work only under certain conditions. Hence governments now tend to tailor their programmes to specific sectors, rotating workers on a regular basis before they build up a financial or social stake in the host country, and keeping them away from urban areas where they might abscond – for example, by housing seasonal workers in special accommodation on or near farms. In many cases, however, these schemes fail to satisfy the demand for low-paid migrant workers, something which has contributed to the flourishing market for irregular immigrant labour.

Excluding Irregular Immigrants

Irregular or illegal immigration is one of the most politically charged aspects of migration policy. Yet irregularity is a fact in most advanced industrial economies, and the combative political rhetoric about 'fighting' it is not always mirrored by reality on the ground. On one level, the failure – if it can be called this – to prevent the complex of activities that lead to irregularity, including visa overstay, unauthorized entry and working without authorization, simply reflects the limits of governments' control capacity. No state can expect to prevent all forms of clandestine or fraudulent entry, let alone identify everyone who overstays their visa or works without authorization. The sheer logistics of policing territorial borders, processing passengers at ports of entry, regulating labour markets, monitoring access to social services, and so on, means that some level of irregular immigration is inevitable, certainly in a free society. Only an island state run on Orwellian lines would come close to preventing all forms of irregular immigration.

But, more than this, the state is profoundly implicated in the *production* of irregularity. As a matter of logic, nothing is illegal until legality is defined. In the case of immigration, policies that stipulate what counts as legal modes of entry, residence and work effectively create their opposite: illegal entry, residence and work. For this reason, irregular immigration is described by Michael Samers (2004: 28) as 'epiphenomenal', a social phenomenon created by laws and rules that seek to define regular immigration. Some forms of irregularity, such as clandestine entry, are produced by states only in the sense that all immigration is produced by the existence of territorially defined states. Yet, for many other types of irregularity, it is the specificities of a particular country's immigration laws that will render a person irregular.

Liberal states are particularly implicated in the production of irregularity. There are at least two dimensions to this, related to the economic and normative dimensions of liberal statehood respectively. As argued in chapter 3, the capitalist economy of liberal states generates pressures for openness towards migrant labour. The most obvious instance of this takes the form of employers lobbying for regular economic immigration, yet it applies to irregularity as well. Some industries have turned to irregular migrant labour because of the lack of legal channels for recruiting workers or, where legal channels exist, on account of the lower labour costs and lack of bureaucracy involved in hiring irregular migrants (Düvell 2011). Irregular migrants both fill labour shortages where legal channels do not match demand and provide cheaper labour even where costly legal channels do exist. The result is that, in certain sectors, particularly those covering low-skill and labour-intensive jobs, and in certain countries, especially those with deregulated labour markets and large informal economies, employers quietly condone irregular practices. One particularly remarkable example is US agribusiness, especially in southern California, which relies heavily on undocumented migrant labour.

Liberal states are also implicated in the persistence of irregular immigration due to their normative commitments. Liberal principles place constraints on the weapons that states may deploy in their 'fight against illegal immigration'. This is because the kinds of measures that are needed to tackle irregularity require invasive powers and regulations that are at odds with freedom and privacy, and which are therefore likely to encounter resistance from citizens and even legal challenges. For example, one instrument used to identify irregular immigrants is checks by public service providers to ascertain whether those accessing public services are authorized to do so. This requires the cooperation of 'street-level bureaucrats', who sometimes resist being co-opted into immigration control functions, especially if they believe this to be at odds with their values or professional norms (Van der Leun 2006). Liberal states also struggle to remove immigrants against their will on account of legal and moral constraints on the exercise of coercive powers (Ellermann 2005, 2009).

In short, to the extent that liberal states are liberal, some level of irregularity is unavoidable. None of this is to say that governments are entirely disingenuous in their opposition to irregular immigration, nor is it to deny that they have adopted increasingly draconian policy measures in an attempt to restrict it. Nevertheless, it is important to recognize that the often illiberal measures taken in the fight against illegal immigration, and the political pressures that produce them, are hedged by liberal constraints.

Before turning to consider exactly how states try to restrict irregular immigration, it is important to outline briefly the scale and complexity of irregularity in advanced economies, since this influences the policies and instruments that governments deploy. The United States has by far the largest number of irregular immigrants of any developed country: in 2010 there were an estimated 11.2 million (slightly down on the peak of 12 million in 2007), which amounts to about 3.7 per cent of the total US population; the majority (58 per cent) were from Mexico (Passel and Cohn 2011: 1). In Europe, the number is probably much smaller, in both absolute and relative terms, though data are far from robust. The EU-funded Clandestino Project estimated the total population of irregular immigrants in 2008 at between 1.9 and 3.8 million (or about 0.4 to 0.8 per cent of the total European population), with the majority living in 'old' EU15 member states (Vogel 2009: 5). Australia has a still smaller irregular immigrant population, largely as a result of its geography as an island continent: the Australian Department of Immigration and Citizenship estimated that, in 2011, the number of visa overstayers was about 58,400, or 0.26 per cent of the Australian population, while the number of irregular maritime arrivals being processed stood at 6,944 (DIAC 2011: 152–5).

There are several different 'routes' or 'pathways' to irregularity (Düvell 2011), including unauthorized entry at land and sea borders, entry through a port using forged documents, visa overstay, violation of visa terms (for example, by working without authorization) and rejection of an asylum claim. The mass media often focus on unauthorized entry, with images of Mexicans making treacherous journeys across remote parts of the Southern border of the United States, and of overcrowded boats crossing the Mediterranean from Africa to Europe. In the case of the United States, there is some foundation to these images. Unauthorized entry is indeed a major route to irregularity in the United States, albeit not by any means the only one: in 2006, the Pew Hispanic Center estimated that, out of a total irregular immigrant population of between 11.5 and 12 million, approximately 6 to 7 million entered the United States by evading border control inspection, while 4 to 5.5 million were visa overstayers (Pew Hispanic Center 2006: 1). In Europe, by contrast, unauthorized entry probably accounts for just 10 to 20 per cent of irregular migrants, with between 80 and 90 per cent entering with authorization, then overstaying or violating the terms of their visa (Düvell 2011).

The diversity of routes to irregularity means that the fight against illegal immigration is necessarily waged on several fronts. The most obvious instruments, which correspond to the popular image of unauthorized entry, are control measures at the state's territorial borders (Koslowski 2011a). A near universal trend across liberal states over the last decade has been the intensification of border controls and increased resources for border control agencies. In the US, the Customs and Border Protection (CBP) agency has grown to be the largest law-enforcement agency in the country, with more than 58,000 employees overall; between 2004 and 2010 it doubled its border patrol personnel from 10,000 to 20,500 (CBP webpage). Parts of the Southwest border with Mexico have become heavily fortified with a network of fences and barriers and the use of military and surveillance technologies such as thermal imaging and drones (Andreas 2000). A similar, if altogether more patchy, intensification of border patrols and technologies is evident at the external borders of the European Union, though complicated by the existence of multiple border control agencies. The creation in 2005 of the EU's External Border Agency, Frontex, was intended to enhance border security by coordinating the activities of the 400,000 border personnel in the different member states, though some parts of the external border, notably that between Greece and Turkey, remain porous.

If measures along territorial borders are principally exclusionary, at air and seaports border agencies have to balance their efforts to prevent unauthorized entry with the need to facilitate authorized passengers. With over 700 million persons crossing the EU's external borders every year, and over 400 million entering the US through ports of entry, identifying suspect movements is like searching for the proverbial needle in a haystack. Moreover, measures such as in-depth passport checks that enable border agencies to intercept 'unwanted' persons (ranging from terrorist suspects to immigration offenders) will typically slow down, and possibly deter, the transit of 'wanted' travellers such as businesspersons and tourists. This 'facilitation-control dilemma' (Hampshire 2009a) is increasingly addressed through so-called smart borders systems, which leverage digital technologies to target interventions on 'high-risk' movements while relinquishing them from 'low-risk' movements. The aim is pre-emptively to identify and sort passengers before arrival at a port of entry, so that immigration officers can concentrate resources on persons of interest.

Smart borders rely upon biometric technologies and large-scale immigration databases to differentiate between various categories of passenger. At one end of the spectrum, passengers are enrolled on trusted traveller programmes, such as IRIS in the UK, Privium in the Netherlands, and NEXUS and SENTRI in the US, which often make use of biometric-based automated border controls (ABCs) to expedite border crossing. At the other end of the spectrum are persons listed on criminal, terrorist and immigration watch-lists, increasingly stored in large databases such as the EU's Schengen Information System (SIS) (Broeders and Hampshire forthcoming 2013). Some governments are also developing systems to analyse advanced passenger information (API) and passenger name records (PNR) that are submitted by carriers in advance of travel. These data can be analysed using risk-profiling techniques to identify persons who have no known 'priors' but who fit certain risk profiles as defined by immigration, customs or police authorities. The UK and the US both operate national border targeting centres for this purpose. Finally, in an attempt to tackle visa overstay, some governments have sought to develop entry–exit systems, so that persons who depart after their visa has expired can be excluded from future re-entry. The US-VISIT programme is a case in point, although it has encountered numerous implementation problems, particularly around the collection of exit data, and presently 'remains a distant goal' (Koslowski 2011a: 1). Undeterred by the US experience, the EU has proposed an entry–exit system of its own.

Closely intertwined with the digitalization of border control systems is the extension of what Aristide Zolberg (2000, 2003) terms 'remote controls': instruments designed to prevent would-be immigrants from reaching a state's territory in the first place. Visa regimes are the classic instrument of remote control, and have become increasingly common for the citizens of some countries and less for others. A citizen of Denmark, for example, can visit 173 countries without a visa, whereas citizens of India, China and Afghanistan can visit just 53, 40 and 24 countries visa-free respectively.[5] Visa requirements as a means to regulate entry to a state are not new; in fact, they constitute one of the earliest forms of immigration control. But they have spread in the age of migration as, broadly speaking, richer countries seek to pre-screen travellers from poorer countries well before they arrive at their borders. A second form of remote control involves 'shifting out' immigration control functions by co-opting non-state actors, such as passenger carriers and transport companies (Guiraudon and Lahav 2000: 184). The principal instrument for co-option of non-state actors is carrier sanctions, which create legal liabilities for carriers to check passengers and impose financial penalties if they are found carrying inadequately documented persons. Introduced by the UK and Germany in 1987, carrier sanctions became ubiquitous during the 1990s. A third dimension of remote control is the growing cooperation between sending and receiving countries to allow immigration officers to be posted overseas at ports of embarkation. Several countries operate networks of 'border security advisers' or 'immigration liaison officers' stationed at airports across the globe, which check that passengers have adequate documentation before embarkation. Some countries, such as the UK and France, operate 'juxtaposed controls', with immigration officers stationed on one another's territory.

Despite the considerable resources now invested by governments, the intensification of border controls has not prevented unauthorized entry. Border control measures may have made irregular entry more difficult and costly, but in many cases they have simply diverted irregular border crossings to other routes or resulted in new strategies on the part of migrants. In a self-reinforcing dynamic of escalation, the fortification of borders is met with increasingly sophisticated attempts by migrants to evade detection, which prompts further fortification, and so on. One notable element of this escalation has been the growing role of organized crime networks in people-smuggling. Indeed, the illicit traffic in people has become big business for criminal organizations that already have expertise in the illicit traffic of goods. The entry of organized crime into irregular migration indicates that border fortification has indeed made irregular entry more difficult (greater resources and organizational capacity are needed to enter rich countries without authorization, hence organized crime moves in to provide this 'service') *and* that these measures are unlikely to be very effective, since criminal organizations often have the resources and the capacity to evade them. Of course, states commit substantial resources to tackling such criminal networks, but, if the war on drugs provides any guide, the fight against organized people-smuggling is unlikely to be winnable.

In any case, external border control measures do not address the other major routes to irregularity. As mentioned above, visa overstaying accounts for the overwhelming majority of irregular immigrants in Europe and a substantial proportion in the United States. In an effort to reduce irregular residence and work, governments have developed internal controls designed to identify, intercept and remove migrants who are already in their territory. These controls take many forms, including random ID checks in public places, routine workplace inspections and raids, reporting requirements for providers of public services, and employer sanctions. Together, these various measures can be understood as controls at the institutional, as opposed to the territorial, borders of states, as they are designed to prevent access to the labour market, welfare, health care and education (Bommes and Geddes 2000). While these measures may deter irregular immigrants from accessing institutions and enable the identification and arrest of a certain number, they probably have only a limited impact, for at least two reasons. First, many of the internal control measures depend on the cooperation of non-state actors, such as employers or public service providers, who, as discussed above, are often reluctant to perform immigration control functions, whether for economic reasons (e.g., employers who do not cooperate with workplace inspections or lobby against the imposition of sanctions) or normative reasons (e.g., doctors who refuse to report undocumented persons who seek treatment). Second, irregular migrants themselves are well aware of internal control strategies and develop their own counter-strategies, avoiding places where they are likely to be identified and arrested (Broeders and Engbersen 2007). Thus, although there is considerable variation in the internal control capacity of different countries – depending for example on the extent of labour market regulation, the size of the informal economy, the existence of ID cards, and the capacity of police and immigration agencies – internal controls are unlikely ever to have a significant impact on irregularity in liberal states because of the limits on governmental intrusion that are the hallmarks of an open economy and society.

A very different way to reduce irregularity is to grant legal status to irregular immigrants. Some governments have developed extensive regularization programmes, others strongly oppose them (although even in these cases practice is often less draconian than official discourse would suggest). Proponents of regularization programmes argue that they incorporate irregular immigrants into the formal economy, which benefits the receiving society through increased tax receipts and the reduction of wage competition, and improve the position of irregular immigrants, who become less vulnerable to exploitation and able to access public services. Opponents of regularization programmes argue that they condone illicit behaviour and act as a pull factor for future irregular migration, since migrants see the possibility of attaining legal status at some future point.

In the EU, between 1996 and 2007 there were some 4.7 million applications to a total of 43 regularization programmes. Of these 4.7 million applicants, about 3.2 million, or approximately 68 per cent, were granted some kind of legal status (ICMPD 2009: 31). The overwhelming majority of applications were lodged in just three member states – Italy (1.5 million), Spain (1.3 million) and Greece (1.2 million). These Southern European countries are all relative newcomers to mass immigration and have not to date developed effective labour migration policies. Partly on account of their large maritime borders and proximity to sending regions, they have been unable to prevent the development of sizeable undocumented populations, attracted to work in their large informal sectors. In these countries, regularization has become a surrogate for legal immigration policy (ibid.: 40) and reflects the failure of government policies to recruit sufficient migrant workers in contexts of structurally embedded labour demand (Baldwin-Edwards 2008). In other European countries, regularization programmes have been more limited, in terms of both their scope (e.g., they are limited to certain categories of migrants such as asylum-seekers or longstanding potential deportees) and their scale. Countries such as Belgium, Denmark and the Netherlands have used limited regularization programmes on humanitarian grounds, especially for persons who have been granted subsidiary or temporary protection through the asylum system. These programmes are numerically much less significant than their equivalents in the Southern European countries and are not integral to immigration policy. Other European governments are either sceptical (e.g., France, the UK) or downright hostile (e.g., Austria, Germany) towards regularization.

In the United States, regularization has been used in the past but has become increasingly contested in recent years. The last major regularization programme, created by the 1986 Immigration Reform and Control Act (IRCA), granted permanent residence to several different categories of migrants: a general amnesty for those with continuous residence since 1982; regularization for seasonal workers in the agricultural sector who could demonstrate a certain number of days' employment in previous years (SAW); and a scheme for Haitians and Cubans. The general amnesty received 1.7 million applicants and the SAW 1.3 million, with acceptance rates of 94 and 85 per cent respectively (ICMPD 2009: 38). Since then there have been no mass regularizations, and recent attempts at immigration reforms that included regularization provisions have been blocked. The 2004 Immigration Reform bill, which granted permanent residency to persons who met six requirements, including payment of a fine, collapsed in the Senate following criticisms from conservative Republicans that it amounted to an amnesty for law-breakers. It remains to be seen whether the most recent proposals for immigration reform will overcome these political obstacles.

The Paradoxes of Asylum Policy

All liberal states uphold the principle of asylum and, as signatories to the relevant UN conventions, all are legally bound to give refuge to those who arrive on their shores and face a 'well-founded fear of persecution' in their country of origin. The refugee system is a core part of the international human rights regime, and liberal states' incorporation into this system reveals their universalistic and rights-based foundations. Yet over the last couple of decades most liberal states have adopted policies that make asylum-seeking increasingly difficult. Indeed, since the 1980s the thrust of asylum policy development has been markedly restrictive. This is partly a result of the increased numbers of asylum-seekers, especially during the 1990s, but it also reflects shifts in geopolitics since the end of the Cold War, changes in the nature of asylum flows, and the often highly politicized and negative character of the asylum debate at the domestic level.

The outcome is that, while liberal states continue to uphold the principle of offering refuge to those fleeing persecution, asylum policy is characterized by an essentially exclusionary logic. Asylum has become what Stephen D. Krasner (1999) calls 'organized hypocrisy' – a longstanding norm that is frequently violated. While the very liberalness of liberal states prevents them from renouncing asylum entirely – for example, by withdrawing from the Refugee Convention – most have nevertheless sought to reduce the number of asylum-seekers through a number of measures. The 'architecture of exclusion' (Gibney 2004: 3) created by liberal states includes measures designed to make it difficult to reach their territories in the first place, legal and administrative changes intended to reduce the number of people that receive refugee status, and measures that make life uncomfortable for those in the process of having their claim assessed.

It was not always thus. For about thirty years after the Second World War, asylum was relatively uncontroversial and refugees were even celebrated by liberal states. At the end of the war there were no fewer than 30 million displaced persons in Europe in need of relief and relocation. In 1949, the United Nations established the United Nations High Commissioner for Refugees (UNHCR) and in 1951 the Convention Relating to the Status of Refugees was signed in Geneva. The Convention defined a refugee as a person who, 'owing to a well-founded fear of being persecuted for reasons of race, religion, nationality, membership of a particular social group or political opinion, is outside the country of his nationality and is unable or, owing to such fear, is unwilling to avail himself of the protection of that country' (Article 1 (A2)). The Convention also established the principle of *non-refoulement* – that no contracting state can return (*refouler*) a refugee to a country where his or her life or freedom would be threatened for the reasons given above (Article 33(1)). Governments that signed the Convention were obliged to establish procedures to determine whether someone claiming asylum qualifies as a refugee and offer refuge to anyone who is determined to qualify. Unauthorized entry is not a bar to claiming asylum, so that anyone who arrives on the territory of a signatory state and makes a claim must be assessed and can only be returned if they are determined not to have a well-founded fear of persecution (though note that many liberal democracies now operate 'safe third-country provisions', which allow a receiving country to return an asylum-seeker to a country they have travelled through if it is on the safe list).

For some years after it was drafted, the Convention received increasing support and the system that it underpinned functioned reasonably well. The geographical and temporal limitations of the Convention were expanded by the 1967 New York Protocol (it originally applied only to persons displaced before 1951 and within Europe), and a growing number of governments ratified it. By 1960, 22 states had signed, by 1970 60 states had ratified either the Convention or Protocol, and by 1980 83 states had done so. Today, 147 countries have signed the Convention, including all countries in the developed world. Despite refugee crises in several countries during the 1970s and 1980s, notably in Bangladesh, Vietnam and Cambodia in the 1970s and in Afghanistan, the Horn of Africa and South America during the 1980s, the refugee system was broadly supported by Western governments during this period for two interrelated reasons. First, the numbers of asylum-seekers that arrived on the shores of rich countries (as opposed to the millions who sought refuge in developing countries) were relatively small and therefore manageable. Second, many of those who did arrive in Western countries were fleeing from communist regimes. Each refugee from communism counted as a small victory in the propaganda battle of the Cold War. Thus the rights enshrined in the Convention were not only consistent with liberal states' norms but also aligned with their interests.

This coupling of norms and interests came under growing pressure in the 1980s as the number of asylum-seekers increased, then really came apart during the 'asylum crisis' of the 1990s. This crisis was prompted by the collapse of communism in the Soviet Union and Central and Eastern Europe, which saw a surge of asylum-seekers in Western Europe. During the mid-1980s, the total number of asylum applicants in industrialized countries was around 100,000 per annum. By 1992 it had reached 850,000, before falling back, then peaking again at 600,000 in 2001, and then falling back once more. There was a very sharp spike in applications in the early 1990s, with EU countries (at that time, fifteen Western European countries) receiving the vast majority of applicants. Germany, which was then at the EU's eastern border, received by far the greatest number of asylum-seekers, with an average of 226,461 applications per annum during 1992–6 (UNHCR ref. H18). The numbers elsewhere were also substantial: the UK peaked between 1997 and 2001 with 76,340 applications per annum and France in 2002–6 with 51,541. Other countries received smaller absolute numbers but larger per capita figures: the Netherlands received 39,773 applicants from 1997 to 2001 (approximately one asylum application per 43 Dutch persons) and Sweden 31,008 in 1992–6 (one application per 276 persons). The sheer numbers involved put asylum systems under strain, but the turn towards restrictive policies was also driven by an increasingly widespread view among governments that asylum-seeking had become a surrogate economic migration channel through which individuals without a well-founded fear of persecution were searching for work.

The combination of an increase in numbers and a perception that the asylum system was being abused prompted several governments to make legislative and administrative reforms. Timothy Hatton (2011: 51) identifies three areas in which new policies were developed: access, processing and welfare. 'Access' refers to measures that affect the ability of asylum-seekers to enter the territory or asylum system of a Geneva Convention state; 'processing' refers to procedures for status determination, including appeal rights; while 'welfare' refers to the rights and benefits to which asylum-seekers and refugees are entitled, both during and after processing. As Hatton (ibid.) and others show, the trend along each of these dimensions has been increased restrictiveness. Although there are cross-national variations in terms of timing (some countries tightened asylum policy earlier than others) and outcomes (some countries are more restrictive than others), the overall direction of travel during the last twenty years has been towards stricter asylum policies.

Many states have tried to restrict access to their territories and asylum determination procedures through 'non-arrival measures' (Gibney 2006). Some of these measures overlap with the wider intensification of border controls discussed above, including the intensification of border surveillance and border patrols to detect and intercept unauthorized entries, as well as the introduction of carrier sanctions and visa requirements. The imposition of visa requirements during the 1990s, for example, was influenced by the potential of particular countries to generate refugees. In addition to these attempts to prevent access to territory as such, several asylum-specific measures have been developed to make access to the asylum system more difficult. The most direct method used is territorial excision, whereby part of a state's territory is excised from its jurisdiction for purposes of asylum law, meaning that asylum claims do not go through the normal procedures and persons can be removed more easily. Several countries have created special airport zones where asylum-seekers can be pre-screened without the full status determination procedure and, crucially, without generating rights of appeal. Australia has gone further still by excising several islands from its territory for the purposes of establishing claims to asylum. Immigrants who land on these islands are not deemed to have landed in Australia for immigration purposes, and, though they may apply for refugee status with the UNHCR, they have no recourse to Australian courts. As mentioned above, other measures designed to create a buffer zone around Geneva Convention states include 'safe third-country' and 'safe country of origin' provisions. These designate countries as places where people are presumed to be safe from persecution, so that the asylum claim of anyone who transits through or originates from one of these countries can be assessed using an expedited procedure for 'manifestly unfounded' claims and the applicant removed.

Since the concept was introduced in 1992, European and other destination countries have adopted safe country provisions into their asylum laws. The effect has been to create a cordon sanitaire around the EU's external borders, making it difficult for a person to claim asylum in an EU country if they have passed through one of the third countries designated as safe. Australia, Canada and the United States also operate safe country provisions.

The second way in which liberal states have sought to reduce asylum-seeking is by making their determination procedures more stringent and thereby reducing recognition rates – i.e., the proportion of applicants who are granted refugee or subsidiary humanitarian status. According to governments, the tightening of status determination became necessary during the 1990s because asylum had become a surrogate channel for economic migration, with many unfounded applicants entering the system and using appeals to delay removal. For human rights NGOs, these procedures have often compromised the integrity of the asylum system. The measures taken to reduce the number of persons granted asylum, as well as the time taken to determine cases, include expedited processing, reduction of the maximum period allowed for decisions, the creation of subsidiary categories that offer temporary protection rather than full refugee status, and reduced rights to appeal negative decisions. Faced with a surge in asylum applications in the early 1990s, Germany revised its constitutional right to asylum in 1993. Other European states also tightened their policies during the 1990s, leading to a 'race to the bottom' as countries sought to ensure their system was at least as stringent as those of others. Asylum flows to other OECD countries were not quite so dramatic, but nevertheless Australia, Canada and the United States also tightened their asylum policies, especially after 2001. Australia adopted some especially draconian measures following the MV *Tampa* incident in August 2001.

Governments have also reduced the rights and benefits that asylum-seekers receive. Measures here include the restriction or abolition of the right to work while an asylum claim is being determined, restrictions on benefits and access to social services, such as the replacement of cash with in-kind benefits, and the dispersal of asylum claimants to reception centres away from urban centres. The most draconian aspect of the toughening of reception conditions has been the growing use of immigration detention. Detention serves at least three distinct purposes: first, it is intended to prevent irregular immigrants and asylum-seekers from absconding, both during the determination process and after a claim has been rejected; second, it prevents immigrants and asylum-seekers from becoming socially integrated into local communities, and thereby minimizes sources of support and networks who can lobby to resist removal; and, third, it is intended to have a deterrent effect on future applicants by signalling a country's toughness. Most OECD countries use immigration detention for certain high-risk categories of asylum-seeker and undocumented immigrants, but since the 1990s the use of detention has become increasingly widespread. In the United States, the use of detention grew during the 1980s in response to inflows of Cuban, Haitian and Central American asylum-seekers, and then increased rapidly after the 1996 Illegal Immigrant Reform and Immigrant Responsibility Act (IIRIRA) made detention mandatory during the process of determining whether an applicant has a credible asylum claim (Gibney 2004: 164). Since then the number of persons in immigration detention has more than trebled, from approximately 95,000 individuals in 2001 to approximately 363,000 in 2010 (DHS 2011). The use of immigration detention has also spread in the UK and other European countries (Silverman 2011).

A final building block in the architecture of exclusion is the growing use of deportation. During the 1980s and for much of the 1990s, only a small percentage of failed asylum-seekers were actually removed (Gibney and Hansen 2003). The resulting 'removal gap' became a source of political embarrassment for governments. Not only did it undermine any claim that they were in control of immigration, it was also believed to act as an incentive for future asylum-seekers, since the chances of being removed if a claim was rejected was so small. As a 'cruel power' (Gibney 2008: 147) that involves the deployment of the state's coercive capacities against often vulnerable persons, deportation is both politically controversial and legally contestable. In liberal states, deportation often encounters political resistance and legal challenges based on both domestic and international human rights law. Deportation is also expensive and time-consuming, as individuals with an obvious interest in evading authorities have to be found and compelled to leave. Even when persons can be found and legal challenges seen off, there are often problems with securing cooperation from the presumed country of origin of the deportee. Sending countries have to agree to accept deportees and cooperate in redocumenting them when, as is often the case, identity documents have either been lost or destroyed or never existed in the first place. These complications have all contributed to deportation traditionally having a secondary status in the state's immigration armoury – a last resort rather than a principal instrument of immigration control.

Yet, according to Gibney (2008: 148), there has been a 'deportation turn' in recent years, in which Western countries have gone to considerable lengths to overcome the obstacles to deportation and close the removal gap. One key element in this has been the increased use of detention, mentioned above. Detention is intended not only to make absconding more difficult but also to isolate failed asylum-seekers from family and social networks who might mobilize to contest their deportation – for example, by lobbying their local representatives or mounting legal challenges. Many liberal states have also negotiated readmission agreements with third countries – essentially agreements to cooperate with deportation, including redocumentation, in return for benefits such as visa facilitation, trade concessions or development aid (Ellermann 2008). The renewed commitment to deportation has certainly had an effect. In Western countries, including the United States, Germany, the Netherlands, Canada and Australia, there has been a substantial rise in the number of deportations of failed asylum-seekers as well as irregular migrants (Gibney 2008: 146). Perhaps the most dramatic example is the UK. Before the asylum crisis of the 1990s, removals and deportations averaged just over 2,000 persons per year. By 1997, the first year of the Labour government, the number of deportations had risen to 7,160 and by 2006 the figure was 16,330 (ibid.: 149).

What effect have these measures had on asylum flows? It is clear that the number of asylum-seekers has declined since 2001–2, as figure 4.1 shows. In 2009, the number of persons who claimed asylum in OECD countries stood at about 363,000, which was about the same as in 2008 and a much smaller number than the peaks of the mid-1990s or early 2000s, when the number peaked at just over 600,000 (OECD 2011: 61). But to what extent has the decline between the early 2000s and the present been caused by more restrictive asylum policies as opposed to non-policy-related factors? Using regression analyses to gauge the impact of different components of asylum policy across nineteen major destination countries, Hatton (2011: 74–6) shows that the various restrictive measures discussed in this section have indeed had a deterrent effect on asylum applications. He estimates that,

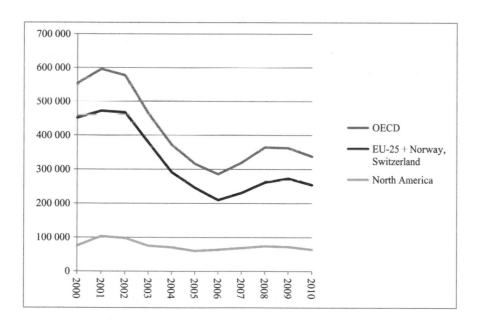

Source: Adapted from OECD (2011: 365), table A.1.3.

Figure 4.1 *Number of asylum-seekers in OECD countries, 2000–10*

between 2001 and 2006, measures designed to restrict access to territory reduced asylum applications by 14 per cent, while tougher processing policies reduced applications by a further 19 per cent (welfare policies, by contrast, had an insignificant effect on applications). Taking all policy measures together, he estimates that, of an overall reduction of 328,139 asylum applications during the period 2001–6, 108,054, or nearly a third, were caused by tougher policies (ibid.: 75).

The deterrent effect of recent policies on the ability to seek asylum redoubles the paradox outlined earlier: while all liberal states profess commitment to the principle of asylum, most have pursued policies that make asylum-seeking more difficult. As we have seen, this tightening was driven both by the belief that many asylum-seekers are in fact economic migrants and by the increasingly politicized debate and negative media portrayal of asylum-seekers. Since the asylum crisis of the 1990s, governments have come under significant pressure to reduce applications and recognition rates, and, unlike economic migration, where there are powerful interests that lobby for expansionist policies and thereby curb populist tendencies, powerful pro-asylum actors are conspicuously absent. Refugee organizations and NGOs have criticized governments for the effects of the exclusionary turn in asylum policy, but their impact on policymaking has been at best modest (Menz 2009: 5). This does not mean that liberal norms are entirely absent from the asylum policy domain. Many of the restrictive measures outlined above have been challenged through the courts and resisted at the implementation stage by coalitions of pro-asylum activists. Yet these constraints notwithstanding, the story of asylum policy since the 1990s has been one of increasing exclusion.

The Turn against Family Migration

Since the 1970s, family-related migration has emerged as an important inflow in most liberal democracies. Across the OECD, 39.6 per cent of all permanent immigration is family-related, making this the largest single category by some margin. Family-related migration has been the dominant legal mode of entry in Europe for the past few decades. In 2009 in France, for example, 76,573 persons, or 42.8 per cent of all immigrants, entered through family routes, the largest single category of admission. In Sweden, the proportion was even higher: 48.7 per cent, or 34,704 in absolute numbers. Yet these figures are dwarfed by the United States, where in that same year 747,413 individuals, or 66 per cent of all permanent immigrants, came through family routes. By comparison, the other settler states have lower levels of family migration, in both absolute and relative terms, but nevertheless family-related admissions in 2009 accounted for about a quarter of total inflows in these countries: 25.6 per cent in Australia, 25.9 per cent in Canada, and 29 per cent in New Zealand (OECD 2011).

Given the political imperatives to restrict immigration, it is perhaps unsurprising that family migration flows have become the subject of increasingly restrictive policies in many though not all liberal states. Yet, as the above figures show, family migration persists as a major category of entry in most of these states. To understand why family migration continues in the face of political opposition once again requires consideration of the interplay between inclusionary and exclusionary dynamics. While elected officials face political pressures to control family migration, other actors are able to mobilize liberal norms and institutions to limit the extent to which it is restricted.

The term 'family migration' encompasses at least three distinct subcategories: family reunification, which involves the admission of family members previously separated by migration; whole family migration, in which various family members migrate together (for example, a migrant on a work visa bringing dependants); and family formation, in which a migrant joins a citizen or previously settled migrant to form a family, often through marriage (Kraler and Kofman 2009: 2). Making these distinctions is important for understanding the evolving political debates and policies, particularly in Europe, where the shift from family reunification to family formation partly accounts for the growing political controversy surrounding family migration.

The fact of family migration is a defining feature of the immigration regimes of liberal states, distinguishing them from immigration regimes in non-liberal states. For example, the large-scale migration of workers to the Gulf region in recent years has not given rise to significant family migration, since these countries typically do not recognize family migration rights. In contrast, liberal states in Europe, North America and Oceania recognize rights to family life, as enshrined in international treaties such as the Universal Declaration of Human Rights (Article 16), in regional treaties (especially Article 8 of the European Convention on Human Rights), and in domestic laws and national constitutions. These liberal rights have enabled various forms of family migration, including secondary flows of migrants following earlier phases of labour migrant recruitment or postcolonial migrations, and more recently as citizens and permanent residents of liberal states seek to bring foreign spouses to their country of residence. In his classic analysis of why liberal states accept so-called unwanted immigration (in which he included family migration), Christian Joppke (1998) argued that family migration to former guestworker countries in the 1970s and 1980s, notably Germany, should be explained by constitutional protections that prevented executives from implementing the restrictive laws that they preferred. In Joppke's influential analysis, family migration, as a form of unwanted migration, occurs because of the liberal state's 'self-limited sovereignty'.

There is much to be said for this argument, but family migration was not always considered to be quite as 'unwanted' as it perhaps suggests. In Europe, the family migrants of the 1970s and 1980s were mostly family *reunification* migrants – the spouses (mostly wives) and children of male migrant workers. While it is true that the numbers sometimes alarmed governments, family reunification migration was not viewed as an inherently negative development. On the contrary, by 'normalizing' largely male migrant cohorts, it was seen as contributing towards the well-being and the integration of existing immigrants. During the 1990s, the composition of family migration shifted from reunification towards marriage migration, especially in those countries with a longer history of immigration and large settled immigrant communities. In the Netherlands, one of the few countries to distinguish between family formation and other forms of family-related admissions in its statistics, family formation rose from 39 per cent of family migration in 1995 to 60 per cent in 2003 (Kraler and Kofman 2009: 3). It was during this period that family migration came to be viewed in increasingly negative terms.

The turn against family migration was of course part of the wider restrictive turn following the collapse of communism. Several of the immigration reforms introduced by European governments during the early 1990s that were not principally about family migrants nevertheless contained provisions to tighten conditions for family admission. This happened in Austria, France and Germany, all of which introduced new rules on family reunification during this period. Most dramatically, in Denmark, the automatic right to family reunification that had been created by the 1983 Alien Law was abolished in 1992 and replaced with conditional administrative decisions. And in the Netherlands, the 1993 immigration reforms introduced income requirements and other conditions for family migrants; they also made a link between family migration and integration by referring to the 'personal responsibility' of those who wished to bring family members into the Netherlands to ensure their integration into the host society. The only European destination country that did not tighten entry conditions for family migrants during this period was the UK, arguably because it already had a comparatively strict framework.

As well as being caught up in the wider restrictive turn since the 1990s, family migration policy began to acquire its own restrictionist dynamics. Unlike the 1970s and 1980s, when family migration was seen as 'secondary' and not wholly undesirable, during the 1990s it came increasingly to be viewed by governments as problematic in several respects. This problematization was related to the changing composition of family migration flows mentioned above, from reunification in the 1970s and 1980s to formation and marriage since the 1990s. As European citizens began to bring foreign spouses to their country of origin, and especially as members of ethnic minority communities sought transnational marriages with spouses from overseas, perceptions about family migration shifted. As Kraler and Kofman (2009: 4) argue, in many European countries family migration became associated with three interrelated problems: first, abuse of the immigration system through marriages of convenience or so-called bogus marriages; second, welfare state burdens as a result of low rates of labour market participation by marriage migrants; and, third, a perception of the 'migrant family' as a patriarchal institution in which unequal gender roles, forced marriages and gender-based violence are prevalent. Thus what was tolerated as a migration flow that would 'normalize' predominantly male labour migrations and potentially facilitate integration came to be seen as an obstacle to integration.

The transformation of family migration into a problem has led European governments to adopt a host of restrictive measures on admission procedures and conditions. Policy measures adopted by European countries include intensified scrutiny of applicants for marriage visas (to identify marriages of convenience), increases in the minimum age of spouses (to limit forced and arranged marriages), greater income requirements for sponsors of family migrants (to reduce welfare costs), and integration measures such as mandatory integration and language courses for family migrants, language requirements for family visas, and pre-entry integration tests (see Kraler 2010: 40–3). The Dutch government pioneered this latter innovation, with a law introduced in 2007 that requires family migrants from certain countries, among them Morocco and Turkey, to pass a test on Dutch language and society in their home country before they can migrate to the Netherlands. Several other European countries, including Denmark, Germany and France, have followed suit (OECD 2011: 118). These developments have a complex relationship to liberalism, since on the one hand they are designed to restrict family migration, which is in tension with rights to family life, but on the other hand they can be, and sometimes are, defended as protecting liberal rights – for example, by preventing coercive and violent practices towards women. On a charitable interpretation, these policies could be viewed as instances of 'repressive liberalism', under which immigrants are required to adopt liberal values (Joppke 2007a); on a less generous interpretation, they are essentially immigration control measures designed to curb numbers.

The United States provides an interesting counterpoint to European developments. As mentioned above, family migration flows to the United States are higher than those in every European country, with family admissions accounting for 747,413 persons, or 66 per cent of all permanent immigrants, in 2009. Two factors, absent in Europe, help to explain these high levels: first, the institutional legacy of a quota system designed in the 1960s and based on family ties; and, second, the role of entrenched ethnic lobby groups, which have successfully opposed reforms to the system. The 1965 Immigration and Nationality Act, which remains the basis of US immigration law to this day, established a country-neutral quota system based on family ties (74 per cent of annual visas), skills (20 per cent) and refugees (4 per cent). Though the 1965 Act has been amended since – for example, the 1990 Immigration Act doubled the number of immigration visas granted for economic and employment reasons (Martin 2004: 66) – the principle of prioritizing entry for relatives of

US citizens and permanent residents persists to this day. Although immigration reform is high on the public agenda, it is one of the most contested issues in American politics, and attempts to change the level and composition of immigration flows have been fiercely resisted. Ethnic lobby groups, often in coalition with humanitarian organizations, have successfully mobilized to oppose restrictive proposals, and the emergence of immigrant voting blocs in key electoral states has given politicians strong incentives to support pro-immigration policies, despite populist opposition (Tichenor 2004: 92). Hence, in the United States, the 'political feedbacks' (ibid.) of immigration sustain expansive policies and prevent the kind of restrictions on family migration that have emerged across Europe.

Conclusion

This chapter set out to map the diverse array of policies and instruments with which governments regulate immigration, and in so doing to illustrate the contrasting dynamics associated with different policy areas. It has shown that the debates and policies associated with authorized labour migrants, irregular immigrants, asylum-seekers and family migrants are very different. Strictly speaking, then, there is no politics of immigration or immigration policy in the singular, rather a diverse array of political processes and policies that give rise to liberal states' apparently paradoxical combinations of openness and closure. The chapter has also shown how migration management is often an unavailing task for governments. Yet recognizing the Sisyphean nature of migration governance is not the same thing as accepting simple narratives of lost control. State policies matter even if they are hardly ever wholly effective.

CHAPTER FIVE

Migration Governance beyond the State

The previous chapters of this book have concentrated on the domestic politics and immigration policies of liberal states. This reflects the fact that immigration policymaking is conducted predominantly at the national level. To ignore developments at the international level would, however, be to miss an increasingly important part of the picture. International migration involves persons moving from one state to another and is therefore inherently a cross-border issue. Yet compared to other cross-border flows, such as international trade or finance, where a set of multilateral institutions and regulations have been developed, migration is notable for the relative absence of multilateral initiatives. There is no unified body of international migration law, nor is there a United Nations (UN) organization for migration.

This is not to say that there are no international institutions or standards that influence states' attempts to regulate international migration. Since the 1990s, the international dimension of migration management has become increasingly important, but, rather than a single multilateral framework, what has developed is 'a complex and fragmented tapestry of overlapping, parallel, and nested institutions' (Betts 2011: 2; see also Koslowski 2011b). These institutions have evolved in an ad hoc and bottom up way, and they are far from integrated or even coherent. Some date back to the immediate postwar period, notably the international refugee system, which was established in the 1950s, but many others have been negotiated more recently by states, existing international agencies and other transnational actors. Thus, while attempts to create a UN forum for global dialogue, let alone action, on migration have foundered in the face of resistance from Northern countries, today there are numerous processes and forums in which migration is debated, as well as a growing number of bilateral and regional interstate agreements.

To analyse this complex terrain, a different conceptual toolkit is needed to that used to examine the domestic level. Unlike domestic politics, where an authoritative rule-maker is able to make and enforce binding laws, the international arena lacks a sovereign ruler. For this reason, scholars of international politics often use the term 'governance', as distinct from 'government', to describe the norms, rules and decision-making procedures that exist at the international level (Betts 2011: 4–5). Global governance includes not only formal institutions at various scales above the national level but also an array of informal processes and procedures that impact on states. A central contention of the wider literature on global governance is that nation-states do not enjoy absolute authority over policymaking, but are shaped by these formal and informal institutions. This chapter examines the extent to which this is true of international migration. What form does migration governance beyond the state take? And to what extent are liberal states constrained by the emerging institutions of global migration governance?

Sovereignty, State Interests and Power

The ability of any state to regulate the entry of immigrants into its territory is an essential aspect of sovereignty. As Stephen D. Krasner (1999) argues, sovereignty is a complex and multidimensional concept, but for the purposes of this chapter it is sufficient to observe that sovereignty both in terms of *capability to rule* (which Krasner labels interdependence sovereignty) and as *exclusive authority to decide* (Westphalian sovereignty) is affected by international migration flows: a sovereign state will want to exercise *de facto* control over movements of people across its borders, as well as to enjoy *de jure* authority to make decisions about the terms upon which entry is or is not permitted. A state that is unable to regulate cross-border flows of people, or which has lost the authority to do so, will have diminished sovereignty. As jealous guardians of their sovereignty, states have therefore been extremely reluctant to create institutions or even engage in negotiations that reduce their capacity or authority to regulate immigration.

This alone is arguably a sufficient explanation of states' reticence about international cooperation on migration. However, there are at least two further reasons why the liberal states that are the subject of this book have been especially reluctant. The first reason is that the inherent connections between immigration controls and sovereignty have been exacerbated by the politicization of immigration across most liberal democracies. As discussed in chapter 2, public opinion towards immigration is generally sceptical, and immigration is an increasingly salient policy issue. In several countries, anti-immigrant sentiments have been mobilized. In this context, governments find themselves under considerable pressure to assert their sovereign powers over immigration, as manifested in promises by politicians to impose 'tough' policies and show that borders are 'under control'. Elected governments are nervous about opening themselves to the charge that they are giving up powers to other states or international institutions because, even though sharing competence with other actors might actually increase a state's capacity to regulate immigration, it is all too easy for political opponents to portray a government that does so as surrendering 'our' powers to keep 'them' out.

In other words, there is an especially strong tendency to national chauvinism over internationalism in this policy area, seen most starkly in the European far right's common allegation that, by surrendering powers to the EU, national governments have lost control of immigration and promoted multiculturalism.

A further reason why liberal states are sceptical of cooperation, and certainly formal multilateralism, are the conflicts of interest that exist between the global North and South. The rich liberal states of Europe, North America and Oceania are predominantly immigrant-receiving countries, while many middle- and low-income countries are predominantly sending countries. This creates conflicts of interest: the governments of Northern countries have an interest in preventing irregular immigration and selectively facilitating a relatively small amount of wanted immigration; Southern countries have comparatively little interest in preventing undocumented emigrants – indeed, they often stand to benefit from their remittances – and they sometimes worry about Northern states poaching their highly skilled workers. These are broad-brush generalizations, and there are undoubtedly exceptions, but countries in the North certainly have rather different priorities for migration governance than countries in the South. In this context, it is to be expected that the powerful states of the North will be opposed to formal multilateral institutions, which would constrain their ability to pursue their interests and give Southern countries greater leverage or even equal standing in negotiations. This is not to say that there are no possible shared interests between the North and South (as we shall see, there are) or that other forms of cooperation might not occur (they do). But countries that are relatively powerful under the status quo are unlikely to endorse multilateralism.

Why Cooperate?

Given these three factors – the importance of migration to state sovereignty, national chauvinism in the domestic politics of immigration, and the opposition of Northern countries to cede powers in an area in which their interests conflict with Southern countries – why would liberal states choose to cooperate on migration? Under what conditions, if at all, should we expect cooperation to occur?

A common explanation for global governance regimes is that they evolve as a response to collective action problems associated with the provision of public goods (see Olson 1965 for a classic statement). A public good is a good that is non-excludable and non-rival: once the good is provided, non-contributors to its production cannot be excluded from enjoying its benefits, and one actor's consumption of the good does not reduce its availability for others. A textbook example is a lighthouse: irrespective of whether they contributed towards the cost of its construction, all passing ships will benefit from the provision of a lighthouse, and one ship's consumption of the light-house's good does not reduce its availability to other ships. Public goods tend to be underprovided on account of free-rider problems. Since potential benefi-ciaries of a public good can enjoy it without contributing to its provision, they look to other actors to incur the costs of providing it; and, since all potential beneficiaries reason in this way, a good that all desire will be under-provided. There are various ways of resolving collective action problems, but all involve mechanisms either to incentivise or to compel actors to produce the good in question. In contemporary global politics, carbon dioxide emis-sions are a good example: all states stand to benefit from reductions in emis-sions, but in the absence of coordinated action states will not want to incur the economic cost of cutting emissions unless they can be sure that others will do likewise. Hence the creation of international institutions to enable collective action on emissions cuts.

Some scholars have tried to argue that migration governance is a public good. James F. Hollifield, for example, maintains that an international migra-tion regime 'can approximate a global public good' by 'achieving orderly, legal movements of people across national boundaries . . . movements that can be beneficial and highly profitable to both the sending and receiving countries require a *degree of international cooperation*' (Hollifield 2011: 230). However, most scholars disagree with this assessment. While public-good reasoning applies to many aspects of global governance, it is far from clear that it can do much work to explain international cooperation on migration. As others have pointed out (e.g., Betts 2011: 25; Hansen 2011: 16–17), migra-tion governance does not meet the criteria of a public good because the costs and benefits of migration are both largely excludable and rival. When a person migrates from country A to country B, the costs and benefits are borne by the sending and receiving countries, with few if any externalities for coun-tries C, D, etc. As an example, if developed country A recruits skilled migrant workers from developing country B, then A will enjoy the labour market benefits and possibly incur some integration costs, while B will incur the costs of losing a worker but potentially stand to receive benefits – for example, in the form of remittance flows. Neither the benefits nor the costs of this migra-tion fall in any significant way on countries C, D, etc. At the same time, given that there are now fewer migrant workers from country B that countries C, D, etc., can recruit, the 'consumption' of the good in question is also rival: country A's admission of migrant workers diminishes the availability of workers from country B for other countries C, D, etc. Refugee protection is arguably closer to a public good (Betts 2011: 25), but this too has been ques-tioned (Hansen: 2011: 17).

If public goods theory can offer little help, how else can international migration cooperation be understood? A more promising explanation looks to governments' pursuit of their national interests, specifically their attempts to maximize the benefits and minimize the costs of migration, while at the same time seeking to retain their sovereignty in this sensitive policy area. The argument is quite simple: many governments have come to believe that their own interests are sometimes best served by cooperation with other states; or, to put it the other way around, they have come to realize the limits of uni-lateral action (Martin 2011: 128). Due to the scale, complexity and inherently transnational character of contemporary migrations, states acting alone have limited capacity to regulate flows in their own interest, whereas cooperation can *sometimes* increase this capacity without significant losses of sovereignty. As Virginie Guiraudon and Gallya Lahav argue, 'by sharing competence, states may have ceded autonomy yet they have done so to meet national policy goals, regaining sovereignty in another sense: capabilities to rule' (2000: 165). In other words, states have not sought to cooperate on migration at the cost of sovereignty, but rather traded some aspects of 'Westphalian sovereignty' in return for increased 'interdependence sovereignty'. A state's decision to shift migration governance 'up' to the international level is done in order to achieve policy objectives that would otherwise be elusive.

In a lucid discussion of these dynamics, Hansen (2011) argues that interna-tional cooperation on migration is 'not natural' for states. Beginning with the assumption that states seek to promote their interests and protect their powers in this highly sensitive area, Hansen contends that states have an in-built preference for unilateral action on migration and will be motivated to cooperate *only* when coordinated action is necessary to achieve their policy objectives. Furthermore, for cooperation to occur, one of two things must hold true: either two or more states must share the same goals or, where they have differing goals, there must be selective incentives for them to cooperate. These incentives can be positive (e.g., state A offers state B a benefit in return for cooperation) or negative (e.g., state A threatens state B with a sanction if it refuses to cooperate). In the case of shared goals, cooperation may evolve relatively easily. For example, when two receiving countries share an interest in preventing irregular immigration from a third country and, crucially, when unilateral action is ineffective and there is reason to believe that coop-eration will be more effective, then cooperation is likely to occur. This align-ment of interests can explain several instances of North–North cooperation, such as on external border controls in the European Union (EU). Even here, however, there needs to be a mechanism to punish non-compliance, other-wise states may find themselves unwilling to cooperate for fear that the other party will not uphold their part of the bargain. Recent controversies over certain member states' ability to regulate the external EU border and thus ensure the security of the free movement area illustrate that this is a very real concern (Brady 2012).

When it comes to North–South relations, the prospects for cooperation are much more limited. Incentives are likely to be essential since, as already mentioned, the policy goals of rich immigrant-receiving states and poor immigrant-sending states are rarely convergent; in fact, they tend to diverge.

As a result of the domestic political dynamics discussed in preceding chapters, rich liberal states have an interest in preventing irregular immigration and facilitating selective labour immigration; whereas immigrant-sending countries in the South typically have an interest in facilitating migration, partly because it creates remittance flows, while at the same time minimizing the 'brain drain' of skilled workers.[6] In this context of divergent interests, incentives and 'issue linkages' are needed. Thus North–South negotiations on migration often link cooperation with other issues such as visa facilitation, trade agreements and development assistance. A typical arrangement involves Northern states offering visa concessions, trade agreements or development aid in return for cooperation from Southern states in preventing irregular migration and readmitting irregular migrants.

Given the unequal power relations that often exist between Northern and Southern states, these negotiations do not take place on a level playing field. The ability to offer benefits and threaten sanctions to induce cooperation is not equal between states. Richer, powerful states have more to offer by way of positive incentives and are better able to impose and credibly threaten sanctions. Broadly speaking, this maps onto the North–South divide: rich immigrant-receiving liberal states in the North – the subject of this book – are typically in a more powerful position than emigration states in the South. Two qualifications to this general claim should be noted. First, there are some very significant exceptions. China and India are both major sending countries, and neither could be considered to lack power in relation to most Northern countries. Second, though many Southern countries are less powerful overall than Northern countries, they are far from powerless in negotiations on migration. After all, they have something that receiving countries want (cooperation on irregular migration), which gives them some leverage (Paoletti 2011). These qualifications notwithstanding, when it comes to North–South cooperation on migration, power inequalities mean that Northern states tend to be policy 'makers' whereas Southern states are often policy 'takers' (Betts 2011: 22).

These arguments about when and why interstate cooperation is likely to occur also have implications for the *form* that migration governance is likely to take. One implication is that cooperation is more likely to take place on a bilateral or regional, rather than a global, basis. Northern states have few incentives to create multilateral institutions, since there is no confluence of interests and limited possibilities for developing selective incentives and enforcement mechanisms on a global scale. Southern states are more likely to support multilateral institutions, since they potentially stand to gain from more coordinated migration governance. Northern states can be expected to oppose developments in this direction. In contrast, shared interests and/or selective incentives are more likely to be found on a regional or bilateral basis.

A second implication is that interstate cooperation is more likely to be informal than formal. Powerful receiving countries will oppose binding agreements on migration that would constrain their sovereignty. Informal non-binding cooperation, by contrast, allows receiving states to engage in negotiations without loss of sovereignty or prior commitments, and the possibility of exit gives them a bargaining chip: accept *x* or we will withdraw from cooperation altogether. For these reasons, Hansen plausibly argues that, when it comes to the institutionalization of migration governance, 'less is more' (Hansen 2011: 14). Lastly, interstate cooperation is more likely to work if it is closed to public scrutiny. Given the highly politicized nature of immigration in liberal states, government officials will be wary of engaging in negotiations with other countries if their deliberations are open to criticism by political opponents or potentially sensationalist media coverage (ibid.: 19).

These claims do not mean that migration governance beyond the state is impossible. But they do imply that there are substantial constraints to international cooperation and that a global migration regime is unlikely ever to emerge. Rather, we should expect to see a complex patchwork of different processes and agreements: some formal bilateral agreements, plus informal negotiations on a regional basis, and few if any global institutions. The remainder of this chapter examines the extent to which these claims are true.

The Shape of Global Migration Governance

Interstate cooperation on migration takes place through a complex, multi-layered and diffuse set of processes and institutions. This patchwork has several distinctive features. First, there is substantial variation in the degree and type of cooperation across different migration policy areas. Koslowski (2011b) distinguishes between three 'global mobility regimes' with varying degrees of cooperation: the refugee regime (most integrated), the labour migration regime (least integrated) and the international travel regime (a middle case). Betts (2011) adopts a more complex schema but also finds substantial variation. Using the four policy categories discussed in chapter 4 – labour migration, irregular migration, forced migration and family migration – the most developed regime is the international refugee system, while labour and family migration are barely regulated at all at the international level, and irregular migration lies somewhere in between. As discussed below, the international refugee system is exceptional insofar as it comprises a formal multilateral framework, enshrined in international law and overseen by a UN agency. Interstate cooperation on irregular migration, including human smuggling and trafficking, is increasingly common, albeit predominantly informal and regional. Various regional consultative processes (RCPs) bring government officials together on an informal basis to share information and identify possibilities for cooperation in tackling irregular migration.

By contrast, interstate cooperation on labour migration is very limited. The International Labour Organization (ILO) has tried to develop international legal standards on labour migration, but most Northern states have refused to sign the relevant treaties. The 1949 Migration for Employment Convention (Revised) has been ratified by a total of 49 countries, while the 1975 Convention concerning Migrations in Abusive Conditions and the Promotion of Equality of Opportunity and Treatment of Migrant Workers has been ratified by 23 states.[7] In both cases, however, the majority of signatory states are sending countries rather than countries of destination. Even more starkly, the 1990 UN Convention on the Protection for the Rights of All Migrant Workers and Members of their Families, which is a comprehensive international treaty dealing with migrants' rights, has been ratified by just 40 states, with not a single Northern destination country among them. While countries of origin supported the treaty on account of their interest in promoting the rights of their overseas citizens, destination countries in Europe, North America and Oceania baulked at its extension of rights to irregular migrants. Thus despite, or in fact because of, its universalist and rights-based logic, liberal states have refused to ratify the Convention. To the extent that there is any international cooperation on labour migration policy, it takes place on a predominantly bilateral basis – for example, individual Northern countries concluding migrant worker schemes with selected Southern countries.

This leads to a second characteristic of global migration governance, namely its 'multi-level' nature. The concept of multi-level governance refers to the dispersal of public decision-making across multiple levels of political authority, which are increasingly interrelated and influenced by one another (Hooghe 1996; Marks 1993). In a system of multi-level governance, policymaking is not vested in a single jurisdiction, whether the nation-state or a global regime, but rather involves 'the articulation of authority across jurisdictions at diverse scales' (Hooghe and Marks 2009: 2). Global migration governance is a case in point. In the absence of a unified multilateral framework, international cooperation on migration takes place on different scales and levels, including bilateral, regional, inter-regional and some multilateral relations. And, as already suggested, the different levels are more significant in some policy areas than in others – thus, largely bilateral relations in the area of labour migration, regional processes on irregular migration, and multilateralism in the refugee regime.

In addition to multiple levels and variations between policy areas, global migration governance is characterized by variation in the degree and intensity of cooperation, ranging from binding arrangements with mechanisms for compliance monitoring at one extreme to informal and non-binding processes at the other. In comparison to many other issues of global import, the tendency in migration governance is clearly towards the latter end of the spectrum. States have tended to prefer the flexibility and conditionality afforded by informal agreements, and they have resisted the construction of international laws and institutions that would significantly constrain their room for manoeuvre. This degree of formality cross-cuts the levels and policy areas already mentioned, adding a further dimension of complexity. Thus there are some limited aspects of formal multilateralism as well as a growing trend towards informal multilateralism; at the same time, both bilateral and regional agreements can be more or less formal, though most instances of formal agreements are bilateral and most regional processes are informal.

A final feature of global migration governance is what Betts (2011: 14) calls its 'embeddedness' in other governance regimes. This refers to the way in which migration-relevant norms, standards and regulations are present in regimes for other policy areas, such as trade, human rights or demography, which are often more developed than the migration regime. Aspects of international human rights law, trade law and maritime law contain migration-related elements that affect state behaviour on migration, either through 'hard law' constraints or 'soft law' norms, and some international lawyers have identified an international migration law emerging from these sources (Cholewinski et al. 2007). In addition, although there is no global migration agency, the mandates of a range of international institutions, including both UN and non-UN agencies, touch upon migration: the World Bank has become involved in discussions about migration, remittances and development; the United Nations Children Fund (UNICEF) is interested in migration as it affects children; the United Nations Population Fund (UNFPA) is concerned with migration as it affects population dynamics; and so on. Betts (2011: 16–17) suggests that this range of pre-existing legal and institutional frameworks is one reason why 'there has been a strong and emerging tendency towards not creating new, binding structures but towards working within the existing ones.' However, though institutional density may be a factor explaining the absence of a single migration agency, it would not be insurmountable if there was a will among states to create such an agency (which, in the case of Northern states, there most emphatically is not). Instead, various coordination mechanisms have been created, notably the Global Migration Group (GMG), which was established by the UN Secretary-General in 2006 (see below).

In sum, migration governance at the international level occurs through a complex and fragmented regime that is characterized by variation in the degree of cooperation between policy areas, multiple levels of cooperation, varying degrees of formality, and a degree of overlap or 'embeddedness' in other international institutions and laws. The remainder of this chapter further examines these claims through four cases of international cooperation on migration: the international refugee system, which is the one instance of formal multilateralism; the rise of informal multilateralism in the migration–development nexus; intergovernmental processes and dialogues on a regional and bilateral basis; and, finally, the European Union's common asylum and migration policy, which is by far the most significant regional migration regime.

Formal Multilateralism: The International Refugee System

The international refugee system is the only example of formal multilateralism in global migration governance. It is based on an international treaty that has been signed and ratified by all liberal states, and indeed by most other states; and it is overseen by a dedicated UN agency with a mandate to ensure refugees' access to protection and develop durable solutions to their plight. The 1951 Convention Relating to the Status of Refugees provides a definition of who qualifies for refugee status and sets out rights to which all refugees are entitled. As discussed in chapter 4, its core principle is that of *non-refoulement* – the right of refugees not to be returned to a country where they risk persecution – which places genuine constraints on state sovereignty. No matter how a person reached a country that has signed the 1951 Convention, its government cannot deport that person to a territory where 'his life or freedom would be threatened on account of his race, religion, nationality, membership of a particular social group or political opinion' (Article 33(1)). Courts in receiving countries have invoked this principle to thwart governments' attempts to remove immigrants forcibly from their territory.

In addition to a well-established body of international law grounded in the 1951 Convention and its 1967 Protocol, the refugee regime is overseen by a UN agency, the Office of the United Nations High Commissioner for Refugees (UNHCR). The UNHCR was created by the United Nations General Assembly in 1950, initially as a temporary organization to address the needs of displaced persons in Europe, but with an increasingly global reach during the 1960s and 1970s (Betts et al. 2012). Today, it is a large and important international agency, with 7,685 staff worldwide and an annual budget in 2012 of $3.59 billion.[8] The UNHCR must chart a difficult course between its humanitarian mission to protect refugees, on the one hand, and its role as a coordinator of individual states' responses to refugees, on the other. It is unique among international migration agencies in terms of its legal mandate, moral authority and expertise. It also has a global scope, with offices in over 125 countries, and the capacity not only to negotiate protection solutions with states but also to conduct operations in the field. Thus UNHCR is a global political actor that engages in a range of activities, including policy advocacy, negotiations with governments on repatriation and resettlement, capacity-building, emergency responses to refugee crises, and longer-term delivery of humanitarian assistance in often dangerous conflict situations.

The existence of such an agency, combined with a binding international treaty that provides rights to forced migrants and constrains state sovereignty, makes the international refugee system quite exceptional. It is not an approach to migration governance that has been, or likely will be, applied in any other area; nor would it be created in the same way today. Both the 1951 Convention and the UNHCR were created at the high tide of formal multilateralism, and both were shaped by very specific historical and regional circumstances. The displacement of millions of people in Europe during the Second World War and the subsequent persecution of dissidents in communist countries generated the political will among Western states to create the refugee system (Hansen 2011: 20). Without the moral imperative to resettle displaced persons (helped along by the labour market needs of war-ravaged countries which were willing to accommodate much needed foreign workers) and the geopolitical advantages of welcoming refugees from communism during the early Cold War, the refugee system would not exist. This was a brief historical moment in which the political and economic interests of liberal states supported rather than conflicted with rights-based universalism and multilateralism, and in which national chauvinism had been temporarily dimmed by the memory of fascism. Yet, even in these unusually propitious circumstances, the United States, which had emerged as the major Western power, wanted to limit the authority and functions of the UNHCR, and most Western governments wanted to restrict the scope of the Convention to pre-1951 European refugees (Betts et al. 2012: 13–16).[9]

Since the postwar years the refugee system has come under increased strain, especially after the collapse of communism and the 'refugee crisis' prompted by the upsurge in asylum-seekers to Europe during the early 1990s. The alignment of economic and political national interests with rights-based universalism that characterized the immediate postwar years came apart during this period (Boswell 2005: 28–30), and since the 1990s states have become reluctant to provide asylum or contribute towards refugee protection. While liberal states remain formally committed to the refugee regime and are obliged to uphold international refugee law, they have increasingly sought to avoid their obligations under the Convention by implementing various restrictive asylum measures (as discussed in chapter 4) and by refusing to accept substantial numbers of refugees under UNHCR auspices.

It is striking that, even in this most formalized and multilateral part of the global migration regime, the discrepancies between North and South are obvious: 80 per cent of refugees (8.5 million persons) are hosted in developing countries, compared to just 15 per cent in Europe and 4 per cent in North America (UNHCR 2011: 6). To a large extent this reflects the fact that most refugees flee to and seek refuge in neighbouring countries, which are overwhelmingly located in the South. Nevertheless, it is clear that the cost of protecting refugees falls disproportionately on some of the poorest countries in the world. While Northern states host a substantial number of refugees who arrived as asylum-seekers, they accept only a tiny proportion of refugees for resettlement in their own territories: during 2010 a total of 98,800 refugees were admitted for resettlement in 22 countries, with the bulk hosted in just nine countries (ibid.: 39).[10] Most European countries do not accept any refugees for resettlement at all.

As the numbers of refugees have grown, and Northern governments have become increasingly reluctant to support them, the UNHCR has found itself trying to persuade states to meet their obligations under the Convention: on the one hand, fighting a rear-guard action on restrictive asylum and border control measures; on the other, advocating for greater responsibility-sharing through resettlement and funding for regional protection solutions. However, without the ability to impose sanctions or compel states to accept refugees, and reliant as it is upon donor states for most of its budget, the UNHCR can only do this through moral suasion and diplomacy. In short, despite the formal multilateralism of the international refugee system, the limits to interstate cooperation on migration are apparent even in this area.

Informal Multilateralism: The Migration–Development Nexus

Beyond the refugee system, multilateral cooperation occurs mostly on an informal basis. While binding treaties are thin on the ground, there is a proliferation of forums in which state representatives meet to discuss international migration, typically with non-binding aims such as seeking common ground, sharing information or identifying 'best practice'. Since the mid-1990s, an increasingly important dimension of informal multilateralism is the North–South dialogue on migration and development. Following discussions about migration at the 1994 International Conference on Population and Development in Cairo, the then UN Secretary-General, Kofi Annan, tried to promote the idea of a global migration conference under UN auspices. Faced with opposition from several Northern states, in 2003 Annan instead set up the Global Commission on International Migration (GCIM), with a mandate 'to provide the framework for the formulation of a coherent, comprehensive and global response to the issue of international migration' (GCIM 2005: vii). The GCIM was made up of nineteen senior politicians from both developed and developing countries. Its 2005 report recommended further development of bilateral and regional interstate cooperation on migration issues and advocated the creation of what it called an 'Inter-agency Global Migration Facility' to coordinate the migration-related activities of various international agencies. This led in 2006 to the establishment of the Global Migration Group, as mentioned above. In the longer term, and much more ambitiously, the GCIM report advocated a 'fundamental overhaul of the current institutional architecture relating to international migration' to include the creation of a single organization with responsibility for migration (ibid.: 75) The exact shape of this organization was not spelled out, though various options were canvassed ranging from the creation of a new migration agency to the incorporation of existing UN agencies (UNHCR and ILO) and possibly the IOM.

Having failed in the late 1990s to persuade states to create a UN forum, Annan was successful in organizing a plenary session of the UN General Assembly to discuss migration and development issues. The UN High Level Dialogue (HLD) on Migration and Development was held at UN headquarters in New York on 14–15 September 2006. In addition to a plenary debate, the HLD consisted of a number of roundtable discussions on issues such as remittances, human smuggling and trafficking, and bilateral and regional partnerships. While most delegates could agree that further informal discussions were warranted, few wanted to go any further than this. Indeed, while the HLD was a significant milestone insofar as it put migration and development at the top of the international agenda for the first time, the outcome of the meeting was a reaffirmation of states' reluctance to commit to formal consultative mechanisms, let alone binding international agreements. In particular, the United States opposed any future consultations taking place through the UN. In response, Annan proposed further dialogues on an annual basis, which would be state-owned and take place outside of the UN framework.

The resulting Global Forum on Migration and Development (GFMD) is now the main consultative mechanism for North–South cooperation on migration. It is an annual intergovernmental meeting which has to date met in Belgium (2007), the Philippines (2008), Greece (2009), Mexico (2010), Switzerland (2011) and Mauritius (2012). As a government-owned process, each year the GFMD is chaired by the hosting state, while a steering group consisting of both developed and developing countries prepares the agenda. The meetings themselves are organized into roundtables that cover topics such as human capital development and labour mobility, remittances, migrants' rights, legal admissions and reducing irregular migration, integration of migrants, and climate change and migration (Martin 2011: 138–9). Each roundtable is normally co-chaired by a developed and a developing country. Alongside the government discussions are so-called Civil Society Days, in which civil society groups meet to discuss the agenda for that year. While there are 'interface' sessions for civil society delegates and government representatives, the forum itself is reserved for the latter, and there is a consensus among governments against opening it to non-governmental actors. Attempts to transform the GFMD into a more formal intergovernmental process, such as the Mexican government's 2008 proposal to integrate it into the UN, have been consistently opposed by Northern countries.

The GFMD is not a decision-making forum: it does not enjoy any powers to conclude agreements between states or to make binding recommendations.

Even its supporters acknowledge that it is a 'vehicle for discussion, not action' (Martin 2011: 142). It is therefore tempting to dismiss it merely as a talking shop, but this would be to underestimate its potential significance. The GFMD has, for example, led to the conclusion of some bilateral agreements: at the first meeting in Brussels, the delegation from Mauritius outlined a programme for circular migration, which led to agreements with Canada and France.[11] And although the forum's online 'Platform for Partnerships' is not exactly brimming with new initiatives, it does provide a mechanism for governments and international organizations to issue calls for action and identify potential partners for cooperative programmes. As this suggests, the GFMD's impact lies more in its facilitative role in bringing government representatives together, which may lead to the diffusion of norms and standards for voluntary adoption rather than to any formal powers. The GFMD itself claims to have 'yielded policy proposals and outcomes, which have been taken forward by participating governments, international agencies and experts, resulting in changes in policy, legislation and institutions in a number of countries', though the evidence cited in support of this claim is fairly modest at present.[12]

Regionalism and Bilateralism: RCPs and Migration Partnerships

Aside from the refugee regime and the migration–development nexus, most interstate cooperation on migration occurs on a regional or bilateral basis. Regional cooperation tends to be informal and consultative, whereas bilateral cooperation more often involves binding agreements between states. Since the mid-1990s, an increasingly common form of regional cooperation on migration is the regional consultative process (RCP). RCPs are state-owned processes made up of governments in the same region or like-minded governments from different regions. They sometimes involve international organizations, though the focus is typically intergovernmental. RCPs involve confidential and informal consultations between government representatives which do not result in binding decisions. Rather, the aim is to share information, identify areas of common interest and disseminate so-called best practices. RCPs do not usually have a substantial administrative staff (the IOM and ICMPD perform the functions of a secretariat for some of the main RCPs), something which participating states value both for the low administration costs and, more importantly, because a smaller secretariat enables direct exchanges between high-level government officials unmediated by an international bureaucracy with a potential agenda of its own.

The first RCP, the Intergovernmental Consultations on Migration, Asylum and Refugees (IGC), was formed in 1985 by a group of seven European states. Today, it has seventeen participating states, plus representatives from the

European Commission, IOM and UNHCR. In its own words, it is an 'informal, non-decision making forum for intergovernmental information exchange and policy debate on issues of relevance to the management of international migratory flows'.[13] The IGC meets annually for a 'full round' and 'mini full round' of consultations, as well as organizing semi-annual meetings of its standing working groups and ad hoc workshops. Discussions initially focused on asylum policy issues, but the IGC broadened its remit during the 1990s to cover entry controls and enforcement, as well as returns, people-smuggling and migration control technologies. Since 2001 it has also discussed labour immigration and integration policies. Strictly speaking, the IGC is not a *regional* process, since it includes the governments of Australia, Canada, New Zealand and the United States, as well as thirteen European states. It in fact involves most liberal states with substantial immigrant populations.

The IGC provided a model for future RCPs, which have proliferated since the 1990s. Three of the most significant are the Budapest Process, the Regional Conference on Migration (RCM), also known as the Puebla Process, and the Bali Process.[14] The Budapest Process is a consultative process established in 1991 for the discussion of 'orderly migration', which means control-oriented policies, including prevention of irregular migration, returns and readmission, and asylum. It began with a focus on Central and Eastern Europe but has expanded eastwards to take in the Commonwealth of Independent States (CIS) and some Asian countries, and now embraces more than 50 governments and ten international organizations. The RCM is the most important North–South RCP in the Americas. Founded in 1996, it involves the governments of Canada, the United States, Mexico and eight other Latin American countries. As with most RCPs, it defines its role in terms of the exchange of information and best practice, with a focus on economic migration policy, human rights and development issues. Lastly, the Bali Process was established in 2002, with a focus on people-smuggling and trafficking in the Asia-Pacific region. It now has 43 members and is co-chaired by Australia and Indonesia. There are also several Southern RCPs, including the Migration Dialogue for Southern Africa (MIDSA), the South American Conference on Migration (SACM or Lima Process) and the Abu Dhabi Dialogue on temporary labour mobility in Asia.

Given their informal and non-binding nature, what impact do RCPs have on states, specifically liberal states in the North? And how do they influence migration policy? The literature on RCPs is far from extensive, but it does offer some tentative answers to these questions. In a discussion of their influence, Thouez and Channac (2006) argue that, despite the proliferation and apparent diversity of RCPs across different regions, they in fact lead to 'convergence in perceptions and expectations' through processes of 'informal socialisation', which in turn leads to 'harmonisation of policies and practices in the field of migration' (2006: 371–2). In other words, by assembling government officials to discuss migration policy and share information, RCPs lead to similar ways of perceiving migration phenomena and thus to common policy approaches. They claim in particular that the 'model of cooperation' characterized by informality, non-binding discussions and a limited administrative structure that was established in the early RCPs in Europe has been emulated by more recently established RCPs across the world.

But it does not necessarily follow that 'common understandings', much less 'policy convergence', will be the result of a transfer of models of cooperation, and Thouez and Channac do not offer empirical evidence to substantiate their claims about policy convergence. It is just as plausible that, rather than RCPs generating common understandings and policy convergence, some measure of common interests is a precondition for their formation (such as the regionally diverse but all-Northern IGC). Equally, transfer of a common model of cooperation may simply fail to generate policy convergence; without more empirical evidence it is not possible to conclude that one leads to another.

In a recent analysis, Jobst Koehler (2011) argues that the effects of RCPs are, as he puts it, more 'subtle'. Drawing on government network theory and evidence from three case studies (the RCM, Bali Process and MIDSA), Koehler argues that the impact of RCPs lies in their 'soft powers' of persuasion and information. Contrary to claims that they induce migration policy convergence, his comparison of the RCM, Bali Process and MIDSA leads him to conclude that their impacts on governance are highly variable and dependent on their composition and follow-up procedures. In particular, RCPs in which ministerial-level officials are regularly involved are likely to have greater impact than those in which only technical levels officials participate (Koehler 2011: 117). For example, he shows that the RCM, in which ministers are 'intimately involved in the process in the form of regular reviews and active leadership' (ibid.), has had much more impact than the MIDSA, which has no ministerial involvement. Moreover, Koehler concludes that the 'policy convergence' thesis is too deterministic: this *may* be an outcome of RCPs, but informed or coordinated policy divergence is also possible. There is little reason to believe that RCPs, as 'loosely coordinated horizontal networks' (ibid.: 119) organized on a voluntary and purely intergovernmental basis, constrain individual states, which can and do persist with 'their' way of doing things if they are at odds with other participating states.

In contrast to RCPs, bilateral migration agreements are not an historically recent phenomenon. Both the European guestworker programmes during the 1950s and 1960s and the US Bracero programme from 1942 to 1964 were based on bilateral agreements with sending countries, while in Asia the Philippines signed labour agreements with numerous countries in the Asia-Pacific region during the late 1970s and 1980s (OECD 2004: 11). Nevertheless, in recent years there has been a trend towards increased bilateralism in migration policy, and most major immigrant-receiving states have negotiated bilateral agreements with sending countries. Unlike regional and global regimes, bilateral agreements are much more likely to be formalized. In bilateral negotiations, it is easier to identify where there are common interests and, where interests diverge, to make issue linkages and negotiate on a quid pro quo basis; furthermore, once a bilateral arrangement has been agreed, it is simpler to monitor compliance and identify defaulters than in complex multilateral arrangements. Bilateral agreements on a North–North or South–South basis are often based on common interests and take a quid pro quo form; one state offers something in return for the same or similar by another state – for example, free movement agreements. In contrast, North–South bilateralism requires issue linkages to overcome conflicts of interest – for example, a Northern state offers trade concessions or development assistance in return for a Southern state's cooperation on border control to deter irregular migration or readmission of irregular migrants. North–South bilateralism often requires difficult negotiations, but the growing number of such agreements shows that these negotiations can succeed under certain circumstances.

Bilateral migration agreements take many forms and are undertaken for different reasons. Space precludes an in-depth analysis of the numerous agreements that exist today. Rather, four ideal types of bilateralism can be identified, with some illustrative examples: bilateral border controls, free movement arrangements, readmission agreements and labour migration agreements – though it should be noted that these categories overlap (i.e., some agreements contain more than one element, often because of the issue linkage mentioned above). The first type of bilateral migration agreement relates to cooperation on border controls: for example, the 2009 Italy–Libya protocol on maritime surveillance and patrols or the UK–France agreement for 'juxtaposed controls' at the Eurostar terminals and ferry ports, where passengers clear passport controls of the destination country before embarkation. A second type of bilateralism covers free movement arrangements for the nationals of two countries: for example, the Trans-Tasman Travel Arrangement between Australia and New Zealand, which allows for free movement of citizens of one nation to the other, or, on a more limited basis, the Polish–Ukrainian multiple entry permits agreement for citizens living within 30 kilometres of their shared border. A third type of bilateral migration agreement is the readmission agreement. As discussed in chapter 4, these arrangements require a sending country to cooperate in the deportation of irregular migrants from a destination country, often in return for visa facilitation. Such agreements have become increasingly common since the late 1990s, as receiving countries have sought to increase their deportation rates. A final type of bilateral arrangement consists of agreements for the recruitment of foreign workers. Bilateral labour agreements are highly diverse and include seasonal employment agreements, especially in agriculture, other temporary or circular labour recruitment programmes, trainee and apprenticeship schemes, and working holidaymaker programmes. Moreover, they can involve high- or low-skilled workers and may or may not be sector-specific. While there is considerable variation between states, most immigrant-receiving countries have concluded bilateral agreements of one form or another; a 2004 study found 176 examples of bilateral labour migration agreements across OECD countries (OECD 2004: 12). While these agreements are obviously shaped by domestic labour market needs, they are also sometimes offered in exchange for readmission agreements and may be informed by wider negotiations and diplomatic relations.

Supranational Regional Governance: The European Union

The European Union's evolving asylum and migration policy is the only example of a supranational migration regime consisting of binding laws and regulations that constrain the sovereignty of multiple member states. Yet despite, or in fact partly because of, its *sui generis* character, the EU regime is essential to a wider understanding of migration governance. As one of the world's main destination regions for immigrants, the EU affects a substantial proportion of the world's international migrants, and the very uniqueness of the EU policy renders it an important test case. If there is anywhere where liberal states' ability to regulate immigration is constrained by a supranational migration regime, then it should be in Europe.

Indeed, at first glance the EU migration regime might appear to contradict the arguments about international cooperation outlined earlier in this chapter. For, while it is far from complete and includes important exceptions, the Common Asylum and Migration Policy (hereafter, the CAMP) is nevertheless a formal and binding migration regime and, moreover, one that is decided not by intergovernmental negotiations in which individual states can wield a veto, but through supranational policymaking processes. Since 1999, when the EU first acquired legal competence in this policy area, and especially since 2009, when the Lisbon Treaty brought all remaining Justice and Home Affairs policies under 'communitarized' policymaking procedures, national governments have been required to adopt asylum and migration legislation that is decided at the European level.[15] Policies that impact on up to 27 European states are now decided using qualified majority voting (QMV) in the EU Council of Ministers (meaning single governments cannot veto legislation if it is endorsed by the votes of sufficient member states weighted according to population size) and using 'co-decision' procedures which require majority support from members of the directly elected European Parliament.

While there is little doubt that the CAMP is an exceptional case of supra-nationalism, on closer inspection, several of the dynamics of international cooperation identified throughout this chapter can also be seen in the EU. As with the wider global migration regime, there is substantial variation in the degree of cooperation or 'Europeanization' of different migration policy areas (see Boswell and Geddes 2011 for a recent overview). There is far more legislation and many more non-legislative initiatives in the areas of asylum and border control, where member states share broadly common interests, than in economic migration policy or immigrant integration, where they have highly divergent approaches. This indicates that common interests are fundamental to shared policies. Indeed, it is important to recognize that the EU is not a free-floating supranational institution that simply 'downloads' policies onto passive member states; rather, national governments also 'upload' their policy preferences and try to shape the European agenda. Some states are, of course, more successful in uploading their preferences than others, but this only reinforces the point that, while EU migration policymaking is no longer formally conducted on an intergovernmental basis, the CAMP nevertheless reflects national interests and power relations between member states. For example, when the then French president, Nicolas Sarkozy, negotiated a Pact on Immigration and Asylum with other European leaders in 2008, it was a clear (and largely successful) attempt to shape the agenda for the upcoming Stockholm Programme, which outlines the EU's policy priorities in the Area of Freedom, Security and Justice (AFSJ) for 2009 to 2014. The European Commission, which drafts policy proposals for consideration by member states in the Council of Ministers, must pre-empt national governments' positions if it is to secure the support of a winning coalition in the Council and not, as has happened on several occasions, propose policies that go beyond what most member states are willing to accept. Finally, when it comes to situating the EU in the context of global migration governance, it is essential to recognize that the CAMP is only viable because of the relative symmetries of interest that exist between European states. Notwithstanding the variations between their labour markets, immigration histories and national cultures, the 27 EU member states are all relatively affluent in global terms and most are, or are in the process of becoming, major destination countries. They therefore share sufficient common interests in most areas of the migration policy field to render cooperation feasible.

These symmetries underlie the EU's free movement area, which is not only central to the CAMP but one of the signal achievements of European integration as a whole. The idea of a free movement area can be traced back to the origins of the EU, specifically the goal of creating a common market to integrate the economies of Europe in a way that would render future wars between European powers all but impossible. As the project of European integration unfolded, it became increasingly clear that economic integration entailed not only a common market for goods and services but also a common labour market in which European workers could move freely between member states. The free movement area began life as an intergovernmental agreement signed in 1985 by Belgium, France, Germany, Luxembourg and the Netherlands on a river-boat near the Luxembourg town of Schengen. The aim of the Schengen Agreement was to further market integration by creating an area without internal border controls while simultaneously improving internal security through better cooperation between participating states, including the creation of a common external border. Over the next decade, several other countries joined Schengen, and in 1999 it was incorporated into the legal framework of the EU as a protocol to the Amsterdam Treaty (Brady 2012; Zaiotti 2011).

The 1997 Amsterdam Treaty provided the legal basis for the CAMP, which was officially launched at a summit meeting in Tampere, Finland, in 1999. At Tampere, the assembled heads of state agreed that the creation of a free movement area without internal borders required both common policies on some aspects of asylum and immigration and improved controls at the shared external borders to prevent illegal immigration. The proposed CAMP would include a Common European Asylum System, partnership with countries of origin, fair treatment of third-country nationals, and management of migration flows. During the five years of the Tampere programme (1999–2003) and the subsequent Hague programme (2004–8), progress was made towards some of the stated objectives, particularly in the areas of border controls and asylum policies, though not surprisingly, given the ambition of the goals set in Tampere, by the time the Stockholm Programme (2009–14) was agreed, a genuinely common policy was still yet to be achieved.

The CAMP therefore remains very much a work in progress. It has four main components, relating to legal immigration, asylum, Schengen provisions and external border controls, and external relations. The area of legal immigration, which includes both economic and family migration, is the least developed element. There has not been a shortage of legislative activity in this area, with several directives, among them those on the admission of foreign students (2004/114/EC) and scientific researchers (2005/71/EC), the Blue Card Directive on highly skilled migrants (2009/50/EC) and, most recently, the Single Permit Directive (2011/98/EU) on the rights of non-EU workers. However, while these directives set out various procedures, statuses and rights for economic migrants, they do not touch upon admissions. None of them transfers any competencies on decisions about the number or profile of economic migrants that member states admit; the number and type of economic immigrants admitted to a given country remain a national competence. This is highly unlikely to change on account of the variable labour market conditions and contrasting immigration histories of European countries, which mean that governments are opposed to transferring control over admissions to the EU. The EU Blue Card Directive is a case in point. It creates a fast-track procedure for issuing a special work and residence permit for highly skilled workers and sets outs rights for Blue Card holders, but it is entirely at the discretion of national governments how many, if any, immigrants they recruit through the scheme.

The other aspect of legal immigration, family immigration, has been the subject of one major piece of European legislation: the 2003 Family Reunification Directive (2003/86/EC), though a revised directive is under consideration. The aim of the 2003 directive is to set common standards for the admission of spouses and children of third-country nationals legally residing in the EU, while leaving member states free to decide on the admission of other family members, such as first-degree ascendants in the direct line, children above the age of majority, and unmarried partners. There were extensive negotiations on this piece of legislation, which was first put forward by the Commission in 1999, with several member states insisting on amendments to allow them to retain existing national legislation, notably on the age of children (Austria and Germany) and requirements for integration and language classes (the Netherlands, Austria, Germany) (Menz 2009: 100–6). As a result, while the final directive establishes some minimal standards, it is much less liberal than the Commission's original proposal.

The second component of the CAMP is the Common European Asylum System (CEAS), which includes the Dublin Regulation, a number of asylum directives, and financial and logistical instruments such as the European Refugee Fund (ERF) and European Asylum Support Office (EASO). Like Schengen, the Dublin system was originally developed as an intergovernmental agreement outside of the EU framework, but it has since been incorporated into European law through the Dublin Regulation. This regulation requires asylum-seekers to make their application for asylum in the first member state that they enter. Thus a person cannot enter the EU through one country then move on to another and apply for asylum. If an asylum-seeker can be shown to have passed through another member state or previously lodged an asylum application in another state, then they can be returned to that country. One aim of the Dublin Regulation was to prevent so-called asylum-shopping, where a person makes multiple asylum claims in more than one country. A less openly admitted aim, at least for some core member states, was to create a buffer zone so that the burden for processing asylum claims would fall on those countries with external EU borders, where the majority of asylum-seekers enter. This has become a source of tension and conflict between member states, with Southern European countries that receive large numbers of asylum-seekers routinely calling for greater 'solidarity' or 'burden-sharing' – calls that have been only partly addressed by the ERF or EASO, the latter established in Malta in 2011. At an operational level, the Dublin Regulation is underpinned by EURODAC, a searchable database that contains fingerprint records of all asylum claimants. When an asylum claim is made, immigration officials routinely check the applicant's fingerprints against the database to ensure that the individual has not lodged an application in another country or previously had an application rejected.

If the CEAS is to be a genuinely common system, then the policies and practices across member states, and indeed the outcomes of asylum applications, should be broadly similar. Yet this is very far from the case today. Despite a number of European laws, there are persistent disparities in the criteria that member states use to make asylum decisions and the protections that they offer. Some countries have more progressive asylum policies while others are more restrictive. As a result of these disparities, recognition rates for asylum-seekers from the same country of origin vary considerably from one member state to another (Neumayer 2005; Vink and Meijerink 2003). For example, in 2011 the Total Recognition Rate[16] for asylum-seekers from Afghanistan ranged from 11 per cent in Greece to 73 per cent in Sweden (UNHCR 2012).

The existing asylum directives – the Reception Conditions Directive (2003/9/EC), the Qualifications Directive (2004/83/EC) and the Asylum Procedures Directive (2005/85/EC) – establish minimum standards, but they have patently not harmonized policies, largely because they allow wide discretion for member states to transpose them into national laws. They are, rather, a 'legislation of minimums' in which European law represents the lowest common denominator between member states (Guild, Carrera and Atger 2009: 3). When the Commission's proposals have extended protections in a way that conflicts with the national status quo, more powerful governments have exacted concessions – for example, the German government successfully demanded an amendment to the Qualifications Directive to restrict labour market rights for beneficiaries of subsidiary protection (Menz 2009: 109) – or, in the case of the UK, have simply not opted in. In 2008, the Commission's Policy Plan on Asylum recommended further harmonization through amendments to the existing directives, and at the time of writing revised versions are under consideration in the Parliament and Council of Ministers.

The third component of the CAMP brings together the Schengen provisions, cooperation on external border controls, and what the Commission calls 'the fight against irregular immigration'. Border controls are, of course, central to state sovereignty, and the EU has consistently upheld the principle that the responsibility for managing the external border lies with member states. Nevertheless, the creation of the free movement area without internal border checks has created a strong shared interest in the security of the external border. Strengthening EU border controls is not, however, a straightforward task. The external border consists of 42,672 kilometres of sea borders and 8,826 kilometres of land borders, and there were 300 million external border crossings in 2009.[17] Eastward enlargement since 2004 has added further challenges, since the external border has shifted closer to sending regions and pre-accession border arrangements in the newer member states were not always functional.

As with other aspects of the CAMP, the European border regime is a work in progress. At present, its core elements are a common visa policy, a European external borders agency, known as Frontex, and a range of coordinated operations on irregular movements and smuggling and people-trafficking. The Schengen countries now operate a harmonized visa regime, which involves a common list of countries for short-stay visas, coordinated conditions for entry, and a single format Schengen visa. At the territorial border, the Schengen Borders Code has created standardized rules and procedures for immigration checks, while within the Schengen zone there is substantial cooperation between immigration and security agencies. Immigration, police and consular officials in Schengen countries have access to EU-wide searchable databases, including the Schengen Information System (SIS), which contains data on lost and stolen identity papers and persons to be refused entry or apprehended, and the Visa Information System (VIS), which contains records of visa applications, issues and refusals, as well as fingerprints and facial scans of visa applicants.

External border controls are conducted by member states but are increasingly coordinated by Frontex. Based in Warsaw, Frontex facilitates operational cooperation between border agencies, including joint operations involving multiple member states, as well as conducting risk analyses, training border guards, and providing technical support to member states. Its staff, budget and activities have grown substantially since it was established in 2005. Joint operations have become a particularly important area of Frontex activities, with numerous operations at sea, land and air borders, notably at the Greek–Turkish land border, which has become the main point for irregular border crossings, as well as joint return operations. Although Frontex's legal mandate is to support member state agencies, its increasingly important presence at the level of strategy and operations is clear. In addition to Frontex, the EU has sought to tighten border security by deploying new technologies. In 2008, the Commission presented an EU 'border package', which contained proposals for a European Border Surveillance System (EUROSUR), an entry–exit system, a registered traveller scheme, and automated border checks to facilitate the movement of 'bona fide travellers' at external borders (Broeders and Hampshire forthcoming 2013).

The final component of the CAMP is the 'external dimension', which refers to relations between the EU and third countries and incorporates a broad range of instruments, including enlargement negotiations, bilateral agreements and a number of regional partnerships and aid programmes. Rather like international cooperation as a whole, the importance of the external dimension has increased as EU and national-level officials have come to recognize the importance of cooperation with sending and transit countries, especially those that lie to the immediate south and east of Europe's external borders. Andrew Geddes (2008: 173) argues that there have been two distinct phases in the development of the external dimension: first, migration and EU enlargement; and, second, migration from Europe's 'neighbourhood'. During the first phase, accession countries were required to adopt EU policies as a condition for entry. This included the development of border controls along what would become the EU's eastern border after enlargement, as well as incorporation into the Dublin system, definition of the applicant states as 'safe third countries' for the purposes of return, and adoption of the Schengen *acquis* into national law. The enlargement dimension persists, now with a focus on accession negotiations in the Western Balkans. The second phase shifted the focus to third countries in Africa and then to the regions to the east and southeast of the EU. The overarching aim of this phase has been to embed cooperation on migration into wider relations with these countries, especially cooperation on irregular migration.

The external dimension took off in December 2005, when the UK presidency of the Council launched the Global Approach to Migration, with the aim of increasing dialogue and cooperation on migration issues between the EU and African countries. Among the range of proposed measures were actions 'to reduce illegal migration flows and the loss of lives, ensure safe return of illegal migrants, strengthen durable solutions for refugees, and build capacity to better manage migration, including through maximising the benefits to all partners of legal migration, while fully respecting human rights and the individual's right to seek asylum' (Presidency Conclusions 15914/1/05). The initial focus on Africa was widened in 2006, when the Global Approach was extended to the eastern and southeastern regions neighbouring the EU (COM(2007) 247 Final). The Global Approach was initially built around three pillars: the organization of legal migration and facilitated mobility; preventing and reducing irregular migration; and migration and development.[18] While these three goals are given equal weight in official discourse, in practice it is the prevention of irregular immigration that drives the European agenda, with the labour mobility and development objectives playing a supporting role. Indeed, Geddes (2008: 177–8) argues that, despite a rhetoric of development and human rights, the predominant 'issue frame' for the external dimension is security, with an 'overriding priority to policies on return, readmission and border controls'. In 2011, the Commission launched a revised and renamed 'Global Approach to Migration and Mobility', which added a fourth pillar to cover the external dimension of international protection, as well as a new emphasis on the wider concept of 'mobility' and migration.

The external dimension has both formal and informal elements. The main concrete instrument of the Global Approach are so-called Mobility Partnerships – agreements with non-EU countries negotiated by the Commission on behalf of member states (who are free to choose whether or not to participate). Like most North–South bilateral relations, these agreements typically offer limited mobility in return for cooperation preventing irregular migration. To date,

Mobility Partnerships have been agreed with four countries: Cape Verde (2008), Moldova (2008), Georgia (2009) and Armenia (2011). The EU has also signed readmission agreements, with Sri Lanka, Albania, Hong Kong, Russia, Pakistan, Ukraine, Moldova and several Western Balkan states. In a remarkably candid evaluation of these agreements, Franco Frattini, the former EU Commissioner for Justice, Freedom and Security, said in 2006 that,

> although these agreements are in theory reciprocal, it is clear that in practise [sic] they essentially serve the interests of the European Community. . . . The successful outcome of negotiations depends therefore to a great extent on 'levers', or should I say 'carrots' that the European Commission has at its disposal, that is to say on incentives that are powerful enough to gain the cooperation of the non-member countries concerned.[19]

As well as measures to reduce irregular migration, the EU has promoted and funded Regional Protection Programmes for refugees in Eastern Europe and Tanzania, and most recently for Syrian refugees, as part of wider attempts to offer durable solutions for refugees in regions of origin, and thereby reduce asylum-seeking. Lastly, as well as these formal initiatives, the Global Approach aims to embed migration as a priority issue in wider EU external relations, such as the European Neighbourhood Policy, and promote informal dialogues through regional processes such as the Rabat Process, the EU–Africa Partnership on Migration, Mobility and Employment, or the EU–LAC Structured Dialogue on Migration with Latin America. However, EU observers have generally been rather sceptical of the Global Approach, one commentator describing it as more 'rhetoric than reality' (Collett 2007). The aim of enabling the EU to 'speak with one voice' on migration is certainly very ambitious given the range and diversity of the 27 different member states' relations with non-EU countries.

In summary, the EU's migration regime is a complex and evolving body of legislation, institutions and norms. Despite its supranational legal foundation, it is a policy shaped by persistent intergovernmental logics and by tensions between European institutions and member states, as well as conflicts between different national governments. Given the size and diversity of the EU, this is far from surprising. But it is nevertheless clear that, so long as conflicts based on national interests persist – and in the current climate they have been increasing rather than decreasing – the CAMP will not become a genuinely harmonized policy.

Conclusion

This chapter began by arguing that unilateralism in migration policy is over-determined. The importance of immigration control to state sovereignty militates against international cooperation, certainly formal multilateralism, and this has been exacerbated by the domestic politicization of immigration in liberal states and the conflicts of interest between the global North and South. Yet, as the chapter has also shown, there is growing international cooperation on migration. The global migration regime is complex, fragmented, far from comprehensive and not especially coherent, but it does represent an important dimension to contemporary migration governance. Nation-states and domestic politics are still where most of the action is, but ignoring international and supranational developments would be a mistake.

However, from the perspective of liberal states in the North, global migration governance has not significantly constrained or diminished their sovereignty, but by and large reinforced it. Liberal states have approached multilateral cooperation warily and have very rarely conceded significant authority to international institutions. Where states have made concessions of Westphalian sovereignty, it has mostly been to strengthen their interdependence sovereignty – in other words, their capability to regulate immigration in their interests. When interstate cooperation or supranational institutions have threatened to undermine those interests, liberal states have refused to participate.

CHAPTER SIX

The Janus Face of Liberal Citizenship

Throughout this book, we have seen how liberal states reveal a Janus face to immigrants, open and inclusive towards some, closed and exclusionary towards others. As the lodestone of liberal state membership, it is perhaps unsurprising that citizenship embodies this paradox; as Rogers Brubaker observed, it is both 'internally inclusive' and 'externally exclusive' (1992: 21). The internal inclusivity of modern citizenship derives from its individualistic and egalitarian character. Starting in the late eighteenth century, citizenship evolved to efface the hierarchical stratifications of feudal societies through the creation of a uniform legal status and equal rights for all members of the political community. Yet the formal equality of citizenship did not, and cannot, extend to everyone. Citizenship of a state necessarily establishes boundaries between insiders and outsiders, between those who are and those who are not citizens. Thus the external face of citizenship is powerfully exclusionary, since it serves precisely to deny access to the equal rights of membership to foreigners.

Both of these dynamics – citizenship's inclusionary and exclusionary dimensions – are fundamental to understanding the politics of immigration. As we saw in chapter 1, international migration is produced by states' dual character as both territorial and membership institutions. As a marker of membership, citizenship constitutes immigration. However, to proceed beyond this basic observation it is necessary to probe more deeply into the complex interrelations between citizenship and immigration. The present chapter examines how citizenship influences immigration and, conversely, how immigration has transformed citizenship. In other words, it takes citizenship as both independent and dependent variable: an institution that powerfully affects immigration, but one that is in turn transformed by it.

Across liberal states, and especially in those European countries that began to experience mass immigration only after their citizenship laws and traditions were already well established, citizenship has undergone profound changes over the last half-century. On the one hand, citizenship has been liberalized, 'becoming more inclusive and universalistic', and its 'internally inclusive core has softened its externally exclusive edges' (Joppke 2010: 31). Yet in recent years there have also been exclusionary counter-trends: in several countries citizenship has become highly politicized, and more demanding citizenship policies have often been the result. Thus, like so many other aspects of immigration in the liberal state, the politics of citizenship is deeply contested and the policy outcomes are complex and even contradictory.

What Is Citizenship?

Answering this question is not as straightforward as might be assumed, since in recent years the word 'citizenship' has been put to a proliferating number of uses. Thus one reads about 'global citizenship' (Carter 2001), 'cosmopolitan citizenship' (Hutchings and Dannreuther 1998), 'urban citizenship' (Holston 1999) and a number of identity-related citizenships, such as 'sexual citizenship' (Evans 1993) or 'cultural citizenship' (Stevenson 2003; for a discussion of these trends, see Heisler 2005; see Hansen 2009 for a highly critical view). The problem with the abundant uses to which the term citizenship is now put is that it threatens to rob the concept of any analytical meaning. It is an acute case of what the political scientist Giovanni Sartori (1970) described as 'conceptual stretching': the extension of a concept to describe divergent phenomena in varied contexts such that it loses any utility for analysis or debate.

Yet, despite the proliferation of meanings attached to citizenship, it is both possible and desirable to delimit the range of uses, even if no one definition is likely to receive universal agreement. The best starting point is to define, or rather reassert, citizenship as membership of a political community, and more specifically as membership of a nation-state. As several scholars have argued, this is the essence of citizenship: a status that 'marks a distinction between members and outsiders based on their different relations to particular states' (Bauböck 2006: 15). Anchoring citizenship in the state achieves a measure of conceptual parsimony and allows for a meaningful discussion of citizenship policies: the laws, rules and regulations that establish how a given state's citizenship is acquired, what the content of citizenship is (the rights and obligations that attach to the formal status), and what is expected from citizens in terms of their identity, allegiance and values. This threefold distinction is borrowed from Christian Joppke's important recent disaggregation of citizenship into status, rights and identity dimensions (Joppke 2007b, 2010). He persuasively argues that these three dimensions have either been insufficiently distinguished in previous analyses or treated in isolation from one another (2007b: 37). By distinguishing between citizenship as status, rights and identity, we can achieve a conceptual framework that is parsimonious yet also sufficiently broad to encompass citizenship's multifaceted character.[20] And we can analyse how the various dimensions interact and vary across different national contexts.

Citizenship *status* is acquired by two principal means: attribution at birth or naturalization. For the overwhelming majority of humankind – some

97 per cent of the world's population – citizenship is a status that is ascribed at birth rather than chosen, according to either where a person is born or the citizenship held by his or her parents. It is for this reason that Joseph Carens ironically describes citizenship as like a feudal privilege since, for all its positive connotations, 'it is assigned at birth and is an inherited status that greatly enhances one's life chances' (Carens 1995: 230). Attribution at birth is determined by two distinct principles: the territorial principle of *jus soli*, under which citizenship is acquired by birth in a state's territory, and the descent-based principle of *jus sanguinis*, under which citizenship is acquired according to the nationality of one's parents. As we shall see, most liberal states incorporate aspects of both *jus soli* and *jus sanguinis* in their citizenship laws, though countries have often been classified according to whether they lean towards one or the other, particularly in relation to the children of immigrants. There have been important changes in this area, generally in the direction of liberalizing access to citizenship.

The second way to acquire citizenship status is through naturalization. In contrast to attribution at birth, this a voluntaristic process typically undertaken by adults who already hold the citizenship of at least one other state, and it is an important mechanism for accessing citizenship by immigrants who have resided in a destination country for a number of years. The requirements for naturalization vary considerably from one state to another; some of the most important criteria are length of residency, toleration of dual nationality and, increasingly, demonstration of language skills and knowledge of the host society. Here too there have been substantial changes in many countries as a result of immigration, both in a liberalizing but also in a restrictive direction.

The second dimension of citizenship is *rights*. In his highly influential study *Citizenship and Social Class* (1950), the British sociologist T. H. Marshall famously specified three types of citizenship rights – civil, political and social – and told a story of how they had evolved over time. In his narrative, citizenship began with civil rights in the eighteenth century, which were supplemented with political rights in the nineteenth century as suffrage was gradually extended, and culminated with social rights in the mid-twentieth-century as the welfare state was established in the aftermath of the Second World War. Though rightly criticized for its Anglocentric account of how citizenship rights evolved, Marshall's contribution remains salient for at least two reasons. First, his threefold typology remains useful for disaggregating citizenship rights. As we shall see, citizenship is of differential significance for each category of rights, with political rights largely the preserve of citizens but many civil and social rights extended to non-citizen residents. Second, Marshall's account reminds us that citizenship is, among other things, an instrument of societal integration. Marshall's argument about how social rights evolve to ameliorate class inequalities and prevent antagonisms from ripping the political community apart reveals the inclusive aspect of citizenship while also hinting at its exclusionary dimension. Citizenship brings members into a circle of protective rights and forges a 'unified civiliza-tion' (Marshall 1950: 47). What Marshall missed was the implication for those situated outside of this 'civilization', for whom the rights of citizenship are more exclusive than integrative.

Finally, in addition to its status and rights dimensions, citizenship is about *identity*. This may be less tangible, but it is no less important. For citizenship has rarely, if ever, been a purely legal status with attached rights. Historically, it has been inextricable from national identity – indeed, it has often been understood as the politico-legal expression of a prior cultural identity. This implies that a given state's citizenship is, or should be, enjoyed only by those who share a national identity, typically based on cultural attributes such as a common language, customs and traditions, and, until at least the mid-twentieth century, also on race and ethnicity. Today, this straightforward association of citizenship with national identity has become increasingly problematic as immigration has resulted in the ethnic and cultural diversi-fication of liberal societies, and citizenship has evolved to reflect this diver-sity. To some extent, then, state membership has been decoupled from shared identity. At the same time, the stubborn persistence of the connection between citizenship and national identity can be seen in the attempts to reassert and renationalize citizenship, especially through the language and civics tests that have been introduced in the naturalization policies of several countries – all of which is discussed further below.

Citizenship Matters

It might seem obvious that, understood as membership of the nation-state, citizenship matters, since the consequences of being or not being a citizen are so profound. If, in Hannah Arendt's resonant phrase, citizenship is 'a right to have rights', then to be stateless, without any citizenship, is to lose the basis for any rights. Though states may violate as well as uphold their citizens' rights, persons who are stateless are 'rightless, the scum of the earth' (Arendt 1951). Assuming that a person *is* a citizen, precisely which citizenship(s) she enjoys fundamentally affect(s) her rights, and indeed her life-chances (Shachar 2009). Citizenship of a rich, stable country such as the United States affords a range of rights and opportunities that are unavailable to citizens of an impoverished, war-torn country such as Somalia. Thus, in one of those paradoxes that haunts citizenship at every turn, the very success of the 'inter-nal inclusivity' of citizenship in rich liberal democracies renders its exclu-sionary dimension all the more significant, since it denies access to rights and opportunities to those who hold the citizenship of more benighted countries.

Surely, then, it is obvious that citizenship matters? Perhaps so. During the 1990s, however, a number of scholars began to argue that the importance of nation-state citizenship in liberal states was actually in decline, precisely as a consequence of increasing immigration. In one of the opening salvoes of this attack on national citizenship, Tomas Hammar argued that immigration to European states had created a large number of permanent residents who were not citizens, yet nevertheless 'enjoy an increasing number of rights and have to fulfil many duties, although they are non-members of the state' (Hammar 1990: 3). Hammar argued that civil and social rights, but also some political rights such as the right to vote in local elections, were becoming decoupled from citizenship and could be accessed by non-citizen residents. He coined the term 'denizenship' to capture the status of persons who, though not citizens, were able to access rights from which aliens had historically been excluded.

Hammar's concept of denizenship blurred the line between citizens and aliens, but other scholars went much further, arguing that immigration and international human rights law were effecting a more radical transformation in national citizenship. According to one exponent of what became known as 'postnationalism', this was nothing short of a revolution: 'what we are witnessing today is the transforming of the state and international institutions, of their function and of their very raison, and human rights provide both the vehicle and object of this revolution' (Jacobson 1996: 3). For Jacobson, as states granted ever more rights to non-citizens, and as immigrants increasingly utilized international law to press states to recognize their rights, citizenship was being devalued:

> Transnational migration is steadily eroding the traditional basis of nation-state membership, namely citizenship. As rights come to be predicated on residency, not citizen status, the distinction between 'citizen' and 'alien' has eroded. The devaluation of citizenship has contributed to the increasing importance of international human rights codes, with its premise of universal 'personhood.' (Jacobson 1996: 8–9)

The most influential statement of this argument, and the one that coined the term 'postnational membership', was Yasemin Soysal's *The Limits of Citizenship* (1994). Soysal argued that national citizenship was being displaced by 'a new model of membership, the main thrust of which is that individual rights, historically defined on the basis of nationality, are increasingly codified into a different scheme that emphasizes universal personhood . . . [and] transcends the boundaries of the nation-state' (1994: 136–7). This 'different scheme' exists through an 'intensifying discourse about the individual and human rights' (ibid.: 41), articulated at a supranational level by international and transnational organizations, such as the UN agencies, and codified into international law, such as the Universal Declaration of Human Rights. This discourse, variously described as trans-, supra- and postnational, 'crystallizes around the idea of personhood' (ibid.: 42), which is to say that it premises rights upon an abstract, universal conception of the person, independent of particular identities and attachments. Moreover, human rights grounded in universal personhood act as a solvent of those identities, since they render them less and less consequential for rights. The implications for the state and national citizenship are clear: the nation-state becomes increasingly irrelevant as a generator of rights, and therefore membership of the nation-state matters less and less. As Soysal put it: 'The change is from a model of national citizenship to one of postnational membership, predicated on notions of personhood' (ibid.: 44).

In the two decades since its publication, Soysal's book has generated a lot of criticism (see Hansen 2009 for an especially withering critique). In the midst of this thoroughgoing critique, it is possible to forget that there were some elements of truth to postnationalism. Soysal did in fact admit the persistent importance of the nation-state when she acknowledged that, 'incongruously . . . post-national rights remain organized at the national level' (Soysal 1994: 157), even if, in Hansen's (2009: 4) phrase, they look like 'policy waiters following the orders of universal persons'. Postnationalists were also right to argue that immigration has driven the liberalization of various aspects of citizenship, although, as discussed below, liberalization has been more marked in policies regulating access to citizenship than rights.

However, as postnationalism's many critics pointed out, the central claim that national citizenship has become increasingly irrelevant for rights is simply not sustainable. The postnationalist thesis always rested on shaky conceptual and empirical ground, and it came to look more and more outmoded as liberal states 'revalued' citizenship during the 2000s. In particular, postnationalism failed to recognize the extent to which certain rights remain the preserve of citizens, including most political rights, many social rights, and even some civil rights. By addressing each in turn, it will become apparent why national citizenship still very much matters.

The most obvious way in which citizenship continues to matter for rights is that national voting rights remain the preserve of citizens. While many liberal democracies have extended local voting rights to non-citizen residents, hardly any have extended national voting rights to this group; just four countries (New Zealand, Malawi, Chile and Uruguay) have a residence-based right to vote in national elections (Bauböck 2005: 684). Some countries extend national voting rights to particular non-citizens, such as the UK, which allows Commonwealth citizens to vote in national elections. But, in general, national voting rights attach to national citizenship. The exclusion of immigrants from voting is highly consequential in both theory and practice. At the level of normative theory, it is problematic, since a core principle of democracy is that all those who are subject to a political authority and its laws should have an equal right to participate and be represented in the making of those laws (see Rubio-Marin 2000). In terms of political practice, it means that immigrants cannot participate in the democratic process unless they naturalize as citizens, which creates a serious obstacle to political influence. As discussed in chapter 2, this helps to explain why pro-immigrant political mobilization is limited at the national level. In addition to national voting rights, the ability to hold high public office is generally restricted to citizens, even in those countries such as New Zealand that have extended the franchise to non-citizens. In short, in the sphere of national-level political rights, the citizen–alien distinction holds firm.

The picture on social rights is more complex. While it is undeniable that some social rights are extended to non-citizens, here too the declining significance of national citizenship has been exaggerated. Contributory benefits such as unemployment compensation and pensions are generally insurance-based and accrue through participation in the labour market. They are therefore independent of citizenship status. However, as Joppke (2010: 89) observes, these benefits have never had any nationality restrictions, so their denationalization is not driven by immigration, as postnationalists claim. Moreover, it is arguable that contributory benefits should be excluded from the ambit of social rights, since they are tied to employment and do not follow the decommodifying and redistributive logics of social citizenship per se. When it comes to non-contributory social programmes such as income support, disability benefits and housing benefits, which *are* redistributive, the relevance of national citizenship persists, since non-citizens are often excluded or entitled only to lower levels of benefit. Many countries place restrictions on access to these non-contributory social programmes (Howard 2006: 445), and in countries such as the UK and the Netherlands legislation since the late 1990s has furthered immigrants' exclusion from welfare.

Furthermore, non-citizens' social rights bear the imprint of alienage because they are so strongly conditioned by their immigration status. As Lydia Morris (2002) has shown, immigrants' rights are highly stratified according to entry categories. This stratification varies significantly between countries, but in general the advanced economies have increasingly sought to differentiate the rights of immigrants according to their entry category in pursuit of policy objectives: wanted immigrants are enticed with attractive packages of rights; temporary immigrants are offered more limited rights; and unwanted immigrants are deterred by restricting their rights. Thus rich countries offer rights to highly skilled migrants, including, for example, permanent residency and the right to bring family members, while low-skilled migrants are typically denied access to permanent residency and are unable to bring family members. Morris argues that the stratification of migrants' rights is integral to migration management, a form of 'monitoring and control' (2002: 9). This analysis further undermines the argument that rights have become decoupled from citizenship, because it reveals the concessionary nature of many aliens' rights, which can be granted to those deemed economically useful and withheld from those who are not.

Nor is stratification a matter only of welfare rights, since access to the labour market is also conditioned by citizenship. As with social rights, access to private-sector jobs is limited to varying degrees depending on a person's immigration status: low-skilled immigrants, for example, may be admitted to work only in particular sectors or even for particular employers. More generally, in European countries employers are legally obliged to conduct a labour market test to show that no domestic worker is available (either a national or other EU citizen) before they may employ a foreigner. There is also substantial variation between countries on whether they allow family migrants to work immediately: Austria and Germany prohibit this, though Britain, France and the Netherlands allow it (Joppke 2010: 87). Access to public-sector jobs is even more restrictive. Marc Morjé Howard (2006: 445) observes that national citizenship is a precondition for employment in a range of public-sector jobs in countries as different as France (hospitals, postal service), Germany (civil service jobs, including public transport and education) and the US (public school teachers, state troopers, probation officers).

While political, social and labour market rights are therefore conditioned by the citizen–alien boundary and stratified by various statuses within the latter category, it might be thought that civil rights would be the least responsive to membership distinctions. After all, these are surely the most universalistic of rights, founded on basic human interests and individual freedoms that are independent of particular identities and attachments. Surely, liberal states do not restrict freedoms of speech, religion and assembly or deny the rule of law for non-citizens?

Since the 9/11 terrorist attacks, even this pillar of liberalism has come into question, as governments on both sides of the Atlantic, notably in the US and the UK, have implemented draconian measures affecting non-citizens in the context of the 'war on terror'. As Hansen (2009: 13) claims, in 'the human rights horror that is Guantánamo Bay', citizenship came to matter rather a lot for those imprisoned without charge by the US authorities. Certain national governments lobbied for and in some cases secured the release of their citizens, but only those who enjoyed citizenship of a country with sufficient political influence in the US were released, revealing both the importance of the citizen right to diplomatic protection and the hierarchical nature of national citizenships. More broadly, the importance of national citizenship became apparent as both the US and the UK government passed legislation that significantly eroded the rights of aliens: in the US, the Patriot Act allowed the government to deport or detain non-citizens without a hearing or trial if the attorney general suspected them of 'terrorist activity'; while, in the UK, the Labour government responded to the US attacks with legislation that allowed for indefinite detention of non-citizens without trial if the home secretary 'reasonably believes' that a person is a terrorist (Hampshire 2009c). In both cases, subsequent court rulings constrained the governments in a way that lends some support to the postnationalist argument about human rights. However, what the response to 9/11 revealed is the contingent and potentially reversible nature of even elementary civil rights such as due process and non-expulsion for non-citizens. While the number of people affected by these laws may have been relatively small, the state's reassertion of its exclusionary powers in the 'war on terror' showed how certain protections that are enjoyed as of right by citizens (or at least those who hold no other citizenship) are altogether more contingent for aliens.

Lastly, and curiously, the postnationalist thesis ignores the fundamental importance of national citizenship for understanding the very process – international migration – that it claims has made national citizenship 'increasingly irrelevant'. For, in addition to the bundle of rights discussed above, which remain wholly or partially the preserve of citizens, both the right and the ability to move across international boundaries is powerfully shaped by national citizenship and barely at all by 'universal personhood'. First, the citizenship that a person enjoys fundamentally affects their rights of international mobility. As distinct from international migration, international mobility refers to persons travelling to another state for a short period of time, typically for work, tourism or to visit family. Citizens of most Southern states are required to apply for a visa to enter most Northern states, whereas citizens from one Northern country can usually travel to another without a visa. Visa regimes are closely correlated to wealth, and citizenship of a rich country with good interstate relations generally affords its holder the opportunity to travel freely to several other states. Some citizenships bestow not only visa-free but also passport-free travel. The most obvious example is the EU, whose free movement rights allow the citizens of one member state to move and indeed permanently reside and work in any of the states of the Union. Other countries have bilateral travel arrangements – for example, the Australia–New Zealand Trans-Tasman Travel Arrangement.

In short, barriers to international mobility are significantly higher for some national citizens than others. Which passport a person holds is rather more important for international mobility than universal personhood. Nor is this entirely separate from immigration, since international mobility is both a source of irregular immigration, through visa overstay, and a bridge to regular immigration – for example, when visits for business, tourism or family reasons generate the desire or means for permanent immigration.

National citizenship is also an important determinant of migration per se. This is because citizenship rights, or their relative absence, underpin the desire and ability to migrate in the first place. Put simply, the equality of human rights that is enshrined in international law (the main source of postnational rights grounded in universal personhood) does not exist in international reality, where there is a clear hierarchy of citizenships: the citizens of highly developed countries enjoy extensive formal rights and institutions that uphold those rights; citizens of transitional countries have fewer formal rights and less robust institutions; while those living in the poorest countries of the South, especially where there is political corruption, abuse of human rights or a lack of basic social services, 'may be citizens in name but not in reality' (Castles 2005: 690–1). Ayelet Shachar (2009) refers to the 'birthright lottery' of citizenship: for the vast majority of human beings, the morally arbitrary fact of birth determines their citizenship, which in turn determines their life chances.

The profound inequalities of citizenship rights, and the capacity or willingness of governments to uphold those rights, constitute an important factor that motivates people to migrate. This is most directly the case when a government actively violates the civil or political rights of its citizens, causing them to flee as refugees, but it is also the case to varying degrees when social rights that are taken for granted by citizens of Northern countries are lacking or absent. In other words, hierarchical citizenship is part and parcel of the differentials that motivate international migration. By focusing on the experience of immigrants living in rich liberal democracies, especially guestworkers in Western Europe, postnationalists wholly ignored the role of persistent inequalities and lack of citizenship rights that motivate migration.

In short, contrary to the postnationalist claim that rights have been decoupled from national membership and anchored instead in a universalistic discourse in which the 'abstract, human person supplants the national citizen' (Soysal 1994: 164), the nation-state remains the pre-eminent generator and guarantor of rights, and national citizenship has if anything become *more*, not less, important in the age of migration.

From National Idioms to Contested Politics

Having established the significance and resilience of national citizenship, a number of avenues of inquiry open up. The first is to explore how national citizenship is shaped. Why is citizenship configured in different ways across liberal states? What factors explain the variation in citizenship between countries? A related set of questions surrounds the impact of immigration on the citizenship policies of liberal states. Although the postnationalist thesis about the decoupling of citizenship and rights is flawed, postnationalists were right to observe that immigration has driven changes in citizenship policies, notably laws that regulate access to citizenship. What is the nature of these changes? And how have states responded to the advent of large numbers of non-citizen residents on their territories? The remainder of this chapter explores these questions.

One of the earliest studies of differences in citizenship regimes was Rogers Brubaker's *Citizenship and Nationhood in France and Germany* (1992). In this path-breaking work, Brubaker argued that citizenship is inextricably bound up with nationhood: 'differing definitions of citizenship have been shaped and sustained by distinctive and deeply rooted understanding of nationhood' (Brubaker 1992: x–xi). Each country had distinctive national self-understandings which were rooted in political and cultural geography, and these self-understandings were 'embodied and expressed in sharply opposed definitions of citizenship' (ibid.: xi). Despite the 'great migratory waves' that were washing over Europe in the early 1990s, these opposed conceptions of citizenship persisted because they were so deeply rooted in national cultural differences. In the case of France, a 'state-centred, assimilationist understanding of nationhood' led to an 'expansive definition of citizenship . . . that automatically transforms second-generation immigrants into citizens', while in Germany an 'ethnocultural, differentialist understanding of nationhood' led to a conception of citizenship that embraced ethnic German immigrants from Eastern Europe and the former Soviet Union but excluded non-German immigrants, notably Turkish guestworkers and their descendants. France's tradition of *jus soli*, according to which citizenship is acquired through birth on French territory, reflected its civic conception of nationhood, whereas Germany's *jus sanguinis* laws reflected its ethnic conception of nationhood. Brubaker's core argument that citizenship laws are formalizations of national cultural idioms which are historically rooted and for that reason relatively resistant to change had obvious implications beyond these two countries.

As insightful as it was, Brubaker's historico-cultural theory of citizenship was problematic for a number of reasons. As Christian Joppke (2010: 18–19) points out, Brubaker's emphasis on the 'politics of identity' leads him to downplay the 'politics of interests' – in other words, the way in which citizenship is fought over for strategic political reasons that have little to do with national culture. For example, when parties of the left and right propose conflicting citizenship policies, as they have in recent years in many European countries including France and Germany, are these plausibly characterized as disagreements about national culture, or are they a matter of strategic political calculation and electoral competition? This leads to arguably the most fatal problem with Brubaker's analysis, which is that it cannot account for the rapid transformations of citizenship that have unfolded in France and Germany, as well as in several other European countries, since the early 1990s. Between 1993 and 1997, the French government placed a restriction on *jus soli* for second-generation immigrants, a move at odds with the supposed civic bent of French nationhood, while in 1999 Germany introduced a major reform of its citizenship laws, including conditional *jus soli* for second-generation immigrants, which overturned its supposed ethnic bias. If Brubaker's argument about national cultural differences was correct, then such a break as occurred in Germany would scarcely have been possible. His analysis suggests institutional inertia and, moreover, implies that reforms to citizenship laws require a prior transformation in a nation's self-conception. Even if this could be said to have occurred in Germany in the years before 1999, the fact that the reforms were so fiercely contested by the main political parties – on the one hand the pro-reform SPD and on the other the opposition CDU/CSU (see Green 2004) – suggests that ideological and interest-based conflicts were as important as national cultural idioms.

Despite these shortcomings, Brubaker was nevertheless right to observe that citizenship is shaped by national historical experiences. Even if he over-stated the case, the fundamental nature of citizenship does indeed mean that citizenship regimes are likely to have a long lineage and to be shaped by often distant historical events. The importance of history is obvious if one compares those countries with a long history of immigration in North America and Oceania with the more recent countries of immigration in Europe. In the former, immigration was a tool of nation-building from the very start. Immigrants arrived as settlers, and they and their descendants were intended to be incorporated into the polity. This led these countries to adopt inclusive citizenship regimes, which would quickly transform newcomers into citi-zens. Thus the United States, Canada, Australia and New Zealand all have citizenship regimes that include *jus soli* attribution at birth and relatively short residency requirements for naturalization. By contrast, European citi-zenship regimes were not originally geared to the incorporation of immi-grants. Indeed, in most European countries, citizenship laws were established long before immigration became a significant phenomenon. As a result, their citizenship policies were often far from inclusive and made naturalization difficult or almost impossible. Since Europe has emerged as the major immi-grant-receiving region of the world over the last few decades, it is here that citizenship has evolved the most.

While this simple comparison between settler states and more recent coun-tries of immigration illustrates how historical legacies of immigration and nation-building shape citizenship, it cannot explain the ongoing differences *within* a region such as Europe. If national cultural explanations of such vari-ation are found wanting, what other historical factors influenced citizenship? The best answer to date is provided by Marc Morjé Howard (2009, 2006). Rather than tying citizenship regimes to national cultural idioms, Howard examines the role of democratization and colonialism to explain whether countries adopted relatively inclusive or restrictive citizenship laws. He argues that European countries that were major colonial powers during the nineteenth century developed deeper relations with non-European countries, and this led them to adopt more open immigration and citizenship policies. Despite the often exploitative nature of colonial relations, major colonial powers such as Britain, France and the Netherlands were themselves shaped by the experience of colonialism: exposure to non-European 'others' had pluralizing effects on their own national identities, and imperialism enabled the movement and mixing of peoples. Through these mechanisms, colonial powers became increasingly open to outsiders and adopted inclusive citizen-ship regimes. This was reinforced during the process of decolonization, as European countries sought to replace their formal powers with an informal sphere of influence by maintaining postcolonial relations and identities, the British Commonwealth being the most obvious example. The construction of inclusive citizenship regimes was an important part of this process. The second part of Howard's explanation of historical variation contends that countries which democratized in the nineteenth century were more likely to develop a civic conception of national identity, which in turn led them to adopt inclusive citizenship regimes. Well before European states became net immigration countries, early democratization led to the inclusion of ethnic minorities, such as Jews, and the establishment of more inclusive civic institutions. Democratization was also associated with the emergence of a 'national identity tied to liberal principles' (Howard 2009: 45). In contrast, countries that democratized only in the twentieth century tended towards a more exclusive conception of national identity and citizenship (Howard 2006: 447).

These two causal factors overlap to a large extent, since most countries that were early democratizers were also colonial powers, although not all colonial powers were democratic. It was those countries that were *both* colonial powers and democratizers that developed inclusive citizenship regimes. As Howard shows in his empirical analysis of fifteen Western European countries (2009: 47–51), this simple theory is well supported: those countries with the historically most inclusive citizenship regimes – namely, Belgium, France and the UK – were all early democratizers and colonial powers; those countries with the historically least inclusive regimes, including Austria, Denmark, Germany, Italy and Luxembourg, were neither. The Netherlands, which was a colonial power but did not democratize during the nineteenth century, falls in between. There are some anomalies, notably Portugal and Sweden, which were neither major colonial powers nor early democratizers in the nineteenth century but nevertheless developed relatively inclusive citizenship regimes. But, overall, Howard's theory offers a persuasive and remarkably parsimonious explanation of historical variation within Western Europe.

These historical legacies set the baseline for contemporary politics, but other factors must be invoked to understand more recent developments. The classic immigration countries of North America and Oceania have not substantially changed their citizenship policies in recent years, but in Europe the onset of mass immigration has prompted substantial changes in several countries. The overall trend in Europe is towards liberalization of access to citizenship (as discussed below), but there has been significant variation in the timing, scope and extent of change. To account for this variation, Howard (2009: 53–60) begins by arguing that various *latent* pressures bear upon European governments, some liberalizing, others restrictive. As immigration unfolded from the 1950s, the need for immigrant incorporation, coupled with liberal norms of inclusion embedded in national and international legal standards, generated liberalizing pressures. At the same time, latent pressures to maintain restrictive citizenship policies come from anti-immigrant and xenophobic sentiment, which creates powerful incentives for elected governments to resist pro-immigrant policies, including the liberalization of citizenship.

Given the existence of these latent pressures across most European countries, what matters is whether they are mobilized. Howard proposes a simple, two-part model. The first part states that liberalization is possible under centre-left governments but unlikely under centre-right governments, because the former are more willing to extend rights to immigrants than the latter. The existence of a centre-left government is not sufficient, however. The second part of the model addresses whether the latent restrictive pressure emanating from public opinion mentioned above is or is not mobilized. This may take the form of a far-right political party, a popular movement or a referendum campaign. If any of these occur, then 'liberalization will essentially be blocked, since no government (whether on the left or right) will be able to overcome the intensity of this mobilization because it has so much resonance in the population' (Howard 2009: 61). In short, citizenship liberalization is put on the agenda by immigration, but it is only likely to occur under a centre-left government and, crucially, in the absence of far-right mobilization to activate latent anti-immigrant pressures.

As with the historical argument, this model is remarkably successful at explaining citizenship liberalization since the 1990s. In his bivariate analysis of far-right parties and citizenship liberalization, Howard shows how countries with high levels of far-right support, such as Austria, Italy and Denmark, did not liberalize their citizenship laws, whereas those that did liberalize, including Finland, Germany, the Netherlands, Portugal and Sweden, all had low levels of far-right support at the time of reform (2009: 65–7). This once more illustrates the contradictions between liberal principles, on the one hand, and anti-immigrant political mobilization based upon nationalist sentiment, on the other. While immigration to liberal states generates functional and normative pressures to liberalize citizenship policies, when these policies become the subject of democratic politics, all too often the mobilization of anti-immigrant sentiment will block reform or even lead to retrenchment, as we shall see further below.

The Liberalization of Access to Citizenship

As already mentioned, in the classic countries of immigration, citizenship policies were geared to integrating immigrants and their descendants from an early stage. The early colonialists who settled these countries imported English traditions of territorially derived birthright citizenship, which ironically enough was a feudal legacy (see Joppke 2010: 37), and later incorporated *jus soli* into their laws and in some cases their constitutions, because it served the integrative needs of nations that were being established through immigration. Thus Australia, Canada, New Zealand and the United States all have longstanding traditions of *jus soli* citizenship. Furthermore, in addition to the automatic incorporation of the children of immigrants through *jus soli*, the

classic immigration countries have comparatively liberal naturalization policies. The residency requirements for naturalization in these countries are
typically lower than in Europe – three years in Canada, four in Australia, and
five in New Zealand and the United States – and all except the United States
officially accept dual nationality. And though the US oath of allegiance
requires naturalizing immigrants to renounce other citizenships, in practice
dual and even multiple nationality is widely tolerated. Given this already
liberal approach to citizenship acquisition, both at birth and through naturalization, it is unsurprising that increased immigration has had few liberalizing effects on citizenship in these countries. As discussed below, if anything,
the trend in some of these countries has been towards a tightening of
requirements.

The situation is very different in Europe. With the notable exception of
Belgium, France, Ireland and the United Kingdom, most European countries
historically did not have liberal citizenship policies. Before the 1990s, most
did not allow for *jus soli* acquisition, allocating citizenship instead on the
descent-based *jus sanguinis* principle, naturalization requirements were often
strict, and many did not tolerate dual nationality. This situation has been
transformed since the 1990s, as European countries, or, to be more precise,
those Western European countries that have become major immigrant destinations, have gradually liberalized access to citizenship for immigrants.
There are three distinct elements to this: the introduction of *jus soli*; an
increased tolerance of dual nationality; and the liberalization of some aspects
of naturalization, notably the reduction of residence requirements and a shift
from discretionary to acquisition as of right.

The most significant liberalization is the introduction of elements of *jus
soli* citizenship to complement traditional *jus sanguinis* citizenship in several
European countries. Automatic or conditional *jus soli* is the most effective way
of incorporating the children of immigrants as citizens, either at birth or
later. It comes in a variety of forms. At birth, and in descending order of
inclusiveness, pure *jus soli* automatically grants citizenship to all children
born in the state; conditional *jus soli* makes some further requirements, often
a period of prior parental residence in the country; and double *jus soli* grants
citizenship at birth to the third generation, based on parental birth in the
country. After birth, *jus soli* can be divided into acquisition during childhood
or at the age of majority, which may be automatic or require a declaration,
and facilitated naturalization, whereby the conditions for naturalization are
less demanding for those born in the country than those required for other
applicants (see Honohan 2010: 5–6).

Whatever form it takes, *jus soli* citizenship is more inclusive of immigrants
than *jus sanguinis*, as its territoriality prevents immigrant-descended populations who have been born and raised in a state from ongoing exclusion from
citizenship, as can occur under descent-based modes of acquisition. A study
of citizenship in 33 European countries by the European Union Democracy

Observatory (EUDO)[21] found that, between 1989 and 2010, *jus soli* in some form was introduced or strengthened in twelve of the countries surveyed, making a total of nineteen with some form of *jus soli* provision by 2010 (Honohan 2010: 9). Major cases of liberalization included Germany (2000), Portugal (2006), Luxembourg (2009) and Greece (2010). The fourteen countries with no *jus soli* provisions in 2010 were Austria, Cyprus, Denmark, Estonia, Iceland, Latvia, Moldova, Malta, Norway, Poland, Slovakia, Switzerland, Sweden and Turkey. In support of Howard's arguments outlined above, it is striking that most of these countries are either not yet major immigrant destinations or have seen a successful far-right party.

It should be noted that, at the same time as historic *jus sanguinis* countries such as Germany have added *jus soli* provisions to incorporate immigrants, so historic *jus soli* countries such as the United Kingdom have added some *jus sanguinis* provisions and conditionality to *jus soli*. Today, no European country operates pure *jus soli* (the last example of this was Ireland, which added parental residence requirements in its citizenship reform of 2004). The result of these trends is a European convergence on mixed citizenship regimes, which are nevertheless generally more inclusive than they were two decades ago.

A second aspect of citizenship liberalization is the increased toleration of dual nationality. Both in Europe and internationally, there has been a steady shift away from hostility towards dual and even multiple memberships (see Faist and Kivisto 2007; Hansen and Weil 2001). The belief that dual nationality results in divided loyalties and potential security threats has slowly given way to a more permissive attitude. In Europe, for example, the shift is clear in the Council of Europe's evolving position, from its 1963 Convention on the Reduction of Cases of Multiple Nationality, which speaks for itself, to the 1997 European Convention on Nationality, which allows for multiple nationality. Today, all European countries allow dual nationality when a child inherits it from parents with different citizenships. However, Europe is deeply divided on the toleration of dual nationality in the context of naturalization: fifteen EU member states allow immigrants who naturalize to retain their previous nationality, while twelve, mostly post-2004 member states without substantial immigrant populations, require renunciation of a previous nationality. In Western Europe, the trend is towards increased tolerance. During the 1980s, just six of the then fifteen EU member states allowed dual nationality for naturalizing immigrants; by 2012, ten of these states officially tolerated dual nationality and, among the five countries that did not, Spain allowed it in practice, since it does not require proof of renunciation of previous citizenship, and there are exceptions in Germany and the Netherlands (Goodman 2010: 10; Howard 2009: 213). The only Western European countries that enforce a blanket prohibition on dual nationality today are Austria and Denmark.

A third dimension of citizenship reform is the partial liberalization of naturalization requirements. In several respects naturalization requirements have become more demanding in recent years, notably with the spread of language and civics tests (see below). But at the same time there has been a modest liberalization of access in some countries, including a reduction of residency requirements and a shift from discretionary to naturalization as of right. The residency requirement for 'ordinary naturalization' – that is to say, the naturalization of an immigrant who has no family, ancestry or other relevant ties to the country – ranges from three (Belgium) to twelve years (Switzerland), with five years being the most common requirement and seven years the median (Goodman 2010: 6–7). Germany, Greece, Luxembourg and Portugal all reduced their residency requirements between 1980 and 2008. During the same period, Denmark (in 2002) and Italy (in 1992) raised theirs. The overall European trend is moderately liberalizing, with some signs of a convergence on five years' residency as a European norm, but there is still variation between countries.

We can see an aggregate picture of how the various aspects of citizenship policy combine to produce liberalizing or restrictive changes from Marc Morjé Howard's (2009) citizenship policy index (CPI). His CPI is based on three main components of citizenship policy (*jus soli*, residency requirements, and toleration of dual nationality) which are each coded on a scale of 0 to 2 according to how liberal or restrictive they are (see Howard 2009: 19–36, 207–15, for details of this methodology). The scores are then adjusted to account for civic integration requirements (discussed further below) and actual naturalization rates, to capture the fact that apparently inclusive policies may be undermined by restrictive use of administrative discretion or other barriers to naturalization. The resulting CPI allocates a score to each country with 0 being the most restrictive and 6 the most liberal. The CPI confirms an overall liberalizing trend across Western Europe, albeit with significant cross national variation. Table 6.1 gives the aggregate CPI score for the EU15 countries in the 1980s and in 2008, the direction and extent of change, and a qualitative classification of that country (note that this last score does not account for changes after 2008, including subsequent liberalizations such as Greece, which reduced its residency requirement from ten to seven years in 2010, but also a restrictive move in Luxembourg, which, after lowering its residency requirement in 2001 from ten to five years, raised it again to seven years with effect from 2009).

The changes in Howard's CPI show clearly that there is a secular trend towards more liberal citizenship policies in Western Europe. While there is cross-national variation in the degree of liberalization, only one country – Denmark – became substantially more restrictive between the 1980s and 2008, and several countries became substantially more liberal. As discussed above, Howard's model explains this outcome, as well as the persistent

TABLE 6.1 Citizenship policies index in the EU15 countries

Country	CPI score in 1980s	CPI score in 2008	Direction of change	Classification
Austria	0.00	0.00	0	Restrictive continuity
Belgium	5.00	5.50	+0.50	Historically liberal
Denmark	1.43	0.00	−1.43	Restrictive continuity
Finland	1.72	4.32	+2.60	Liberalizing change
France	4.22	4.97	+0.75	Historically liberal
Germany	0.00	2.04	+2.04	Liberalizing change
Greece	1.25	1.00	−0.25	Restrictive continuity
Ireland	4.36	4.86	+0.50	Historically liberal
Italy	0.72	1.50	+0.78	Restrictive Continuity
Luxembourg	0.50	2.25	+1.75	Liberalizing change
Netherlands	2.72	4.22	+1.50	Liberalizing change
Portugal	1.75	4.32	+2.57	Liberalizing change
Spain	1.25	1.38	+0.13	Restrictive continuity
Sweden	1.72	5.22	+3.50	Liberalizing change
UK	5.47	4.97	−0.50	Historically liberal

Source: Adapted from Howard (2009: 27–31)

restrictiveness in Austria, as a consequence of successful far-right parties preventing liberalization. But these countries are the exceptions. Elsewhere the direction of change is almost all in one direction, even where the far right has been successful, such as in the Netherlands. The UK registers a small restrictive shift, caused by its introduction in 2002 of citizenship tests, but it remains liberal in terms of its overall score. As a result of the changes captured in table 6.1, the historically liberal countries of Belgium, France, Ireland and the UK have been joined by Finland, Germany, Luxembourg, the Netherlands, Portugal and Sweden as having relatively liberal citizenship policies. Five countries are classified by their restrictive continuity, but this becomes four when Greece's 2010 reforms are taken into account. In an era of mass immigration, it would appear that, while countries liberalize at different paces and extents according to domestic political factors, there is an underlying logic, possibly even a functional inevitability, of eventual liberalization.

Reasserting Exclusionary Citizenship?

These findings may strike some readers as odd, given the often illiberal tone of political debates about citizenship and immigration in recent years. It is certainly true that, while immigration has created pressures to liberalize citizenship policies, this has often been resisted, and in some cases the outcome has been to limit reforms or even introduce new restrictions. This is true not only of countries such as Austria or Denmark, where the far right has made the running on citizenship. In the UK, for example, one of the liberal countries in Howard's classification where the far right has no national representation, there have been extensive debates about 'reinvigorating' citizenship which have led to more, not less, demanding requirements for naturalization. And in Germany, where a historically restrictive policy was partially liberalized in 1999 by introducing conditional *jus soli*, the original centre-left SPD–Green government's proposals to tolerate dual nationality were abandoned following fierce opposition by the centre-right CDU/CSU party, which mobilized hostile public opinion through a petition campaign (Green 2005). More recently, several Western European countries have instituted controversial citizenship tests. Meanwhile, in the newer EU member states, most of them former communist countries, citizenship policies remain restrictive and, in the absence of significant immigrant flows to date, there has been little by way of liberalization. Looking beyond Europe, in 2007 Australia made its naturalization policy more, not less, demanding. Is, then, the story of immigration-driven citizenship liberalization wholly accurate?

Despite the liberalizations examined in the previous section, the most widely discussed trend in European naturalization policies in recent years has been the introduction and strengthening of language requirements and civic integration tests. Citizenship tests have long been established in Canada and the United States, but they are novel in Europe, and, as Sara Wallace Goodman (2010: 13) argues, 'no other changes have been as widespread and consequential to the future of national citizenship and the identity that citizenship formally institutionalises as those concerning language skills, country knowledge, value commitments, and general integration requirements.' In the 2010 EUDO Citizenship survey of 33 European countries, all except six countries (Belgium, Cyprus, Ireland, Italy, Poland and Sweden) had an explicit language requirement for ordinary naturalization, assessed in various ways such as a written test, educational certification or an interview. Of those countries that have language requirements, there is a clear trend towards formal testing: in 1998, just six countries in the EUDO study operated formal language tests (and, of these, five were former Soviet bloc countries without significant immigrant populations), but, by 2010, nineteen countries operated formal tests, among them most of the major immigrant-receiving countries (ibid.: 16). Language requirements are often justified in terms of integration (whether as an instrument of integration or as a sign of integration already achieved), but it is worth noting that they can have the opposite effect, most blatantly in the specific cases of Estonia and Latvia, where language tests are a barrier to the naturalization of Russian-speaking minorities.

The second innovation in European naturalization policies is the introduction of country knowledge or civics tests. The trend towards this type of test is not as strong as that towards language testing, but it is still significant. In 1999, just four European countries (Hungary, Latvia, Estonia and Lithuania), none of them major immigrant destinations, operated formal country knowledge tests. By 2010, twelve European countries used such tests, including major immigrant destination countries such as Austria, Denmark, Germany, the Netherlands and the United Kingdom. As with language tests, the trend is linear, with no country to date having removed a country knowledge requirement. A further five countries (France, Greece, Luxembourg, Norway and Turkey) operate informal tests through a naturalization interview or require attendance at a civics course without a test (Goodman 2010: 15–16).

In the five major immigration countries that have introduced tests there has been considerable debate about their form and content. In general, the new European tests are more demanding than those in classic immigration countries, with more questions and a higher threshold for a pass (Goodman 2010: 16). The content of the tests varies considerably. In some cases, such as the British and German federal naturalization tests, the emphasis is more on civic than cultural or historical knowledge; in others, for example in Denmark, questions focus on national history and culture; and, in the infamous case of the interview guidelines issued by the German *Land* of Baden-Württemberg, naturalization officers were expected to assess the 'inner disposition' of applicants from member states of the Islamic League through questions about their personal beliefs on topics such as gender, sexuality, religion and terrorism.

Looking beyond Europe to those countries where citizenship tests are well established, there have also been reforms, though not always in the same direction. In 2008, the United States revised the content of the federal naturalization test that had been in place since the 1980s, although surprisingly, given the heightened American nationalism post-2001, the new test was neither more difficult nor appreciably more nationalistic (Joppke 2010: 124–5). More in tune with European developments was the 2007 citizenship reform in Australia, which introduced a formal naturalization test that emphasizes English-language abilities and so-called Australian values. As in Europe, populist fears about multiculturalism, Muslims and terrorism influenced the centre-right government of John Howard to promote a test that is supposed to reassert Australian identity and patriotism (Betts and Birrell 2007; Johnson 2007).

Naturalization tests, especially country knowledge tests, polarize opinion. In Europe especially, the introduction of tests is justified with reference to

immigrant integration, with language tests supposed to encourage the acquisition of skills necessary for employment and country knowledge tests supposed to ensure that naturalizing immigrants have sufficient knowledge and
identification with the host country to participate as citizens and, more con-
tentiously, to ensure that they endorse its putative values. However, the barriers that such tests raise are also argued to stymie rather than further
immigrant integration, and on a normative level they may be construed to
be inconsistent with liberal values (see the debate in Bauböck and Joppke
2010). Whether tests act as an incentive to acquire the required skills and
knowledge or as a deterrent to naturalization is not presently well understood, but most likely depends on the nature and stringency of the requirements. The normative issue depends partly on the content of the tests, with
tests of applicants' values and personal beliefs on issues such as gender equality and homosexuality being particularly problematic from a liberal perspective (Hampshire 2011: 967).

However, it is far from clear that instrumental objectives of immigrant
integration – whether language skills or civic knowledge – are the real driver
of these policies. The introduction of tests has undoubtedly been influenced
by anti-immigrant populism, most directly in those countries such as Austria,
Denmark and the Netherlands where the far right has joined coalition governments, elsewhere through an increasingly xenophobic and often anti-
Muslim discourse about multiculturalism, national identity and security. In
this regard it is notable that all of the tests in major immigrant-receiving
countries have been introduced since 2001. There is more than a hint of
political symbolism and exclusionary nation-building in these measures,
with the aim at least partially to reassure voters who hold anti-immigrant
and anti-Muslim sentiments. In the case of the Netherlands, tests are also used
for immigration control purposes, with certain categories of would-be immigrants required to pass a test before they can receive a visa (Scholten et al.
2012). Whatever interpretation is put on them, it is clear that tests raise the
bar for naturalization, requiring immigrants to demonstrate language skills
and country knowledge, and in some cases expend considerable time and
money taking the requisite courses.

If language and civic integration requirements are the most visible aspect
of more stringent citizenship policies in Europe, they are not the only examples of immigration-driven restrictions. Although the aggregate story of liberalization is irrefutable, it can overshadow a few important cases in which
exclusionary dynamics came to the fore, including the introduction of
increased residency requirements for naturalization and limitations to *jus
soli*. Among the classic countries of immigration, the only state that has
engaged in significant reform of its citizenship policy in recent years is
Australia, and that was in a restrictive direction. The Australian Citizenship
Act of 2007 doubled the residency requirement for naturalization from two
to four years, as well as introducing the naturalization test discussed above.

In Europe, changes to residency requirements have not always been in a liberalizing direction. In Denmark, the far-right Danish People's Party, which campaigns on a virulently anti-immigrant platform, has successfully pushed for a tightening of citizenship as well as immigration and integration policies, notably in 2002, when the residency requirement for naturalization was increased from seven to nine years (Ersbøll 2010: 20–1). More recently, and without the influence of a far-right party, Luxembourg's 2008 Citizenship Act partially undid a 2001 reduction of the residency requirement from ten to five years by increasing it to seven years.

In two of the historically liberal countries, the United Kingdom and Ireland, the onset of mass immigration even spurred restrictions on highly inclusive *jus soli* regimes. The 1948 British Nationality Act had created the category of Citizenship of the United Kingdom and Colonies (CUKC), which, as its name implies, granted a single citizenship status and rights on a *jus soli* basis to all persons born throughout the British Empire. The 1948 Act was not passed with immigration in mind, and it was certainly not intended to facilitate the transformation of Britain into a multi-ethnic country (rather, it was a response to a unilateral move by the Canadian government to redefine British subjecthood; see Hansen 2000: 37–45), but its implications for immigration were profound: literally millions of persons across the globe were granted the right to settle in the United Kingdom, and their children would automatically become *jus soli* British citizens. As immigration from colonial and postcolonial countries increased during the 1950s and 1960s, the consequences of CUKC became increasingly apparent. Resolved to control this immigration, but wary of antagonizing fledgling governments during and after decolonization, successive British governments used immigration policy to carve a line within CUKC, a move justified by the Conservative Home Secretary Rab Butler as making a distinction between 'citizens who belong' and 'citizens who do not belong' (see Hampshire 2005: 25–42). To effect this distinction, an element of descent-based citizenship – 'patriality' in the terms of the 1971 Immigration Act – was smuggled into the law through the back door of immigration legislation.

In 1981, the Conservative government passed the British Nationality Act (BNA 1981), which repealed the 1948 legislation and defined a distinct British citizenship to the exclusion of former colonies; it also abolished pure *jus soli*. Today, British citizenship is acquired at birth through a combination of territory and descent: a child born in the United Kingdom acquires British citizenship automatically only if either of its parents is a British citizen or is settled in the United Kingdom (Hansen 2000: 214). Thus, while the United Kingdom's citizenship policy remains comparatively liberal insofar as it allows for conditional *jus soli*, the history of immigration from the 1950s to the early 1980s illustrates how it can also have restrictive effects on citizenship.

In other words, whereas immigration creates pressure for the liberalization of exclusionary *jus sanguinis* citizenship (as in the case of Germany), it also tends to hedge pure *jus soli*, which is highly – some would argue overly – inclusive. The story of CUKC is admittedly a special case, but the point remains that immigration can have exclusionary effects on citizenship.[22]

A more recent example of immigration curtailing a highly inclusive citizenship regime is the 2004 reform in Ireland. Before that year, Ireland was the last example of a pure *jus soli* regime in Europe. In the context of the politicization of immigration, allegations began to circulate that pregnant unauthorized immigrants, mainly from Nigeria, were coming to Ireland solely to give birth to a baby who would thus acquire Irish (and hence EU) citizenship. This prompted a public debate about so-called citizen tourism, which further fuelled anti-immigrant sentiment. A referendum held on 11 June 2004 found that 80 per cent of Irish citizens supported a change to the constitution to restrict the country's historic tradition of pure *jus soli*. The resulting Irish Nationality and Citizenship Act introduced the condition that a child born in Ireland to non-citizens will automatically acquire Irish citizenship only if at least one parent has been resident for three of the preceding four years. As with the United Kingdom, post-2004 Irish citizenship policy remains liberal in comparative terms, but once again the Irish case illustrates the potentially restrictive effects of immigration on inclusive citizenship regimes.

Conclusion

The widespread introduction of naturalization tests, as well as increased residency requirements and restrictions on pure *jus soli* in some countries, illustrates that immigration is not always and everywhere a trigger for more inclusive citizenship policies. The trend towards citizenship liberalization is irrefutable, but amid the inclusionary dynamics there are exclusionary counter-forces. The real question is not whether there are exclusionary tendencies in contemporary citizenship politics, but how to interpret them in the light of the immigration-driven liberalization of the last half-century. Are these counter-trends mere 'nuances within, not a roll-back to, the overall liberalization of access to citizenship', as Joppke (2010: 32) argues, or are they more substantive than this? What explains the often contrasting direction of travel in different countries?

Certainly, we should avoid a teleological narrative, in which immigration inevitably drives citizenship towards an inclusive end point. The various counter-examples discussed in this section should suffice to establish this. When citizenship is put on the political agenda, and especially when it is framed as an issue of national identity, it has proven quite possible to mobilize opposition to liberalization. Howard's analysis of the influence of far-right parties shows that, where they achieve political success, such as in Austria and Denmark, the effect on citizenship is almost invariably restrictive. However, given the number of cases where restrictions of one kind or another have occurred in the absence of the far right – for example, it was not a significant factor in Australia (2007), Ireland (2004), Luxembourg (2008) or the United Kingdom (1981) – it cannot be considered a necessary condition for more restrictive policies. As with immigration policy more broadly, mainstream political parties do not need to be pushed by the far right, as they often have their own incentives for politicizing citizenship.

Immigration is thus something of a double-edged sword for citizenship. It has clearly created pressures for liberalization but it has also engendered the conditions in which liberalization can be held back, or even undone. One of the most important impacts of immigration on citizenship policymaking is to have transformed it from a low-key, relatively technical issue into a matter of high political contention. In the process, the liberalizing driver of immigration paradoxically becomes its own fetter as it stokes illiberal counter-forces. If this is correct, then we should not be complacent about the future of citizenship liberalization.

A lot will depend on whether and how citizenship becomes embroiled in the increasingly contested debates about integration. In Europe, and also to some extent in the classic countries of immigration, the perceived failure of immigrant integration underlies the reassertion of citizenship (Hansen 2009: 15–17). The effect of socio-economic exclusion among certain immigrant communities – measured in terms of educational outcomes, unemployment and wages – can be seen in the introduction of language requirements, which are supposed to improve labour market participation as well as wider social integration, while concerns about Islamist terrorism and the identification of Muslims with liberal democratic values partly motivate country knowledge and values tests. These policies are inextricable from attempts to shore up unity in increasingly diverse societies. All of which leads to the politics of immigrant integration, the topic of the next chapter.

CHAPTER SEVEN

Integration in the Liberal State

Few aspects of the immigration debate generate more controversy than the issue of integration. From the extent to which immigrants are integrated, to how they should be integrated and what the state should do about it, almost every aspect of integration is contested. In North America and Oceania, integration has been a matter of debate for well over a century, in the former case since nineteenth-century nativist movements opposed first Catholic, then Chinese and Jewish immigration on the grounds that these groups were alien to the supposedly Protestant European identity of the United States. In Europe, the integration debate is altogether more recent. Not only because immigration is more recent but also because serious consideration of integration had to wait until governments finally accepted that immigrants were here to stay, which happened in some countries in the 1960s but in others only as recently as the 1990s. Notwithstanding these different histories, in liberal states across all three regions, integration has become increasingly politicized since the 1990s. Popular anxieties about the impact of immigration on national identity and security are partly responsible for the ascent of integration on the public agenda, but so too is evidence of discrimination, residential segregation and unemployment among immigrants.

What is integration? We can begin with a simple definition: integration is a process or set of processes by which immigrants become full members of the host country. But this immediately begs as many questions as it answers. What does full membership consist of? What is required of immigrants and of host societies for the former to become full members? And where should the burden of adaptation lie? Assimilationist approaches to integration place the burden of adaptation squarely upon immigrants themselves; as newcomers, it is immigrants who should assimilate to the practices, traditions and customs of the host society. Multicultural approaches, by contrast, demand more of the receiving societies so as to tolerate, recognize and even encourage the expression of cultural difference. An increasingly common *via media* is to describe integration as a two-way process: as the European Union put it in its 2004 Common Basic Principles, 'integration is a dynamic, two-way process of mutual accommodation by all immigrants and residents of Member States.' Yet, whether integration is spoken of in terms of assimilation, multiculturalism or mutual accommodation, all too often the political debate is structured around simplistic assumptions and a binary opposition between a supposedly integrated 'us' and an allegedly unintegrated 'them'.

Beyond these clichés of the integration debate lies a complex reality. Immigrants to liberal states are enormously and in most cases increasingly diverse in terms of their national origin, language, religion and culture, not to mention their socio-economic profile. What integration means for a lowly educated person who migrates from a rural region of a developing country must be different from what it means for a highly skilled immigrant moving from one global city to another. Furthermore, integration itself is a multidimensional process, with economic, social, cultural and political aspects. And it is not only the targets of integration policy and the process of integration that are complex; so too is the entity into which immigrants are supposed to become incorporated, since, as discussed below, modern societies are highly differentiated. Thus integration is a dizzyingly complex issue, belied by the clichés of much popular debate.

The Problem of Unity in Liberal States

Even if immigration could be factored out of the equation (which it obviously cannot) the maintenance of unity in modern societies is far from straightforward. One of the defining characteristics of modern societies is their functional differentiation. In contrast to the stratified or segmented societies of the pre-modern world, in which status or place were the organizing principles, modern societies are organized into distinct realms or subsystems based on functional specifications, such as economics, politics, law, science, art, and so on. In modern societies issues are defined principally as 'political' or 'economic' or 'legal', and only secondarily in terms of status or location – for example, as 'upper class' or 'working class', 'urban' or 'rural'.

The two most influential theorists of functional differentiation, the American sociologist Talcott Parsons and his student Niklas Luhmann, both explored the significance of functional differentiation for social theory. Parsons (1937) argued that differentiation is a process which drives traditionally integrated societies apart and therefore requires the promotion of a collective identity and shared norms to maintain social order. Luhmann (1982) conceived of society as being nothing other than the various subsystems and the interdependencies that they generate, and he took issue with Parsons's account of the separateness of the subsystems. Whereas for Parsons they are empirically observable realms which may overlap and mutually influence one another, for Luhmann they are ontologically distinct and closed 'autopoietic' systems based on their own binary codes. Despite these differences, both Parsons and Luhmann agreed that the functional subsystems of modern societies are more or less autonomous and operate according to their own logics. Modern societies are thus fragmented and lack a hierarchical ordering that organizes their various parts into a unified whole.

It is not necessary to go further into the complexities of social systems theory to see the significance of functional differentiation for understanding how (indeed, whether) integration is achievable. If modern societies are fragmented into autonomous subsystems, then the apparent production and maintenance of a harmonious social order is far from straightforward. Functional differentiation implies that distinct and potentially conflicting logics are inherent to modern societies, and thus the achievement of institutional and normative integration, let alone social harmony, is problematic. As the basic structures of complex societies embody values that are in inherent conflict, the maintenance of social order entails some level of reconciliation of conflicts through shared normative frameworks to guide social conduct. But, given the absence of an overarching order or set of organizing principles, these reconciliations are necessarily contingent. According to Parsons's more optimistic account, modern societies can achieve integration, but only through the institutionalization of a common value framework that specifies social roles and the rewards attached to those roles; and this framework must be accepted and shared by members as motivation for their actions.

Integration is particularly problematic in liberal societies. As is well known, liberalism is committed to individual freedom and the equal moral worth of individuals. Among other things, this entails a commitment to allow individuals to pursue and revise their own conception of the good, so long as a given conception is consistent with the freedom and equality of others. These core liberal values, which are often institutionalized in the constitutions of liberal states, give rise to what John Rawls called 'reasonable pluralism' (1993: xviii; 2001: 33–4). Since the exercise of human reason does not lead to a single conception of the good, individuals living under free institutions will come to affirm different conceptions, and liberal society is therefore inevitably characterized by moral and religious diversity (Rawls 2001: 34). This is a permanent feature of liberal societies, which cannot be undone without violating the basic rights of citizens. Liberal states must remain neutral on the question of the good – in other words, not try to promote or restrict any particular conception – so as to respect citizens' freedom and equality. This makes the achievement of unity especially difficult because the inherently universalistic nature of liberal values cannot give content to a particular identity around which diverse citizens can coalesce. Indeed, it is one of the hallmarks of liberalism that its commitment to universal freedoms constrains efforts to check centrifugal tendencies through the promotion of particular identities or comprehensive doctrines.

Historically, Western states have nevertheless tried to shore up unity through nation-building: standardizing languages, promoting national symbols and myths, inculcating national values in school curricula, enacting ethnically discriminatory immigration policies, and so on. But this nation-building response to diversity became increasingly untenable in the latter half of the twentieth century. Partly this was because, in an era of globalization, government-led attempts to spell out, let alone promote, a shared national identity were progressively undercut by the emergence of trans- and sub-national identities, which are themselves both cause and consequence of greater international mobility. Furthermore, the constraints imposed by liberal norms, which were at best dormant and at worst actively undermined for much of the twentieth century, started to bite in the latter half of the century, first, as the fallout out from the Second World War and, later, as the rights revolution of the 1960s unfolded. As liberal constraints have become more actual than theoretical, the governments of liberal states have become ensnared in paradoxical attempts to ground particularistic identification with the nation-state using universalistic values.

Thus liberal states face a problem of integration. Functional differentiation and moral pluralism generate powerful centrifugal tendencies in modern societies, and liberal values place constraints on what governments can do to counter these tendencies. Liberal modernity is a solvent of unity, and the elusive nature of integration in liberal states is not solely or even principally a problem of *immigrant* integration. To be sure, when immigration *is* entered into the equation this problem is exacerbated, since immigrants tend to increase diversity and further problematize the classic nation-building response. But the point remains that the problem of integration in liberal states pre-exists the problem of immigrant integration.

The Multidimensionality of Immigrant Integration

Given the complex and differentiated nature of the societies to which immigrants come, it should not be surprising that the processes of integration are complex and differentiated. The range of processes that are often grouped together under the single term 'integration' are in fact multifaceted, with economic, social, political and cultural dimensions (Joppke and Morawska 2003). Economic integration entails *inter alia* participation in the labour market and educational outcomes; social integration involves residential patterns, friendships with members of the host society, and intermarriage rates; political integration includes participation in the public life of the receiving society – for example, voting, party membership or other forms of political activism; while cultural integration embraces language acquisition and convergence with the majority's values and beliefs. Given this diverse range of processes involved as newcomers and host societies interact, the factors that shape integration outcomes will be equally diverse.

The multidimensionality of immigrant integration is further complicated by the fact that immigrants and their children are themselves diverse. It is now well established that different immigrant groups integrate at different rates and to different extents across the various dimensions. Some groups integrate across several or all dimensions, adopting majority customs, participating in the labour market, forming social relations with natives, and actively participating in politics; others are relatively less integrated. In the UK, for example, there is a stark contrast between Indians and Sri Lankans, on the one hand, and Pakistanis and Bangladeshis, on the other. These groups are often lumped together under the umbrella term 'Asians', but, whereas Indians and Sri Lankans are socially mobile and actually outperform the 'white British' population on a number of educational and economic indicators, Pakistanis and Bangladeshis have lower levels of education and employment and are concentrated in deprived urban areas. Other groups may be more integrated on some dimensions but not on others. For example, Britons of Caribbean ancestry have relatively high rates of intermarriage but lower levels of education attainment and employment (Saggar and Somerville 2011: 6–7).

There are also intra-group variations in integration processes and outcomes. In fact, it is debatable whether measures of integration should focus on nationally and ethnically defined groups at all, as opposed to individuals, locations or immigration statuses. The example of the category 'British Asian' masking variation between Indians and Pakistanis illustrates that outcomes depend on how groups are defined. At the individual level, meaningful comparison becomes all but impossible. Is a first-generation Turkish-speaking shopkeeper who devoutly practises Islam 'more' or 'less' integrated than the German-born son of Turkish guestworkers who is unemployed but German-speaking? One contributes to the economy while retaining his distinctive cultural and religious identity; the other claims welfare benefits but would be no more at home in rural Anatolia than his ethnic German peers. That a meaningful assessment of integration at this level can hardly be made reminds us that integration is complex and that it depends to a large extent on how analytical boundaries are drawn.

The overlay of multidimensionality with individual- and group-level diversity means that the immigrant side of the integration equation is just as complex as the side of the receiving society. It may be the case that integration outcomes on the various dimensions are closely interrelated, so that, for example, integration into the labour market is positively correlated with integration into the culture of the host society. But there are reasons to doubt that this is the case. In an intriguing recent analysis, Rahsaan Maxwell (2012) argues that immigrant integration involves trade-offs. An integration trade-off occurs when a positive outcome on one dimension promotes a negative outcome on another, or vice versa (ibid.: 3). Maxwell disaggregates integration into three dimensions – social, economic and political – and shows that social integration can have trade-offs with both economic and political integration. Under certain conditions, immigrant groups that are *more* socially integrated become *less* economically and politically integrated. The mechanism Maxwell posits to explain this surprising outcome is group mobilization. Immigrant groups that are more socially integrated have less capacity for group mobilization precisely because they experience greater interaction with mainstream society, and therefore they have less need for strong co-ethnic networks for survival. Their relatively weak capacity for group mobilization undermines their ability to exert political pressure and respond to adverse economic circumstances. Conversely, groups that are socially segregated rely more upon co-ethnic networks, which leads to better group mobilization, and thence greater political influence and resources that further economic integration (ibid.: 4). This means that groups that are more residentially integrated, that intermarry more, and that become culturally assimilated will, under certain conditions,[23] have *worse* educational and employment outcomes, as well as *lower* levels of political participation and representation, compared to less socially integrated groups.

Maxwell's argument is based on a detailed empirical analysis of the integration outcomes of different immigrant groups in Britain and France, as well as some more tentative findings in the Netherlands and the United States. He shows, for example, that differences in the economic and political integration outcomes of Caribbean, Indian, and Bangladeshi and Pakistani immigrants in Britain reveal trade-offs with social integration. Caribbean immigrants are more socially integrated than the latter groups, but have worse economic outcomes than Indians and lower levels of political influence than all the other groups. In France, the greater social integration of Caribbean compared to Maghrebian immigrants does not extend to economic or political integration.

The idea that 'successful' integration in one dimension may hinder integration in others has profound implications for understanding integration processes, not to mention for the design of integration policies. Integration research and integration policymaking has often worked with an implicit assumption that integration is a single process or at least a set of processes that are mutually self-reinforcing. If in fact 'positive' outcomes on one dimension can produce 'negative' outcomes on another, then integration policies must recognize the possibility of trade-offs and seek to ameliorate them. When *the* problem of integration or *the* failure of integration policies is debated, it is worth asking where the problem lies and which aspects of policies are deemed to have failed.

In Search of Integration Models

Unfortunately, the complexity of integration is not always adequately reflected in research on integration policies in liberal states. The literature too often pays insufficient attention to both the functional differentiation of receiving societies and the multidimensionality of integration. Instead, a dominant theme is the attempt to identify distinct national 'models' of integration: unified and coherent frameworks for integration policymaking. This tradition takes its cue from Rogers Brubaker's (1992) classic study of citizenship, in which he argued that citizenship laws in France and Germany reflected distinct conceptions of national community (see chapter 6). The search for national integration models typically proceeds by sketching a theoretical typology – sometimes deductively, more often inductively – and then placing individual countries in that typology. The emphasis tends to be on the degree of cultural adaptation expected of immigrants vis-à-vis natives.

A textbook case – literally, given its location in a widely read migration textbook – is Castles and Miller's (2009: 247–8) identification of four models of 'immigrant incorporation' in Western democracies: assimilation, which they describe as a one-sided process of adaptation that requires immigrants to relinquish their linguistic and cultural characteristics so as to become incorporated into the host society; differential exclusion, which entails temporary incorporation into the labour market but exclusion from citizenship and political participation; integration, which they see as a soft form of assimilation, with some mutual accommodation but still a final goal of absorption into the dominant culture; and multiculturalism, which pursues the inclusion of immigrants without an expectation that they give up their own culture, religion or language. While intuitively plausible and with some empirical resonance, this typology lacks theoretical specification, and therefore the criteria for classifying countries as fitting into one model or another are far from clear (Freeman 2004: 947).

A more sophisticated approach is provided by Adrian Favell's (2001) comparison of 'philosophies of integration' in Britain and France. Favell argues that these two countries have developed divergent integration policy frameworks informed by

> two contrasting and seemingly incompatible sets of ideas about the correct frame for policy responses to ethnic dilemmas in liberal democracies: the integration of *immigrés* into the universalist national community, via access to full participatory political *citoyenneté* in France; the integration of *ethnic minorities* into the tolerant multi-national state, via the management strategy of *race relations* and *multiculturalism* in Britain. (Favell 2001: 26)

These distinct 'public philosophies' provide a language and theoretical scheme – embodying epistemological, explanatory and normative claims – through which political debates on integration and integration policies are conducted. Once consolidated, a public philosophy 'structures and constrains political actions and policy interventions that take place within the accepted frame' (ibid.). Since the national particularities and idiosyncrasies that are embedded in these frameworks tend to be self-reproducing, they lead countries that are facing apparently similar integration problems to persist with very different policy solutions, even when a given framework may appear pathological to an external observer.

The contrasting public philosophies that Favell dissects are well illustrated by the fact that, whereas in Britain 'race' and 'ethnicity' are formally recognized, in France they have been consistently denied in the name of a 'colour-blind' and universalist republicanism. Although Favell argues that the concept of public philosophies should be understood not as equivalent to 'a rooted historical tradition which determines the language and outcomes of present-day politics' but rather as 'a series of contingent political constraints' (2001: viii) within which domestic political struggles are fought out, he maintains that these philosophies are articulated at the national level and exhibit a level of coherence and unity to frame what is perceived as possible and desirable within a particular national context. The public philosophies that Favell discusses do not encompass the full gamut of integration, however, as they are essentially ideational frames for cultural and political integration, with relatively little to say about economic integration.

Other researchers have focused on institutional and organizational structures, and in so doing come closer to explicitly multidimensional models of immigrant integration. In her book *Limits of Citizenship*, which paradoxically became best known for its argument about postnationalism, Yasemin Soysal compared national-level 'immigrant incorporation regimes' in Europe using a two-dimensional 'membership model'. Her first dimension relates to the 'legitimized locus of action and authority', with some polities locating more authority in the state, others in society, either with individuals or corporate groups. The second dimension relates to the 'organizational configuration' of the polity, in terms of whether public space and authority are centralized or decentralized (Soysal 1994: 36–41). These two dimensions combine to produce four membership models: corporatist (centralized organizational configuration combined with society as the locus of action and authority), liberal (decentralized organizational configuration with a societal locus of authority), statist (centralized organizational configuration combined with a state-oriented locus of authority) and fragmental (decentralized and statist). Examples of the fragmental model cannot be found in the Western democracies (the illustration Soysal gives is the Gulf oil countries), but within Europe she identifies examples of each of the other three models: Sweden and the Netherlands represent the corporatist model, Britain and Switzerland the liberal model, and France the statist model. Some countries are ambivalent, notably Germany, which in Soysal's account exhibits elements of both corporatism and statism. Soysal's major contribution was to analyse how the membership structure of national polities, including institutions and discourses that were not developed with immigrant integration in mind, nevertheless shape integration processes. Specific instruments and discourses of integration are embedded in these wider membership models. Thus liberal Britain seeks to incorporate immigrants as individuals into the labour market, corporatist Sweden and the Netherlands incorporate immigrants as collective groups, while France refuses to recognize collective identities, pursuing an individualist yet centralized approach (ibid.: 45–83).

An alternative two-dimensional model, focused more on 'field-specific' institutions and discourses, is advanced by Ruud Koopmans, Paul Statham, Marco Giugni and Florence Passy (2005) in their analysis of how citizenship and integration policies influence patterns of political contention on immigration and cultural diversity. In a study of five European countries, Koopmans and his colleagues argue that cross-national variation in political mobilization depends on 'different conceptions of national identity and their crystallization in nation-specific integration and citizenship policies. These national self-understandings and policies act as institutional and discursive opportunities and constraints' (Koopmans et al. 2005: 6). Institutional opportunity structures include formal rights and duties, as well as resources and institutional channels that are available to immigrants and their opponents; discursive opportunity structures include cultural notions of citizenship and national identity that determine what claims are seen as feasible and legitimate in the public sphere. Koopmans et al. map variation in these opportunity structures along two axes. On one axis is equality of individual access to citizenship, which ranges from conceptions of citizenship based on ethnicity to conceptions based on equal civic rights and territorial attribution. On the other axis are cultural difference and group rights, which range from support for cultural pluralism to an insistence on conformity to a single cultural identity. As with Soysal's approach, this yields four ideal-typical configurations: segregationism, under which migrants are excluded from an ethnic conception of citizenship and are not expected to give up their own cultures; assimilationism, which operates an ethnic conception of citizenship but encourages or even requires citizens to assimilate to the majority culture as a condition of membership; universalism, which combines a civic-territorial conception of citizenship but denies cultural or ethnic group differences as a legitimate policy category; and multiculturalism, which is also civic territorial but recognizes ethnic, racial and cultural differences as the basis for policies – for example, on discrimination.

Koopmans et al. stress that their typology does not assume 'fixed or uniform national coordinates' (2005: 16), and they use it not only for cross-national comparison but also to track changes of particular countries over time. Using a number of indicators to plot the five countries' location in this space during the period 1980 to 2002, they categorize Germany and Switzerland as assimilationist, though with some movement away from the ethnic and cultural monist poles during the 1990s, particularly in Germany; France sits within the universalist quadrant, with just a small amount of movement; Britain hovers between universalism and multiculturalism, moving towards the latter in the 1990s; while the Netherlands sits in the multicultural quadrant, moving increasingly towards both civic territorial access to citizenship and cultural pluralism (ibid.: 71–3).[24]

Despite the recognition of institutional complexity and the multidimensionality of integration in these studies, the attempt of Koopmans and his colleagues to identify coherent policy frameworks remains something of an oversimplification. As Gary Freeman argues in a powerful critique of these more nuanced approaches:

> no state possesses a truly coherent incorporation regime. Instead, one finds ramshackle, multifaceted, loosely connected sets of regulatory rules, institutions, and practices in various domains of society that together make up the frameworks within which migrants and natives work out their differences. . . . The partly deliberate, partly accidental character of incorporation frameworks defeats efforts to identify national models or to construct abstract typologies of incorporation regimes. Although one may find idiosyncratic incorporation mechanisms in particular countries, these cannot be labelled national models because they do not represent self-conscious, deliberate choices so much as the unintended consequences of subsystem frameworks that are weakly, if at all, coordinated. Attempts to stipulate more general and abstract typologies of incorporation regimes that produce cells into which particular states may more or less easily fit oversimplify an extremely messy reality. (Freeman 2004: 946)

An important insight here is that integration outcomes are influenced as much, if not more, by 'rules, institutions and practices' that were constructed without immigrant integration in mind. Instead of an integration policy framework or model, Freeman proposes a multisectoral approach, which disaggregates immigrant incorporation into four domains – state, market, welfare and culture – and does not seek to identify any overarching logic across the domains. Rather, incorporation into each of these subsystems is influenced by a complex range of institutions, regulations and discourses, some of which are explicit integration policies, many of which are not. Economic integration is shaped by the market and welfare sectors. An immigrant's likelihood of finding employment, starting a business, or accessing social benefit programmes is fundamentally shaped by the structure of the national economy and its welfare system. Differences in labour market regulations will influence participation in the labour market, and welfare institutions will affect incentives to work. Hence different varieties of capitalism are more significant for immigrant integration than the comparatively paltry range of dedicated economic integration policies. Differences between 'liberal market economies' (LMEs) and 'coordinated market economies' (CMEs) (Hall and Soskice 2001) are likely to affect immigrants' participation in the informal sector, the level of protections that immigrants enjoy relative to national workers, the level of migrant self-employment, and anti-discrimination in the labour market (Freeman 2004: 954). Similarly, welfare institutions and social benefits will have a profound effect on economic and social integration, influencing the marginal utility of work and the level of migrant welfare.

Even the culture domain, in which there has been the most extensive debate about integration in recent years, is profoundly influenced by institutions and ideas which have little to do with immigration, and were certainly not constructed as integration policies. While 'state policies on cultural recognition and expression produce critical incentive structures for the retention or loss of immigrant cultural characteristics' (Freeman 2004: 958), these processes are also shaped by national identities and self-understandings that are everywhere broader than immigration and integration debates. Of course, these identities are partly forged by immigration and reactions to immigration – most obviously when one compares the national self-definitions of settler states with those of European countries – but national identity is nowhere made through cultural integration policies alone. In fact, these policies tend to draw upon and institutionalize prior cultural discourses about identity and belonging.

Given the breadth and relative independence of the different sectors, Freeman concludes that, although we might be able to identify loose patterns of subsystem configurations, or 'national syndromes', these are nowhere near as cohesive, intentional or interdependent as the language of national models suggests (ibid.: 961).

Where does this review of the integration policy literature leave us? First, it suggests that we should drop the language of national models. Since integration is shaped by myriad institutions, regulations and discourses that are uncoordinated and fragmented, the idea of national models is misleading at best (see Bertossi and Duyvendak 2012 for a recent critique). Following from this, a second conclusion is that any attempt to measure or compare integration regimes must reflect the multidimensionality of integration. One recent policy index, the Migrant Integration Policy Index (MIPEX), does attempt to do this.[25] This leads to a third conclusion, which is that many of the institutions – such as labour markets and welfare systems – that decisively influence integration processes are not integration policies at all. As discussed below, the impacts of these deep-seated structures are not easily changed, and certainly not by means of integration policies alone.

A Question of Employment?

Of all the various dimensions of immigrant integration, two have come to predominate in recent years. The economic integration of immigrants is a cause of growing concern among governments, as there are significant and persistent disparities in employment and wages between immigrants and natives in most OECD countries. And cultural integration has become an increasingly salient policy issue, especially since the rise of Islamist terrorism prompted heated debates about the compatibility of Islam with liberal democracy and the place of Muslims in liberal societies.

Governments have good reason to be concerned about the economic integration of immigrants. Bearing in mind the caveats discussed earlier about inter- and intra-group level diversity, in the aggregate immigrants tend to have lower levels of employment, lower wages, and less social mobility than native workers. This is especially the case in Western Europe. As table 7.1 shows, in every major receiving country in Europe, immigrants have higher levels of unemployment than native-born workers. In 2010, the unemployment rate for foreign workers was 14.7 per cent compared to 8.9 per cent for native-born workers (OECD 2011: 84), though the disparity varied considerably from one country to another: while foreign/native unemployment rates were 9.1/7.8 in the UK, in Belgium they were 17.6/7.0. The best way to capture these disparities is through the relative unemployment rate of foreign-born workers (the immigrant unemployment rate divided by the native-born unemployment rate). This is reported for the period 2008 to 2010 in the last three columns of table 7.1. In 2010, the relative unemployment rate of foreign-born workers across all OECD European countries was 1.65. In other words, immigrant unemployment was 65 per cent higher than native-born unemployment in wealthy European countries. The discrepancy between foreign-born and native-born unemployment was smallest in the UK, where the relative unemployment rate was 1.17. In Germany, Europe's largest economy, it was 1.82. Elsewhere it was as high as 2.13 in the Netherlands, 2.30 in Sweden and 2.51 in Belgium. In these latter countries, immigrants are more than twice as likely as natives to be inactive in the labour market. In the classic immigration countries in North America and Oceania the disparities are much smaller, and in the United States immigrants are *less* likely to be unemployed than natives. The 2010 relative unemployment rate in these countries was 0.99 in the United States, 1.06 in Australia and 1.32 in Canada. On the basis of these data, Randall Hansen makes a powerful case that the obsession with cultural integration in Europe is entirely misdirected. As he puts it, 'work, not culture, needs to be the basis of immigration policy in Europe' (2012: 8).

The evidence to support this claim is compelling. But the reasons behind the high levels of immigrant unemployment in many OECD countries, and hence the policies required to improve labour market outcomes, are complex. Both supply- and demand-side factors play a role. On the one hand, characteristics of immigrants themselves, such as their levels of education, skills and training and their ability to speak the majority language of the host society, affect labour market outcomes. On the demand side, factors such as labour market regulations, the residential concentration of immigrants in depressed post-industrial regions, non-recognition of foreign qualifications, and racial discrimination play a role to varying degrees across countries. Thus tackling immigrant unemployment is a highly complex matter that requires many policy levers, some of which are politically difficult to pull.

At the aggregate level, one striking feature of the cross-national variation is that most of the countries with lower levels of immigrant unemployment

TABLE 7.1 Unemployment rates for native- and foreign-born workers and relative unemployment rates, selected OECD countries, 2008–10

| | Unemployment rate (%) | | | | | | Relative unemployment | | |
| | 2008 | | 2009 | | 2010 | | 2008 | 2009 | 2010 |
	Native-born	Foreign-born	Native-Born	Foreign-born	Native-born	Foreign-born	Foreign/native	Foreign/native	Foreign/native
Australia	4.2	4.6	5.3	6.7	5.3	5.6	1.10	1.26	1.06
Belgium	5.9	14.6	6.6	16.2	7.0	17.6	2.47	2.45	2.51
Canada	6.0	7.2	7.9	10.2	7.6	10.0	1.20	1.29	1.32
Denmark	3.0	7.1	5.7	9.9	6.9	13.6	2.37	1.74	1.97
France	6.8	11.8	8.5	14.3	8.6	14.6	1.74	1.68	1.70
Germany	6.7	12.3	6.9	12.8	6.5	11.8	1.84	1.86	1.82
Italy	6.6	8.5	7.5	11.0	8.1	11.2	1.29	1.47	1.38
Netherlands	2.3	5.8	2.9	6.8	3.8	8.1	2.52	2.34	2.13
Spain	10.2	16.7	18.0	27.2	18.1	29.1	1.64	1.51	1.61
Sweden	5.3	12.2	7.2	15.4	7.1	16.3	2.30	2.14	2.30
UK	5.5	7.1	7.5	8.9	7.8	9.1	1.29	1.19	1.17
USA	6.0	5.9	9.4	9.7	9.9	9.8	0.98	1.03	0.99

Source: Adapted from OECD (2011: 94, table I.B1.2).

have immigration policies that are explicitly designed to respond to labour market needs. Both Australia and Canada operate points-based systems that select immigrants according to human capital criteria, including education, skills and age. And the country in Europe with the best immigrant employment outcomes, the United Kingdom, also has a points-based system. In contrast, in those European countries where immigrant employment outcomes are worse, family or forced migrants make up a larger proportion of inflows. All this implies that economic integration is as much about immigration policy – who gets in – as it is about integration policy. Selecting immigrants according to labour market needs would, not surprisingly, appear to result in higher levels of labour market participation. However, the United States is a glaring exception to this otherwise apparently neat explanation. Its immigration policy is based on family ties rather than skills, and the overwhelming majority of immigrants to the United States are family migrants (see chapter 4). Yet it has the lowest levels of immigrant unemployment of any OECD country. Thus, while they play a role, immigration policies are not the whole story.

As Gary Freeman suggests, it is necessary to consider how non-immigration policies and institutions affect the labour market outcomes of immigrants. It is striking in this regard that the OECD countries with the lowest relative unemployment for immigrants (the United States, Australia, the UK and Canada) are all Anglo-Saxon liberal market economies with deregulated labour markets and less generous welfare provisions. By contrast, the countries with the highest relative levels of immigrant unemployment (including Belgium, the Netherlands, Germany and the Nordic countries) all have coordinated market economies with greater labour market regulation and more generous welfare systems. It would seem, therefore, that national political economy is crucial to explaining immigrant integration. Independent of the effect of different 'varieties of capitalism' on absolute levels of unemployment, it seems that immigrants are integrated more easily into the labour markets of liberal than of coordinated economies. This certainly helps to explain the case of the United States, which, although operating an immigration system that is not skills-based, is a liberal market economy with deregulated labour markets and residual welfare protections. Further research is needed to prove the effect of political economy structures on immigrant integration, but it seems highly likely that this, combined with immigration policies, can do a lot of the work in explaining why some countries do so much better than others in integrating immigrants into their labour markets.

This raises a crucial problem for those seeking to improve the economic integration of immigrants in Europe. If labour market incorporation is influenced mainly by factors that have little to do with integration policies per se, and more by labour market regulations and welfare systems, then improving immigrant employment entails striking out onto policy terrain that is politically fraught – even more so than integration narrowly construed. The institutional differences between liberal and corporate market economies are deep-seated and resilient, and their defining elements are highly interrelated. Reforming institutions that are deeply embedded in a nation's political economy is exceptionally difficult due to their 'stickiness' and also the institutional complementarities that knit together the financial system, industrial relations system, and education and training system into more or less cohesive modes of capitalism (Hall and Soskice 2001). Any attempt to change these institutions – for example, to move from a coordinated to a more liberal approach – will have wide-ranging impacts, affecting *inter alia* corporate strategies, modes of production, employment and income distribution, and hence a wide range of interests. All of which makes the economic integration of immigrants look a good deal more difficult than it might appear at first glance; it is certainly not a matter of simply pulling a few integration policy levers.

In his plea for a greater focus on economic aspects of integration, Hansen (2012: 6–7) identifies three policy areas that must be levered to increase labour market participation of immigrants: education, welfare and (rather nebulously) economic growth. Education policy, he argues, must address the often poor schooling and training opportunities available to immigrants and their children; in the area of welfare policy, consideration should be given to reforming both direct and in-kind benefits, including income support, to ensure that they are no higher than market wages and do not create an incentive structure which 'encourages migrants and residents to opt for welfare rather than work' (ibid.: 6); and, finally, a resolution of the banking and sovereign debt crisis is essential for the resumption of economic growth, without which immigrants, as well as natives, face a bleak employment future. Whatever the independent merits of these arguments, the point to be made here is that none of these proposals are immigrant integration policies in the narrowest sense. And none are easily achievable. Targeted education policies, particularly language training, are the most narrowly tailored and perhaps attainable, but reforming welfare benefits and increasing economic productivity are much larger issues, with a wide range of affected interests entailing difficult political calculations for governments which embark on this path. What all this means is that immigrant integration policy, at least in the economic domain, is embroiled in a much wider politics of economic and welfare reform.

This is not to say that nothing can be done to influence the labour market participation of immigrants using targeted integration policies. Aside from refocusing immigration policies on skills-based selection, there are at least two types of policies that governments have adopted in recent years. First, strongly influenced by the UK experience of race relations legislation dating back to the 1960s, in 2000 the European Union adopted a Race Directive, requiring national governments to pass anti-discrimination legislation and create monitoring bodies. To the extent that racial discrimination is a factor in hiring, this should be expected to reduce a major obstacle to the employment of ethnic minorities. The second trend in economic integration policies focuses on the supply side of the equation and consists of language requirements or classes. As discussed in chapter 6, several countries now require demonstration of proficiency in the majority language or attendance at language classes as a condition of naturalization, and some have extended this to grants of permanent residency as well. These measures are among the few targeted integration policy tools that are likely to have substantial positive effects on immigrant employment rates.

The Politics of Cultural Integration

While there is a strong evidence-based case for a greater focus on the economic aspects of immigrant integration, this is not the direction in which the public debate has been heading. In most liberal states there is, rather, a growing emphasis, bordering on an obsession in some cases, with the cultural integration of immigrants. Across Europe, far-right populists have made especially strident demands in this area, but mainstream politicians have also increasingly argued that immigrants should do more to become culturally integrated. In late 2010, Thilo Sarrazin's polemic *Deutschland schafft sich ab* (Germany Does Away with Itself) alleged that Muslim immigrants were reluctant to integrate, leading to a heated national debate in which the German chancellor, Angela Merkel, claimed that Germany's supposedly 'multikulti' approach to integration had 'utterly failed'. In February 2011, at a security conference in Munich, the British prime minister, David Cameron, similarly claimed that what he called 'the doctrine of state multiculturalism' had failed, and called for shift from 'passive tolerance' towards a 'more active, muscular liberalism' (Cameron 2011). On the other side of the Channel, the French government had already flexed its muscles by banning religious face coverings in August 2010, which were described by then President Nicolas Sarkozy as 'not welcome' in republican France. In the classic countries of immigration, there has also been anxious debate about immigration and cultural diversity. In Australia, where an official policy of multiculturalism persists, there was nevertheless a 'downscaling' in the 1990s (Joppke 2004) under the centre-right government of John Howard. And in the United States, conservatives have attacked the supposed threat that cultural diversity and Latino immigration (Huntington 2004) pose to American national identity.

In this most symbolic of areas, the hardening of tone is significant in itself, but, as the French case dramatically illustrates, the tougher language has also been accompanied by policy shifts in many countries. In fact, cultural integration has become the dimension of integration policy where most concrete initiatives are to be found. Since the late 1990s, the direction of travel has been away from broadly multicultural policies – at least where they existed in the first place – towards more assimilationist approaches. Christian Joppke argues that there is growing convergence across liberal states on a two-pronged approach, which combines demanding civic integration policies with anti-discrimination legislation (Joppke 2004, 2007a, 2007b; see also Joppke and Morawska 2003). It is the first prong of this approach that has seen a turn against policies that officially recognize or institutionalize immigrants' cultural differences towards policies that seek to narrow the cultural distance between immigrants and natives, with the burden of adaptation falling upon the former. These integration policies include language requirements as a condition of residency permits as well as naturalization, requirements for immigrants to demonstrate country knowledge and, most controversially, requirements that immigrants adopt the supposed norms and values of the host society.

Probably the most dramatic shift in this direction occurred in the Netherlands, where an 'ethnic minorities' policy, which funded separate immigrant organizations, media and schools, was replaced from the late 1990s by an increasingly harsh approach that made permanent residence permits conditional upon passing a civic integration exam. Several other European countries have followed a similar, if less draconian, trajectory. Germany introduced *Integrationskurse* (integration courses), which focus on German-language acquisition, with non-attendance or failure of the exam leading to a loss of social benefits. France adopted *contrats d'accueil et d'intégration* (contracts of welcome and integration), which require non-francophone immigrants to attend state-paid language lessons and other immigrants to attend a civics class, albeit without sanctions for non-attendance. In Britain, language and country knowledge requirements that were first introduced for the naturalization procedure were gradually extended to applications for permanent settlement: most applicants who are English speakers must now pass a 'Life in the UK' test, while non-English speakers must pass an English-language and citizenship course. Going further still, several countries have introduced pre-entry or 'integration from abroad' tests: the Netherlands (2006), Germany (2007), the UK (2010) and Austria (2011) have all made *entry* for certain categories of immigrants conditional on demonstrating language proficiency, country knowledge or, most controversially, commitment to liberal values (Scholten et al. 2012).

The second dimension of the emerging integration model is anti-discrimination legislation. This too grew out of a perceived failure of immigrant integration, but, unlike civic integration requirements, which place the responsibility with immigrants, anti-discrimination policies seek to tackle racism and prejudice in the host society. In the United States and the United Kingdom, legislation outlawing racist discrimination has been on the books for several decades, but in many European countries no such legislation existed and, indeed, in several cases it was wholly alien to the legal tradition. The passage in 2000 of the EU Race Directive, which requires all member states to outlaw direct and indirect discrimination, was thus a major milestone, requiring significant adaptation by countries such as France and Germany where (for rather different reasons) such legislation was novel. Although transposition of this directive into national law allows states a certain amount of leeway, which means ongoing variation in anti-discrimination laws and institutions across member states, the overall result has been a greater harmonization of practice in this area.

Joppke's argument about integration policy convergence is broadly persuasive, but it should be noted that significant differences between states do remain. Despite the spread of civic integration and anti-discrimination policies, individual countries' policies and their wider public discourses about integration continue to have national inflections. Returning to Favell's comparison of Britain and France (see pp. 137–8), despite some policy convergence it is clear that these countries still have distinct 'philosophies of integration' (Favell 2001). For several decades, Britain has framed immigrant integration in terms of 'race relations' (Bleich 2003; Hampshire 2009b) and for several centuries it has had an established Church. British authorities routinely classify and collect data on their citizens according to their 'race' or ethnicity, and have moved to ensure equal treatment of religions not by abolishing the Church, but by recognizing minority religions. France, by contrast, has a strong republican tradition of citizenship and a related tradition of laïcité (secularism). The collection of ethnic data remains controversial, and the government has adopted a hard-line stance on religious expression in the public sphere, most dramatically in the ban on religious face coverings, targeted at the Muslim veil.

It is thus not surprising that the European Union's 2004 Common Basic Principles on Integration are both non-binding and lacking in specific details; they simply had to be so in order to secure agreement across member states with such different traditions of citizenship and nationhood. Similarly, the 2011 European Agenda for the Integration of Third-Country Nationals is presented as a 'flexible toolbox' from which national governments can 'pick the measures most likely to prove effective in their specific context, and for their particular integration objectives'.[26] Beyond Europe, national differences are also marked in the classic countries of immigration. Canada and, to a lesser extent, Australia have adopted official discourses on multiculturalism, the former recognizing Canada's 'multicultural heritage' in its Charter of Rights and Freedoms and the 1988 Canadian Multiculturalism Act. In contrast, the United States has evolved a sense of nationhood that recognizes group distinctions and identifications, but it has avoided a federal policy of multiculturalism, instead moving from the famous 'melting pot' metaphor to what one scholar calls a 'post-multiculturalist settlement' (King 2005: 167).

These caveats about cross-national variation notwithstanding, the rise of demanding civic integration policies, especially in Europe, raises interesting questions about normative integration in the liberal state. At first glance, the two sides of the new civic integration policies seem to pull in different directions: anti-discrimination legislation is unambiguously liberal, but cultural integration requirements appear illiberal, since they often promote a set of values and a vision of nationhood that could be thought inconsistent with the freedom to pursue one's conception of the good and with state neutrality. There is little doubt that these measures are controversial, but they are arguably less an illiberal development than a shift *within* the liberal tradition away from a tolerant, neutralist liberalism towards a perfectionist liberalism which promotes autonomy. The governments of liberal states are effectively trying to delimit legitimate diversity and nation-build using a liberal vocabulary. This is a paradoxical exercise, as it deploys universal values to forge particular attachments and identities. Yet it does have an exclusionary edge since, by setting requirements for citizenship, and now entry and residence, the intention is to deny membership to persons who are perceived to hold illiberal beliefs.

Whatever the normative justification of civic integration requirements, there remains an efficacy problem. As one of the founding liberal philosophers, John Locke, argued in his 1689 *Letter Concerning Toleration*, governments may coerce obedience, but they do not have the necessary instruments to inculcate belief. In the context of the European wars of religion, Locke observed that, while dissenters could be coerced to conform outwardly, their 'inward persuasion of mind' was untouchable by the civil magistrate: 'such is the nature of the understanding, that it cannot be compelled to the belief of anything by outward force. Confiscation of estate, imprisonment, torments, nothing of that nature can have any such efficacy as to make men change the inward judgement that they have framed of things' (Locke 2003 [1689]). Much the same can be said today of integration tests. Applicants for citizenship or residency may be required to demonstrate knowledge or even express certain views, but it is doubtful that this will inculcate liberal beliefs, much less trip up an ideologue bent on promoting illiberal values or murdering liberal citizens.

It is therefore worth asking why cultural integration has become the focus of so much attention. It should first be said that the most ubiquitous aspect of cultural integration policies – language requirements – in fact overlaps with economic integration, and there is little doubt that policies in this area have been influenced by a desire to improve the labour market outcomes of immigrants. Language requirements are one of the few accessible policy levers to improve immigrant employment, so it is hardly surprising that governments have begun to pull them. However, if this can help explain governments' enthusiasm for language tests, it cannot do much to explain the other aspects of cultural integration, which have little or nothing to do with labour market participation. The attempt to narrow the supposed cultural distance between immigrants and natives through policies that require demonstration of country knowledge or adoption of liberal values requires consideration of other factors.

One such factor is a growing concern about the impact of immigration on social cohesion and trust. There are a variety of different arguments here. Some left-leaning critics of multiculturalism have argued that policies which seek to recognize group differences – for example, by creating group-based exemptions from certain laws or granting minority groups special privileges or subsidies – have misdiagnosed the problems faced by immigrants and minority groups and, moreover, undermined the pursuit of equality and social justice by deflecting attention from socio-economic disadvantage (see Barry 2001 for a robust statement of this position). In a different vein, liberal nationalists have argued that well-functioning democracies rely upon a shared sense of national identity, which liberal states should therefore seek to promote (Miller 1997; Tamir 1993). Others have argued that the social trust and common identification necessary to maintain support for a welfare state are undermined by rapid cultural diversification, and for this reason governments should seek to promote a shared identity in an era of increased migration (Goodhart 2004; see Putnam 2007 for empirical support of the idea that social capital and ethnic diversity are negatively correlated). These debates have contributed towards a perception that multicultural policies have 'failed', because they place too much emphasis on cultural difference and not enough on commonalities, and to the idea that governments should foster unity and let diversity take care of itself.

There is, however, a more potent spectre haunting the integration debate in Europe: the spectre of Islam. This Marxian metaphor is appropriate not only because a small number of extremists believe Islam to be every bit as revolutionary as Marx wanted communism to be, but because, like communists before them, Muslims have become a source of fear and anxiety in the imaginary of parts of the Western public. Since the 9/11 terrorist attacks, followed by Islamist bombings in Bali in 2002, Madrid in 2004 and London in 2005, immigrant integration has become entangled in a wider debate about the place of Muslims in liberal societies. The integration of Muslims was an issue before 2001, but the rise of Islamist extremism has intensified popular anxieties about cultural change by juxtaposing them with perceptions of an imminent security threat. This concatenation of security and culture is powerful indeed, as it creates an existential politics that is at once about protection against terrorism and defence of a way of life. This linkage is made by many of the far-right parties that have been gaining ground across Europe and their violent fellow travellers, such as the Norwegian mass murderer Anders Breivik. Moreover, concern about Muslim integration is not the preserve of far-right extremists. The opposition to 'state multiculturalism' and calls for more 'muscular liberalism' emanating from mainstream politicians such as David Cameron are clearly directed at Muslims. It was no coincidence that Cameron used these phrases in a speech delivered to a conference on security and counter-terrorism, not integration.

While Islamist terrorism has undoubtedly spurred anxieties about Muslim cultural integration, this is not a debate that is narrowly focused on extremism. It encompasses a much wider perception that Muslims hold values and beliefs that are incompatible with those of liberal societies, including latent support for political violence, opposition to free speech, intolerance of homosexuality, anti-Semitism, and oppressive cultural practices towards women such as veiling, honour abuse and forced marriage. Public opinion surveys do lend support to some of these perceptions. A 2006 Pew Research Center survey, one of the largest of its kind to date, found that sizeable minorities of Muslims in France, Spain and Britain believed violence against civilian targets in order to defend Islam could be justified (16, 16 and 15 per cent, respectively, said 'sometimes' and 19, 9 and 9 per cent said 'rarely'; though in Germany the respective percentages were much lower, at 7 and 6 per cent). The same survey found that in Germany and Britain only 38 per cent and 32 per cent of Muslims had a favourable attitude to Jews, compared to 69 per cent and 74 per cent of the general public in those countries, though notably in France the difference was much smaller, at 71 versus 86 per cent (Pew Research Center 2006; also Pew Research Center 2011). A 2009 Gallup survey found that there was a significant gap between Muslims and non-Muslims over whether homosexuality is 'morally acceptable': in France, 35 per cent versus 78 per cent; in Germany, 19 per cent versus 68 per cent; and in Britain, 0 per cent versus 58 per cent (Gallup 2009).

Probably more important still in terms of fostering a popular perception of a values gap between Muslims and non-Muslims have been the number of highly politicized controversies about blasphemy and free speech that have erupted in recent decades. The controversy surrounding Salman Rushdie's *The Satanic Verses*, published in 1988, was the first case. Rushdie's novel contains sections about the life of Muhammad which some Muslims argued were blasphemous. There were calls for the book to be banned and for Rushdie to be punished as an apostate. After Ayatollah Khomeini, the Supreme Leader of Iran, issued a fatwa calling for his death, Rushdie was forced to live in hiding under police protection for the next decade. Several others who translated or published the book were later attacked, including Hitoshi Igarashi, the book's Japanese translator, who was stabbed to death in 1991.

Among other incidents was the murder of the Dutch film-maker Theo van Gogh, who was killed by a Dutch Moroccan Muslim on 2 November 2004 in revenge for a provocative film he had made with the Somali-born Dutch politician Ayaan Hirsi Ali which criticized the treatment of women in Islam (Buruma 2006). The most recent controversy that put Muslim integration on the front pages (quite literally) was the Danish cartoon affair. In September

2005, a right-wing Danish newspaper, *Jyllands-Posten*, published several cartoons of Muhammad, the most provocative of which depicted him wearing a turban shaped as a bomb. The newspaper claimed it wanted to elicit a debate about self-censorship after a children's book author had been unable to find an illustrator for her book about the Prophet. After complaints by several ambassadors of Muslim countries to the Danish government were rebuffed, a tour of the Middle East by two Danish imams succeeded in generating outrage and a demand for sanctions. *Jyllands-Posten* responded by defending its right to publish the cartoons but also apologizing for any offence caused. Across Europe, several other newspapers then republished the cartoons, citing freedom of speech. By early 2006, what had begun as a provocative act by a small newspaper had escalated into a global event. Protests across the Islamic world led to over 100 deaths, Danish embassies were set alight, boycotts of Danish goods were launched, and the editor and cartoonists became the targets of death threats and assassination attempts (Klausen 2009).

In the wake of Islamist terrorist attacks, these controversies have further stoked an angry debate about Muslims in Europe (Bawer 2006; Caldwell 2010; Phillips 2006). Though the contributors to this debate often adopt a sensationalist tone, it would be wrong to deny that there is a legitimate issue of integration here: the data cited above suggest that there is a values gap between European Muslims and non-Muslims, and a small minority of Muslims (mostly young men) have turned to violent extremism. At the same time, anti-immigrant politicians and commentators have all too often used these events to demonize Muslims and denounce the supposed failure of multiculturalism.

The history of immigration suggests that, over time, differences between immigrants and natives subside, and any values gaps will either close or come to a negotiated settlement. As for the current civic integration policies, it is doubtful that they will do much to assist processes of mutual accommodation, and, when accompanied by tough rhetoric denouncing multiculturalism, they may even retard them by contributing towards a perception that there is a problem of incompatibility. In any case, the tools that governments have at their disposal to effect value change are extremely limited, especially in liberal states, with their self-imposed constraints on what can legitimately be demanded of citizens in terms of identity and belief. Naturalization and residency requirements are unlikely to affect a fundamental shift in values among Muslims – not only because they will not affect the many Muslims who are now born in European countries, but because there are inherent limitations to their efficacy, as discussed above.

But the new integration policies are not precision instruments calibrated to facilitate immigrant integration. Rather, in a climate of growing anxiety about immigration in general, and Muslim immigration in particular, they are better understood as performative utterances than as tools to effect attitudinal and behavioural change. This is a performance conducted by governments partly for immigrants, but above all for native voters. To immigrants, civic integration policies say 'this is who we are and what we expect of *you*'; just as importantly, to native citizens they say 'this is who we are and what we expect of *them*'. It is an exercise in shoring up national identity in an era of greater mobility and increasingly fragmented identities. Nicolas Sarkozy admitted as much when, just a few days after David Cameron had called for more 'muscular liberalism', he too weighed in to denounce the 'failure' of multiculturalism: 'the truth is', he told *Libération* newspaper, 'that in all our democracies we have taken care, more than we should have, of the identity of the arriving person and not enough of the identity of the receiving country' (cited in Bertossi and Duyvendak 2012: 244).

Contrast this populist appeal with the dry tone of the European Commission's 2011 European Agenda for the Integration of Third-Country Nationals, which focuses on labour market participation, and it becomes clear how differently integration discourse is conducted when votes are at stake. Indeed, the only real point of contact between these two discourses is language acquisition, as this serves both the instrumental function of socio-economic integration and the symbolic function of identity-building. But, otherwise, these are separate universes. Improving educational or employment opportunities for immigrants may do more to improve objective integration indicators, but the current politics of integration is less about these indicators than a rhetoric of identity and belonging.

There is, however, a gap between political rhetoric, on the one hand, and the everyday reality of accommodating diversity in a liberal society, on the other. The case of France starkly illustrates the point. On the one hand, public-facing government statements assert a strict interpretation of republicanism that sometimes spills over into calculated intolerance, most obviously in the campaign against the burka. Face coverings were first banned in public schools in 2004, then in 2008 the Conseil d'État denied a female Muslim French citizenship for wearing a burka. In 2009, a parliamentary inquiry led the following year to legislation which banned face coverings in all public places. The bill passed the National Assembly by a vote of 335 to 1 and the Senate by 246 to 1, with 100 abstentions, and polls showed that a large majority of the French public supported the law. Yet, out of the public spotlight, French authorities adopt a notably more pragmatic and inclusive approach to Muslims. The French state has helped establish a confederation of Muslims in France (CFCM), supported the construction of mosques, and subsidized the education of French imams at the Institut Catholique in Paris (Joppke 2012: 4). Hence, behind the scenes, it appears much less wedded to hard-line secularism than its public policies would suggest. The French debate has its particularities, of course, but the gap between what is said by politicians for public consumption and how the accommodation of Muslims works in practice can be found in other countries as well.

This gap between rhetoric and practice reflects the way in which civic integration policies and discourses are a kind of nation-building in a liberal idiom. True, it is all but impossible to construct a plausible narrative about nationhood using the liberal language of rights, freedom and equality. By definition, these principles cannot distinguish *this* people or *this* nation, which is why 'stories of peoplehood' so often rely upon 'an account of unchosen, inherited, usually quasi-ethnic identity' (Smith 2003: 65). But liberal universalism *is* exclusionary of those who do not accept liberal principles. To the extent that Muslims are believed to hold illiberal beliefs, civic integration is directed at this group. Dutch 'integration from abroad' tests that seek to establish visa applicants' attitudes towards supposedly Dutch (read liberal) values and norms, including gender and sexual equality, are targeted at family migrants from Turkey and Morocco (Scholten et al. 2012: 12). At the same time, nation-building of a more traditional kind is not dead, as the new liberal exclusions are often conjoined to civic integration policies that openly promote a particular account of national history, culture or traditions. While countries such as Germany or the classic countries of immigration have adopted a more practical, civic knowledge test, thus largely avoiding the murky waters of national identity, countries such as Denmark openly promote a view of national culture. And significantly, in Britain, which was one of the first European countries to introduce citizenship tests, the current government has announced that the 'Life in the UK' test will be revised so that it focuses less on practical knowledge and citizens' rights and more on British culture and history.[27]

Conclusion

Immigrant integration is complex because liberal societies are differentiated, immigrants are diverse, and the processes involved in becoming a full member of a host country are multidimensional and potentially divergent. The literature on integration policy and politics has seldom paid sufficient attention to these complexities, instead seeking to identify distinct national models of integration which are then used to explain a wide range of outcomes. Once integration processes are disaggregated, it becomes apparent that a national models approach is unable to account for a messy reality. As this chapter has argued, many of the institutions that influence integration processes – for example, labour markets – are not integration policies at all and are not easily amenable to change. To the frustration of governments, integration is not something that can be facilitated, or for that matter hindered, by pulling a few clearly labelled policy levers.

The relative prominence of cultural compared to economic integration in public debate may be regrettable, but it is far from insignificant. The emphasis on cultural integration has been driven by an unease about Islam and

Muslim immigrants in liberal societies and a wider anxiety about national identity in an era of increased mobility and fragmenting allegiances. Civic integration policies have become the liberal state's chief weapons in a struggle to maintain this identity. While the vehemence with which this battle is often fought reveals the persistent importance of nationhood to liberal states, the weakness of those weapons reveals the inherent limitations in the ability of liberal states to shore up national identity. Thus immigrant integration once again exposes the contradictions of the liberal state. The prominence of identity in integration debates reminds us that liberal states are not (and possibly cannot be) simply contractual associations for mutual advantage but are political communities reliant upon affective ties and allegiances that are becoming increasingly elusive in an age of mass migration.

CHAPTER EIGHT

Conclusion: Living with Contradictions

We live in an age of international migration and mobility, with more people living outside their country of birth or citizenship than at any time since territorially bounded states came into existence. Despite the worst economic crisis for almost a century, international migration flows have continued at historically unprecedented levels. Although the upward trend in migration flows came to a halt in 2008 – notably labour and free movement migration – migration has proved remarkably resilient. In particular, there is little indication of a collapse in immigration to the rich liberal democracies. While permanent migration to the OECD declined by 3 per cent between 2009 and 2010, the third consecutive year a reduction had been recorded, net migration remained positive, and preliminary data for 2011 show that immigration started to increase again in most European countries, as well as in Australia and New Zealand (OECD 2012a: 3). Immigration to the advanced economies is almost certain to resume its upward trajectory for years to come on account of persistent inequalities in wealth and stability between the global North and South, demographic ageing in the former, and a host of facilitating factors such as cheap international transportation, information communication technologies, and transnational social networks. For rich liberal states, then, immigration is here to stay.

Yet, as this book has shown, governments have found it difficult to adapt to the age of migration by developing effective or coherent immigration policies. Some commentators have argued that this is because the only way to manage migration flows effectively is to establish an international migration regime (e.g., Ghosh 2000). Whatever the merits of this argument, it is largely moot since, as we saw in chapter 5, such a regime is not going to evolve in the foreseeable future. Immigration is so closely tied to state sovereignty and national interests that governments are exceptionally reluctant to cede powers to international organizations, and the conflicting interests of Northern and Southern countries mean that formal cooperation on a global scale is little more than a utopian fantasy. Such international cooperation as does exist is limited, often informal, and mostly regional or bilateral. The one glaring exception to this rule – the international refugee regime – was the product of a uniquely propitious historical moment; it is certainly not seen as a model for wider cooperation by governments today. Hence the nation-state and domestic politics will persist as the principal arena in which migration policy is made.

In chapter 1, four facets of the liberal state – representative democracy, constitutionalism, capitalism and nationhood – were outlined. It was argued that each facet is associated with different constellations of actors, institutions and ideas, and that the politics of immigration cannot be understood without taking account of the complex ways in which they interact. Exactly how these factors influence immigration varies across countries, depending *inter alia* on a given country's model of representative democracy, constitutional arrangements, model of capitalism and self-understanding of national identity. But, notwithstanding this variation, there are striking similarities across liberal states in how these four facets influence the way in which governments attempt to govern immigration.

In the area of immigration policies proper – those policies which deal with the number of immigrants who are admitted, the criteria used for their selection, and the rights they receive once in the country – there is a powerful conflict between the outputs from the democratic system, on the one hand, and the embedded demand for migrant labour and constraints imposed by liberal rights, on the other. Democratic politics typically generates pressure on governments to adopt more restrictive policies, especially (though not exclusively) when anti-immigrant parties successfully articulate a nationalist discourse about the supposed threat posed by immigration and multiculturalism. Even when anti-immigrant parties are not a significant political force – as, for example, in Britain and the United States – negative public opinion and sensationalist media coverage still give elected politicians plenty of reasons to talk tough on immigration. To understand how this restrictionist public discourse does not translate into equally restrictive policy outcomes requires attention to different factors depending on the kind of immigration in question. Human rights play a key role in explaining openness towards so-called unwanted immigrants such as asylum-seekers and family migrants, while employer demand plays a more important role in explaining openness towards labour migration. The impact of the different factors depends on the relative power of the actors who mobilize to counteract restrictive majoritarian policies. Thus powerful business interests have generally found more success in lobbying for the admission of labour migrants than have migrant NGOs and charities that seek to prevent draconian measures towards asylum-seekers and undocumented migrants. Though, even here, action through the courts to mobilize rights can sometimes constrain government attempts to control and exclude.

Citizenship and integration policies also reveal contradictory imperatives arising from liberal institutions and norms. Citizenship itself embodies a liberal paradox insofar as it is at once an inclusionary and an exclusionary status. Citizenship extends rights to its bearer which non-citizens do not enjoy. Yet, partly as a result of immigration, the bright line between citizens and aliens has become blurred, as many rights have been extended to permanent residents. At the same time, citizenship still very much matters for national voting rights, mobility rights and security of residence. In many countries, citizenship policies have been liberalized in recent years as *jus soli* acquisition has become increasingly common, while residency requirements for naturalization have been reduced in several countries and dual nationality is increasingly tolerated. At the same time, new barriers to citizenship have been erected. Many European countries have introduced country knowledge tests and language requirements, while some have actually increased residency requirements. The direction of travel varies across and even within individual countries, and each case requires attention to the specific debates surrounding citizenship. But, once again, a clear tension can be identified between the exclusionary tendencies of democratic politics and the inclusionary thrust of liberal rights. Liberal norms of equality cannot long tolerate persons being excluded from access to rights, hence there is an inherently inclusionary logic at work in liberal states. But as Howard (2009) gloomily concludes, when citizenship is put on the political agenda, and especially when it is framed as an issue of national identity, it has proven quite possible to oppose and roll back liberalization.

Recent trends in immigrant integration policies reveal even more starkly how populist anti-immigrant mobilization, drawing from the well of nationalist sentiment, can counter liberal universalism. Integration is an enormously complex matter. Modern societies are highly differentiated, and liberal principles of equal treatment and public neutrality place constraints on what governments can do to promote integration. Furthermore, immigrants are diverse and the process of integration into a host society is multidimensional. Amid this complexity it is striking how myopic the political debate about integration has become in many countries. While there is substantial, if variegated, evidence of poor educational outcomes and high relative unemployment among immigrant groups, especially in mainland Europe, the integration debate has increasingly fixated on identity and culture. Partly this is because rhetorical denouncements of multiculturalism are easier to conjure up than difficult labour market and welfare reforms. But this also reflects heightened anxieties about national identity in a globalizing world, which have been exacerbated in the post 9/11 climate by the perception that Muslim immigrants in particular pose a threat to liberal values (though a lot of the opposition from far-right activists has more to do with racism and xenophobia than liberal principles). The new civic integration policies, which are partly intended to assuage these concerns, seek to shore up unity not through the particularistic language of nationhood but through the universalistic language of liberalism.

This book has tried to show how the conflicts surrounding immigration, citizenship and integration are rooted in the liberal state itself, specifically the tasks that the governments of liberal states must perform if they are to govern effectively and achieve legitimacy. As Christina Boswell (2007a) has argued, states are engaged in an ongoing effort to sustain their legitimacy, which requires them to perform certain political actions and meet the expectations of the public, including both the state's own citizens and actors in the wider international arena, such as other states. She maintains that, for a liberal state to be perceived as legitimate, it must meet four criteria: protection of territorial integrity and physical security of its citizens; competent economic management to facilitate the accumulation of wealth; fairness in the distribution of goods; and conformity to formal conditions of democracy and liberty, such as the rule of law and civil liberties. Each of these 'functional imperatives' informs immigration policies because immigration flows have profound effects on the ability of the state to meet those imperatives and therefore secure legitimacy.

Boswell's analysis is not identical to the framework outlined at the start of this book. Her four criteria – security, accumulation, fairness and institutional legitimacy – do not map directly onto the four facets outlined earlier.[28] Moreover, Boswell collapses representative democracy and constitutionalism under what she calls 'institutional legitimacy'. The argument of this book would suggest this to be mistaken, as it obscures the tensions between majoritarian modes of legitimation through representative politics (elections, parties, and so on) and rights-based legitimation through fidelity to constitutional standards (rule of law, individual rights and due process). These are distinct bases of legitimacy that can come into conflict. In Alexis de Tocqueville's memorable phrase, untrammelled democracy risks a 'tyranny of the majority', which is precisely why liberal states set constraints on majoritarian decision-making through constitutional checks and balances and individual rights. As we have seen, majoritarian legitimation and rights-based legitimation form an important fault-line in the politics of immigration. Time and again populist demands to restrict the number of immigrants or limit their rights come up against 'hard' national and international legal constraints as well as 'soft' normative constraints; and activism on the street and in the courts has mobilized these norms in ways that have limited populist demands.

Focusing on these conflicting imperatives helps to explain why immigration policymaking is so intractable. Each of the four facets of liberal statehood is associated with a different mode of state legitimation: majoritarian, rights-based, accumulative and nationalistic. In the sphere of immigration policy, these imperatives cannot be satisfied simultaneously. It is exceedingly difficult, perhaps even impossible, to design migration policies that will command majority support and fully respect the rights of migrants; nor is it easy to imagine popular consent for labour migration policies that maximize economic growth. Similarly, citizenship and integration policies that offer equivalent rights, especially welfare rights, to migrants compared to natives conflict with the idea that states should prioritize the interests of their nationals, and are therefore susceptible to populist opposition. Thus the intractable nature of immigration policymaking is not a quirk of history or the product of a contingent set of political circumstances, but an inherent feature of liberal statehood. So long as liberal states remain liberal, immigration policymaking will be compelled by mutually incompatible demands.

If there is no obvious way to resolve these contradictions, there are strategies that governments can adopt to try to smooth them over. Faced with irreconcilable objectives, one strategy is to mobilize support behind one imperative (Boswell 2007a: 93). This is unlikely to prove very stable, however. Mobilizing behind one imperative will almost always generate a powerful counter-reaction, as actors associated with other imperatives will be able to articulate their opposition in terms that question the legitimacy of the policy direction. For example, politically motivated promises to cut the number of immigrants – as the current British government has vowed to do – will meet with resistance from employers (who will argue that it threatens economic growth) and migrants' rights groups (who will argue that it violates liberal norms). Both are potentially effective counter-mobilizations precisely because they appeal to liberal state legitimacy. Certainly in the British case the promise by the coalition government to cut net migration by over half has met with opposition from employers and education providers, who have succeeded in extracting concessions that frustrate the original policy (Bale and Hampshire 2012). Equally, an open labour migration policy that satisfies employer demand for cheap labour will likely encounter resistance from anti-immigrant actors, who can mobilize popular opposition around claims that the government is failing to protect the interests of nationals for jobs, housing and welfare or is debasing the national culture. But then pandering to populist sentiments through draconian policies often faces challenges in the courts and moral condemnation from civil society. And so it goes on. The point is that privileging one imperative to the detriment of others is inherently contestable and therefore unlikely to be sustainable for extended periods of time.

Perhaps this picture of inevitable legitimacy conflicts is too deterministic, however. The most potent conflicts that can be found running through immigration policy – the conflict between majoritarian and nationalist sentiments, on the one hand, and liberal rights and capitalist accumulation, on the other – are contingent on the fact of popular opposition towards immigration. Given that public opinion is not immutable, these conflicts could potentially be resolved if public attitudes were more receptive towards immigration. Softening public opinion would render majoritarian legitimation more consistent with rights-based or accumulative legitimation. While theoretically possible, there are strong reasons to doubt that representative democracy will ever generate sustained demand for immigration policies of the sort mandated by universal rights or capitalist accumulation. The public opinion data discussed in chapter 2 show substantial opposition towards immigration across most liberal democracies. And the history of opposition towards immigration suggests that this is not a contemporary quirk, nor is it restricted to countries with no prior experience of immigration. In the United States, the classic 'nation of immigrants', anti-immigrant sentiment has been a part of public discourse for centuries: Protestant nativists opposed Irish Catholic immigration during the mid-nineteenth century; Irish immigrants attacked Chinese immigrants in the 1870s; and, in the early twentieth century, opposition to Eastern European and Jewish immigration led to the infamous National Origins system. Contemporary opposition to Latino immigration is thus part of a long American tradition of nativism. European opposition to immigration may be more recent, but there is no good reason to think that it is likely to ease anytime soon.

In short, the range of countries and periods in which negative attitudes towards immigration prevail in public debate suggests that there is an inherently exclusionary tendency in popular attitudes towards newcomers. While the form, content and intensity of anti-immigrant sentiment certainly vary, depending partly on the behaviour of anti-immigrant actors, it is tempting to draw the conclusion that latent popular scepticism towards immigration is something of a historical constant. But, even if this is a conclusion too far, it is difficult to see how more positive public attitudes towards immigration could be generated in the political climate of most major destination countries today.

What then is the likely future? If mobilizing behind one imperative is inherently unstable, and public opinion is unlikely to align with the economic imperatives and moral norms of liberal states, then governments must persist with contradictory policies. As Peter Hall argues:

> a state faced with multiple tasks and well-defined conflicts of interest among the social classes it governs, or the groups within these, may find it necessary to maintain a degree of deliberate malintegration among its various policy-making aims so that each can mobilize consent among its particular constituencies by pursuing policies which, even if never fully implemented, appear to address the needs of these groups. (Quoted in Boswell 2007a: 92–3)

In other words, governments must pursue contradictory policies in an attempt to manage contradictory demands. This is a particularly difficult trick to pull off in the immigration policy area because of the depth of conflict generated by majoritarian versus economic and rights-based imperatives. It certainly means that there is little hope of immigration politics becoming consensual or immigration policymaking becoming less intractable. Rather, the governments of liberal states will have to muddle through, buffeted by the headwinds of anti-immigrant and nationalist sentiments, while swept along by capitalist demand and liberal norms.

Notes

1 Though note that migration is not the same as mobility. Entry or exit for the purposes of a short visit, say a business trip or tourism, is not normally classified as migration. The standard UN definition of an international migrant is someone who is outside their country of citizenship or birth for a year or more.

2 The relationship between liberalism and capitalism, unlike that between liberalism and democracy and constitutionalism, but like that between liberalism and nationhood, is contingent. On the one hand, some argue that liberalism does not necessitate capitalism (e.g., the later Rawls); on the other hand, it is clear that many countries with capitalist economic systems are not liberal. For the purposes of this book I make no theoretical claim about the nature of the relationship between liberalism and capitalism. Rather, the discussion is based on the empirical observation that all contemporary states commonly defined as liberal have some form of capitalist economic system.

3 Speech to the Dutch Parliament, 6 September 2007, accessed at http://web.archive.org/web/20080614074737/http://www.groepwilders.com/website/details.aspx?ID=44.

4 For permanent residence visas only. The revised version of the theory holds that temporary work visas are characterized by concentrated benefits and concentrated costs, which yields an 'interest group' rather than a 'client' mode of politics (see Freeman 2006: 230).

5 See https://www.henleyglobal.com/citizenship/visa-restrictions/.

6 The national interests of a given state are defined through domestic political processes. In democratic countries, a state's interests emerge through political mobilization and contestation in democratic institutions, as discussed in the preceding chapters. In non-democratic countries, a state's interests are more likely to be shaped by political elites without regard to public opinion.

7 See www.ilo.org/ilolex/english/convdisp1.htm.

8 See www.unhcr.org/pages/49c3646c2.html.

9 The temporal and geographical limits of the Convention were amended by the 1967 Protocol.

10 These countries are the United States, Canada, Australia, Sweden, Norway, Finland, New Zealand, Denmark and the Netherlands.

11 See www.gfmd.org/en/pfp/practices/item/180-mauritius-circular-migration-case.

12 See www.gfmd.org/en/recommendations-follow-up-actions.html.
13 See www.igc.ch/.
14 This is a far from comprehensive list. Other RCPs are the 5+5 Dialogue on Migration in the Western Mediterranean, the Mediterranean Transit Migration Dialogue (MTM) and the Inter-Governmental Asia-Pacific Consultations on Refugees, Displaced Persons and Migrants (APC).
15 Though note that the governments of Denmark, Ireland and the UK negotiated the right to opt in to legislation on a case-by-case basis.
16 The Total Recognition Rate includes those granted full refugee status as well as complementary forms of protection, such as temporary humanitarian status.
17 See www.frontex.europa.eu/.
18 http://ec.europa.eu/home-affairs/policies/external/external_ga_en.htm.
19 Lecture by Franco Frattini before the French Senate, March 2006, quoted in an open letter about readmission agreements to Mirak Topolanek, President of the Council, and José Manuel Barroso, President of the Commission, by Migreurop, 29 January 2009. Accessed at www.migreurop.org/article1350.html.
20 Admittedly this threefold approach omits a possible fourth dimension: citizenship as participation.
21 The 27 EU member states plus Croatia, Iceland, Moldova, Norway, Switzerland and Turkey.
22 As Howard's CPI takes the 1980s as its baseline, it omits this case; however, Howard does discuss the qualification of *jus soli* in his discussion of the UK case (2009: 158–161).
23 Three intervening variables affect whether this trade-off occurs or not: the size of the immigrant group, its vulnerability to discrimination, and its access to independent financial resources (see Maxwell 2012: 22–5 for elaboration).
24 These findings may strike some readers as odd, but note that their dataset ends in 2002, and it is highly likely that the countries have moved again since then. For example, if the orthodox view in the wider integration literature is correct, then since 2002 the Netherlands would be seen to have moved away from cultural pluralism towards cultural monism on the cultural difference and group rights axis, and thus towards a more universalist configuration.
25 The MIPEX is essentially a benchmarking exercise. On the basis of how close a given policy component is to 'best practice' (as defined by the MIPEX investigators) it awards up to 3 points against 148 indicators in seven integration policy areas. The scores are then aggregated to produce an overall score and ranking for each of the 31 countries covered by the index. A discussion of the pros and cons of this method is beyond the scope of this chapter, though it is worth noting that, although MIPEX explicitly recognizes the multidimensionality of integration, its focus on integration policies necessarily omits wider institutions and ideas that influence integration processes, such as labour market structures or national identities. See the MIPEX website for details: www.mipex.eu/.
26 See http://ec.europa.eu/dgs/home-affairs/what-we-do/policies/immigration/integration/index_en.htm.

27 See Alan Travis, 'UK Migrants to Face "Patriotic" Citizenship Test', *The Guardian*, 1 July 2012, at www.guardian.co.uk/uk/2012/jul/01/uk-migrants-patriotic-citizenship-test.

28 Two of them, accumulation and institutional legitimacy, map closely onto capitalism and constitutionalism, respectively. The security criterion has not been discussed separately here primarily because it is not a distinguishing feature of liberal state legitimacy (it is generic to all modern states), though security is an important driver of immigration policy. The criterion of fairness is not treated here as a single mode of legitimation as it arguably includes distinct and potentially conflicting elements: equality before the law versus the idea that liberal states derive legitimacy by protecting the privileged rights of their own nationals.

References and Bibliography

Aalberg, Toril, Shanto Iyengar, and Solomon Messing (2012) 'Who is a "Deserving" Immigrant? An Experimental Study of Norwegian Attitudes', *Scandanavian Political Studies* 35:2, 97–116.

Akkerman, Tjitske (2012) 'Comparing Radical Right Parties in Government: Immigration and Integration Policies in Nine Countries (1996–2010)', *West European Politics* 35:3, 511–29.

Anderson, Benedict (1991) *Imagined Communities: Reflections on the Origins and Spread of Nationalism*. 2nd edn, London: Verso.

Andreas, Peter (2000) *Borders Games: Policing the U.S.–Mexico Divide*. Ithaca, NY: Cornell University Press.

Arendt, Hannah (1951) *The Origins of Totalitarianism*. New York: Schocken Books.

Baldwin-Edwards, Martin (2008) 'Towards a Theory of Illegal Migration: Historical and Structural Components', *Third World Quarterly* 29:7, xx.

Bale, Tim (2003) 'Cinderella and her Ugly Sisters: The Mainstream and Extreme Right in Europe's Bipolarising Party Systems', *West European Politics* 26:3, 67–90.

Bale, Tim (2008) 'Politics Matters: A Conclusion', *Journal of European Public Policy* 15:3, 454–64.

Bale, Tim, and James Hampshire (2012) 'Easier Said Than Done? The Conservatives, the Coalition, and Immigration Policy', in T. Heppell and D. Seawright (eds), *Cameron and the Conservatives*. Basingstoke: Palgrave.

Bale, Tim, Christoffer Green-Pedersen, André Krouwel, Nick Sitter, and Kurt Richard Luther (2010) 'If You Can't Beat Them, Join Them? Explaining Social Democratic Responses to the Challenge from the Populist Radical Right in Western Europe', *Political Studies* 58:3, 410–26.

Barry, Brian (1996) 'Political Theory, Old and New', in R. Goodin and H.-D. Klingemann (eds), *A New Handbook of Political Science*. Oxford: Oxford University Press.

Barry, Brian (2001) *Culture and Equality: An Egalitarian Critique of Multiculturalism*. Cambridge: Polity.

Bauböck, Rainer (2005) 'Changing Citizenship: Theory and Practice', *PS: Political Science & Politics* 38:4, 667–99.

Bauböck, Rainer (2006) *Migration and Citizenship: Legal Status, Rights, and Political Participation*. Amsterdam: Amsterdam University Press.

Bauböck, Rainer, and Sara Wallace Goodman (2010) *Naturalisation*, EUDO Citizenship Policy Brief no. 2, available at: http://eudo-citizenship.eu/publications/policy-briefs.

Bauböck, Rainer, and Christian Joppke (eds) (2010) *How Liberal are Citizenship Tests?*, EUI Working Papers RSCAS 2010/41. Florence: European University Institute.

Bawer, Bruce (2006) *While Europe Slept: How Radical Islam is Destroying the West from Within*. New York: Broadway Books.

Bertossi, Christophe, and Jan Willem Duyvendak (2012) 'National Models of Immigrant Integration: The Costs for Comparative Research', *Comparative European Politics* 10:3, 237–47.

Betts, Alexander (ed.) (2011) *Global Migration Governance*. Oxford: Oxford University Press.

Betts, Alexander, Gil Loescher, and James Milner (2012) *The United Nations High Commissioner for Refugees (UNHCR): The Politics and Practice of Refugee Protection*. New York: Routledge.

Betts, Katherine (1999) *The Great Divide: Immigration Politics in Australia*. Sydney: Duffy & Snellgrove.

Betts, Katherine (2000) 'Immigration: Public Opinion and Opinions about Opinion', *People and Place* 8:3, 60–7.

Betts, Katherine, and Robert J. Birrell (2007) 'Making Australian Citizenship Mean More', *People and Place* 15:1, 45–61.

Betz, Hans-Georg (1994) *Radical Right-Wing Populism in Western Europe*. Basingstoke: Macmillan.

Bhagwati, Jagdish (2006) 'Borders beyond Control', in Anthony M. Messina and Gallya Lahav (eds), *The Migration Reader: Exploring Politics and Policies*. Boulder, CO: Lynne Rienner, pp. 552–7.

Bigo, Didier (2002) 'Security and Immigration: Toward a Critique of the Governmentality of Unease', *Alternatives* 27, 63–92.

Billig, Michael (1995) *Banal Nationalism*. London: Sage.

Bleich, Erik (2003) *Race Politics in Britain and France: Ideas and Policymaking since the 1960s*. Cambridge: Cambridge University Press.

Bleich, Erik (2011) *The Freedom to be Racist: How the United States and Europe Struggle to Preserve Freedom and Combat Racism*. Oxford: Oxford University Press.

Bommes, Michael, and Andrew Geddes (2000) *Immigration and Welfare: Challenging the Borders of the Welfare State*. London: Routledge.

Boswell, Christina (2005) *The Ethics of Refugee Policy*. Aldershot: Ashgate.

Boswell, Christina (2007a) 'Theorizing Migration Policy: Is There a Third Way?', *International Migration Review* 41:1, 75–100.

Boswell, Christina (2007b) 'Migration Control in Europe after 9/11: Explaining the Absence of Securitization', *Journal of Common Market Studies* 45:3, 589–610.

Boswell, Christina, and Andrew Geddes (2011) *Migration and Mobility in the European Union*. Basingstoke: Palgrave.

Brady, Hugo (2012) *Saving Schengen: How to Protect Passport-Free Travel in Europe*. London: Centre for European Reform.

Broeders, Dennis (2007) 'The New Digital Borders of Europe: EU Databases and the Surveillance of Irregular Migrants', *International Sociology* 22:1, 71–92.

Broeders, Dennis, and Godfried Engbersen (2007) 'The Fight against Illegal Migration: Identification Policies and Immigrants' Counterstrategies', *American Behavioral Scientist* 50:12, 1592–609.

Broeders, Dennis, and James Hampshire (forthcoming 2013) 'Dreaming of Seamless Borders: ICTs and the Pre-emptive Governance of Mobility in Europe', *Journal of Ethnic and Migration Studies*.

Brubaker, Rogers (1992) *Citizenship and Nationhood in France and Germany*. Cambridge, MA: Harvard University Press.

Brubaker, Rogers (1995) 'Comments on "Modes of Immigration Politics in Liberal Democratic States"', *International Migration Review* 29:4, 903–8.

Brubaker, Rogers (2001) 'The Return of Assimilation? Changing Perspectives on Immigration and its Sequels in France, Germany, and the United States', *Ethnic and Racial Studies* 24:4, 531–48.

Buchanan, Patrick J. (2004) *Where the Right Went Wrong: How Neoconservatives Subverted the Reagan Revolution and Hijacked the Bush Presidency*. New York: Thomas Dunne Books.

Buchanan, Patrick J. (2006) *State of Emergency: The Third World Invasion and Conquest of America*. New York: Thomas Dunne Books.

Burns, P., and J.G. Gimpel (2000) 'Economic Insecurity, Prejudicial Stereotypes, and Public Opinion on Immigration Policy', *Political Science Quarterly* 115:2, 201–26.

Buruma, Ian (2006) *Murder in Amsterdam: The Death of Theo van Gogh and the Limits of Tolerance*. New York: Penguin.

Buzan, Barry, Ole Waever, and Jaap de Wilde (1998) *Security: A New Framework for Analysis*. Boulder, CO: Lynne Rienner.

Calavita, Kitty (2004) 'Italy: Economic Realities, Political Fictions, and Policy Failures', in Wayne A. Cornelius, Takeyuki Tsuda, Philip L. Martin and James F. Hollifield (eds), *Controlling Immigration: A Global Perspective*. 2nd edn, Stanford, CA: Stanford University Press, pp. 345–80.

Caldwell, Christopher (2010) *Reflections on the Revolution in Europe: Immigration, Islam and the West: Can Europe Be the Same with Different People In It?* London: Penguin.

Cameron, David (2011) 'PM's Speech at Munich Security Conference', 5 February, available at: www.number10.gov.uk/news/pms-speech-at-munich-security conference/.

Carens, Joseph H. (1995) 'Aliens and Citizens: The Case for Open Borders', in Ronald Beiner (ed.), *Theorizing Citizenship*. New York: SUNY Press, pp. 229–53.

Carter, April (2001) *The Political Theory of Global Citizenship*. London: Routledge.

Carter, Elisabeth (2005) *The Extreme Right in Western Europe: Success or Failure?* Manchester: Manchester University Press.

Castles, Stephen (1985) 'The Guests who Stayed: The Debate on "Foreigners Policy" in the German Federal Republic', *International Migration Review* 19:3, 517–34.

Castles, Stephen (2005) 'Changing Citizenship: Theory and Practice', *PS: Political Science & Politics* 38:4, 667–99.

Castles, Stephen, and Mark J. Miller (2009) *The Age of Migration: International Population Movements in the Modern World*. 4th edn, Basingstoke: Palgrave.

Caviedes, Alexander A. (2010) *Prying Open Fortress Europe: The Turn to Sectoral Labor Migration*. Lanham, MD: Lexington Books.

Cerna, Lucie (2009) 'The Varieties of High-Skilled Immigration Policies: Coalitions and Policy Outputs in Advanced Industrial Countries', *Journal of European Public Policy* 16:1, 144–61.

Cerny, Philip G. (1997) 'Paradoxes of the Competition State: The Dynamics of Political Globalization', *Government and Opposition* 32:2, 251–74.

Cholewinski, R., R. Perruchoud, and E. MacDonald (eds) (2007) *International Migration Law: Developing Paradigms and Key Challenges*. The Hague: T. M. C. Asser.

Citrin, J., D.P. Green, C. Muste, and C. Wong (1997) 'Public Opinion toward Immigration Reform: The Role of Economic Motivations', *Journal of Politics* 59:3, 858–81.

Collett, Elizabeth (2007) *The 'Global Approach to Migration': Rhetoric or Reality?* Brussels: European Policy Centre.

Cornelius, Wayne A., Takeyuki Tsuda, Philip L. Martin, and James F. Hollifield (eds) (2004) *Controlling Immigration: A Global Perspective*. 2nd edn, Stanford, CA: Stanford University Press.

DHS (US Department of Homeland Security) (2011) *Immigration Enforcement Actions: 2010*, DHS Office of Immigration Statistics, available at: www.dhs.gov/xlibrary/ assets/statistics/publications/enforcement-ar-2010.pdf.

DIAC (Department of Immigration and Citizenship) *Department of Immigration and Citizenship Annual Report 2010–11*. Canberra: DIAC.

Düvell, Franck (2011) 'Paths into Irregularity: The Legal and Social Construction of Irregular Migration', *European Journal for Migration and Law* 13:3, 275–95.

The Economist (2009) 'The Battle for Brains', available at: www.economist.com/ blogs/lexington/2009/03/the_battle_for_brains.

Ellermann, Antje (2005) 'Coercive Capacity and the Politics of Implementation: Deportation in Germany and the United States', *Comparative Political Studies* 38:10, 1219–44.

Ellermann, Antje (2006) 'Street-Level Democracy: How Immigration Bureaucrats Manage Public Opposition', *West European Politics* 29:2, 293–309.

Ellermann, Antje (2008) 'The Limits of Unilateral Migration Control: Deportation and Inter-State Cooperation', *Government and Opposition* 43:2, 168–89.

Ellermann, Antje (2009) *States against Migrants: Deportation in Germany and the United States*. Cambridge: Cambridge University Press.

Ellinas, Antonis A. (2010) *The Media and the Far Right in Western Europe*. Cambridge: Cambridge University Press.

Ersbøll, Eva (2010) *Country Report: Denmark*. Florence: EUDO Citizenship Observatory, European University Institute.

Eurobarometer (2012) *Eurobarometer 71.3 Variable Report: Globalization, Personal Values and Priorities, European Identity, Future of the European Union, Social Problems and Welfare, and European Elections June–July 2009*. Luxembourg: Publications Office of the European Union.

European Commission (2008) *Communication from the European Commission . . .: A Common Immigration Policy for Europe: Principles, Actions and Tools*, COM(2008) 359. Luxembourg: Publications Office of the European Union.

European Commission (2011) *Demography Report 2010: Older, More Numerous and Diverse Europeans*. Luxembourg: Publications Office of the European Union.

Eurostat (2008) 'Population Projections 2008–2060', STAT/08/119, available at: http://europa.eu/rapid/press-release_STAT-08-119_en.htm.

Evans, David T. (1993) *Sexual Citizenship: The Material Construction of Sexualities*. London: Routledge.

Fahrmeir, Andreas, Olivier Faron, and Patrick Weil (eds) (2003) *Migration Control in the North Atlantic World: The Evolution of State Practices in Europe and the United States from the French Revolution to the Inter-War Period*. Oxford: Berghahn.

Faist, Thomas, and Peter Kivisto (2007) *Dual Citizenship in Global Perspective: From Unitary to Multiple Citizenship*. Basingstoke: Palgrave.

Favell, Adrian (2001) *Philosophies of Integration: Immigration and the Idea of Citizenship in France and Britain*. 2nd edn, Basingstoke: Palgrave.

Favell, Adrian, and Randall Hansen (2002) 'Markets against Politics: Migration, EU Enlargement and the Idea of Europe', *Journal of Ethnic and Migration Studies* 28:4, 581–601.

Fitzgerald, Keith (1996) *The Face of the Nation: Immigration, the State, and the National Identity*. Stanford, CA: Stanford University Press.

Freeden, Michael (1996) *Ideologies and Political Theory: A Conceptual Approach*. Oxford: Oxford University Press.

Freeman, Gary P. (1979) *Immigrant Labor and Racial Conflict in Industrial Societies: The French and British Experience, 1945–1975*. Princeton, NJ: Princeton University Press.

Freeman, Gary P. (1995) 'Modes of Immigration Politics in Liberal Democratic States', *International Migration Review* 24:4, 881–902.

Freeman, Gary P. (2004) 'Immigrant Incorporation in Western Democracies', *International Migration Review* 38:3, 945–969.

Freeman, Gary P. (2006) 'National Models, Policy Types, and the Politics of Immigration in Liberal Democracies', *West European Politics* 29:2, 227–47.

Gallie, W.B. (1956) 'Essentially Contested Concepts', *Proceedings of the Aristotelian Society* 56, 167–98.

Gallup (2009) 'U.S., Canada Show More Interfaith Cohesion than Europe', available at: www.gallup.com/poll/118273/canada-show-interfaith-cohesion-europe. aspx.

GCIM (Global Commission on International Migration) (2005) *Migration in an Interconnected World. New Directions for Action: Report of the Global Commission on International Migration*. Geneva: GCIM.

Geddes, Andrew (2003) *The Politics of Migration and Immigration in Europe*. London: Sage.

Geddes, Andrew (2008) *Immigration and European Integration. Beyond Fortress Europe?* 2nd edn, Manchester: Manchester University Press.

Ghosh, Bimal (ed.) (2000) *Managing Migration: Time for a New International Regime?* Oxford: Oxford University Press.

Gibney, Matthew J. (2004) *The Ethics and Politics of Asylum: Liberal Democracy and the Response to Refugees*. Cambridge: Cambridge University Press.

Gibney, Matthew J. (2006) 'A Thousand Little Guantanamos: Western States and Measures to Prevent the Arrival of Refugees' in K. Tunstall (ed.) *Displacement, Asylum, Migration: The Oxford Amnesty Lectures 2004*. Oxford: Oxford University Press, pp. 139–69.

Gibney, Matthew J. (2008) 'Asylum and the Expansion of Deportation in the United Kingdom', *Government and Opposition* 43:2, 146–67.

Gibney, Matthew, and Randall Hansen (2003) *Deportation and the Liberal State: The Forcible Return of Asylum Seekers and Unlawful Migrants in Canada, Germany and the*

United Kingdom, New Issues in Refugee Research, Working Paper no. 77. Geneva: UNHCR.

Gibson, Rachel (2002) *The Growth of Anti-Immigrant Parties in Western Europe*. Lewiston, NY: Edwin Mellen Press.

Givens, Terri E. (2005) *Voting Radical Right in Western Europe*. Cambridge: Cambridge University Press.

Givens, Terri E., Gary P. Freeman, and David L. Leal (eds) (2008) *Immigration Policy and Security: US, European, and Commonwealth Perspectives*. London: Routledge.

Goodhart, David (2004) 'Too Diverse?', *Prospect*, no. 95, February.

Goodman, Sara Wallace (2010) *Naturalisation Policies in Europe: Exploring Patterns of Inclusion and Exclusion*. Florence: EUDO Citizenship Observatory, European University Institute.

Goot, Murray (2000) 'More "Relaxed and Comfortable": Public Opinion on Immigration Under Howard', *People and Place* 8:3, 46–60.

Green, Simon (2004) *The Politics of Exclusion: Institutions and Immigration Policy in Contemporary Germany*. Manchester: Manchester University Press.

Green, Simon (2005) 'Between Ideology and Pragmatism: The Politics of Dual Nationality in Germany', *International Migration Review* 39:4, 921–52.

Guild, Elspeth (2009) *Security and Migration in the 21st Century*. Cambridge: Polity.

Guild, Elspeth, Sergio Carrera, and Anais Faure Atger (2009) *Challenges and Prospects for the EU's Area of Freedom, Security and Justice: Recommendations to the European Commission for the Stockholm Programme*, CEPS Working Document No. 313. Brussels, Centre for European Policy Studies.

Guild, Elspeth, Kees Groenendijk, and Sergio Carrera (eds) (2009) *Illiberal Liberal States: Immigration, Citizenship and Integration in the EU*. Farnham: Ashgate.

Guiraudon, Virginie (2000) *Les Politiques d'immigration en Europe*. Paris: Harmattan.

Guiraudon, Virginie, and Christian Joppke (eds) (2001) *Controlling a New Migration World*. London: Routledge.

Guiraudon, Virginie, and Gallya Lahav (2000) 'The State Sovereignty Debate Revisited: The Case of Migration Control', *Comparative Political Studies* 33:2, 163–95.

Gurowitz, Amy (1999) 'Mobilizing International Norms: Domestic Actors, Immigrants, and the Japanese State', *World Politics* 51, 413–45.

Hainmueller, Jens, and Michael J. Hiscox (2010) 'Attitudes toward Highly Skilled and Low Skilled Immigration: Evidence from a Survey Experiment', *American Political Science Review* 104:1, 61–84.

Hall, Peter A., and David Soskice (eds) (2001) *Varieties of Capitalism: The Institutional Foundations of Comparative Advantage*. Oxford: Oxford University Press.

Hammar, Tomas (1990) *Democracy and the Nation State: Aliens, Denizens and Citizens in a World of International Migration*. Aldershot: Avebury.

Hampshire, James (2005) *Citizenship and Belonging: Immigration and the Politics of Demographic Governance in Post-War Britain*. Basingstoke: Palgrave.

Hampshire, James (2009a) 'The Future of Border Control: Risk Management of Migration in the UK', in Heinz Fassmann, Max Haller and David Lane (eds), *Migration and Mobility in Europe*. Cheltenham: Edward Elgar.

Hampshire, James (2009b) 'Race', in Matthew Flinders, Andrew Gamble, Colin Hay and Michael Kenny (eds) *The Oxford Handbook of British Politics*. Oxford: Oxford University Press.

Hampshire, James (2009c) 'Disembedding Liberalism? Immigration Politics and Security in Britain since 9/11', in Terri E. Givens, Gary P. Freeman and David L. Leal (eds) *Immigration Policy and Security: US, European, and Commonwealth Perspectives*. London: Routledge.

Hampshire, James (2011) 'Liberalism and Citizenship Acquisition: How Easy Should Naturalisation Be?', *Journal of Ethnic and Migration Studies* 37:6, 953–71.

Hansen, Randall (2000) *Citizenship and Immigration in Post-War Britain*. Oxford: Oxford University Press.

Hansen, Randall (2002) 'Globalization, Embedded Realism and Path Dependence: The Other Immigrants to Europe', *Comparative Political Studies* 35:3, 259–83.

Hansen, Randall (2009) 'The Poverty of Postnationalism: Citizenship, Immigration, and the New Europe', *Theory and Society* 38:1, 1–24.

Hansen, Randall (2011) 'Making Cooperation Work: Interests, Incentives and Action', in Randall Hansen, Jobst Koehler and Jeanette Money (eds), *Migration, Nation States, and International Cooperation*. London: Routledge, pp. 14–28.

Hansen, Randall (2012) *The Centrality of Employment in Immigrant Integration in Europe*. Washington DC: Migration Policy Institute.

Hansen, Randall, and Jobst Koehler (2005) 'Issue Definition, Political Discourse and the Politics of Nationality Reform in France and Germany', *European Journal of Political Research* 44, 623–44.

Hansen, Randall, and Patrick Weil (eds) (2001) *Dual Nationality, Social Rights and Federal Citizenship in the US and Europe: The Reinvention of Citizenship*. Oxford: Berghahn.

Hatton, Timothy J. (2011) *Seeking Asylum: Trends and Policies in the OECD*. London: Centre for Economic Policy Research.

Hatton, Timothy J., and Jeffrey G. Williamson (2002) *What Fundamentals Drive World Migration?*, available at: www.cepr.org/meets/wkcn/3/3516/papers/hatton. pdf.

Heisler, Martin O. (2005) 'Introduction: Changing Citizenship Theory and Practice: Comparative Perspectives in a Democratic Framework', *PS: Political Science and Politics* 38:4, 667–70.

Higham, John (1955) *Strangers in the Land: Patterns of American Nativism, 1860–1925*. New Brunswick, NJ: Rutgers University Press.

Hollifield, James F. (1992) *Immigrants, Markets, and States: The Political Economy of Postwar Europe*. Cambridge, MA: Harvard University Press.

Hollifield, James F. (2004) 'The Emerging Migration State', *International Migration Review* 38:3, 885–912.

Hollifield, James F. (2007) 'The Politics of International Migration: How Can We "Bring the State Back In"?', in Caroline B. Brettell and James F. Hollifield (eds), *Migration Theory: Talking Across Disciplines*. 2nd edn, London: Routledge, pp. 183–238.

Hollifield, James F. (2011) 'Migration as a Global Public Good', in Rey Koslowski (ed.), *Global Mobility Regimes*. New York: Palgrave.

Holston, James (ed.) (1999) *Cities and Citizenship*. Durham, NC: Duke University Press.

Honohan, Iseult (2010) *The Theory and Practice of Ius Soli*. Florence: EUDO Citizenship Observatory, European University Institute.

Hooghe, Liesbet (ed.) (1996) *Cohesion Policy and European Integration: Building Multi-Level Governance*. Oxford: Oxford University Press.

Hooghe, Liesbet, and Gary Marks (2009) 'A Postfunctionalist Theory of European Integration: From Permissive Consensus to Constraining Dissensus', *British Journal of Political Science* 39:1, 1–23.

Howard, Marc Morjé (2006) 'Comparative Citizenship: An Agenda for Cross-National Research', *Perspectives on Politics* 4:3, 443–55.

Howard, Marc Morjé (2009) *The Politics of Citizenship in Europe*. Cambridge: Cambridge University Press.

Huntington, Samuel P. (2004) *Who Are We? The Challenges to America's National Identity*. London: Simon & Schuster.

Hutchings, Kimberly, and Roland Dannreuther (eds) (1998) *Cosmopolitan Citizenship*. Basingstoke: Palgrave.

Huysmans, Jef (1995) 'Migrants as a Security Problem: Dangers of "Securitizing" Societal Issues', in Robert Miles and Dietrich Thranhardt (eds), *Migration and European Security: The Dynamics of Inclusion and Exclusion*. London: Pinter, pp. 53–72.

Huysmans, Jef (2000) 'The European Union and the Securitization of Migration', *Journal of Common Market Studies* 38, 751–77.

Huysmans, Jef (2006) *The Politics of Insecurity: Fear, Migration and Asylum in the EU*. London: Routledge.

Huysmans, Jef, and Alessandra Buonfino (2008) 'Politics of Exception and Unease: Immigration, Asylum, and Terrorism in Parliamentary Debates in the UK', *Political Studies* 56:4, 766–88.

ICMPD (International Centre for Migration Policy Development) (2009) *REGINE: Regularisations in Europe: Study on Practices in the Area of Regularisation of Illegally Staying Third-Country Nationals in the Member States of the EU*. Vienna: ICMPD.

Ignazi, Piero (2003) *Extreme Right Parties in Western Europe*. Oxford: Oxford University Press.

IOM (International Organization for Migration) (2010) *World Migration Report 2010: The Future of Migration: Building Capacities for Change*. Geneva: IOM.

Ivarsflaten, Elisabeth (2005) 'Threatened by Diversity: Why Restrictive Asylum and Immigration Policies Appeal to Western Europeans', *Journal of Elections, Public Opinion and Parties* 15:1, 21–45.

Jacobson, David (1996) *Rights across Borders: Immigration and the Decline of Citizenship*. Baltimore: Johns Hopkins University Press.

Johnson, Carol (2007) 'John Howard's "Values" and Australian Identity', *Australian Journal of Political Science* 42:2, 195–209.

Joppke, Christian (1998) 'Why Liberal States Accept Unwanted Immigration', *World Politics* 50:2, 266–93.

Joppke, Christian (1999) *Immigration and the Nation State: The United States, Germany, and Great Britain*. Oxford: Oxford University Press.

Joppke, Christian (2004) 'The Retreat of Multiculturalism in the Liberal State: Theory and Policy', *British Journal of Sociology* 55:2, 237–57.

Joppke, Christian (2005) *Selecting by Origin: Ethnic Migration in the Liberal State*. Cambridge, MA: Harvard University Press.

Joppke, Christian (2007a) 'Beyond National Models: Civic Integration Policies for Immigrants in Western Europe', *West European Politics* 30:1, 1–22.

Joppke, Christian (2007b) 'Transformation of Citizenship: Status, Rights, Identity', *Citizenship Studies* 11:1, 37–48.

Joppke, Christian (2010) *Citizenship and Immigration*. Cambridge: Polity.

Joppke, Christian (2012) *The Role of the State in Cultural Integration: Trends, Challenges, and Ways Ahead*. Washington, DC: Migration Policy Institute.

Joppke, Christian, and Ewa Morawska (2003) *Towards Assimilation and Citizenship: Immigrants in Liberal Nation States*. Basingstoke: Palgrave.

Jupp, James (1998) *Immigration*. 2nd edn, Melbourne: Oxford University Press.

Jupp, James (2007) *From White Australia to Woomera: The Story of Australian Immigration*. 2nd edn, Cambridge: Cambridge University Press.

Kessler, Alan E., and Gary P. Freeman (2005) 'Public Opinion in the EU on Immigration from Outside the Community', *Journal of Common Market Studies* 43:4, 825–50.

Kindleberger, Charles (1967) *Europe's Postwar Growth: The Role of Labour Supply*. Cambridge, MA: Harvard University Press.

King, Desmond S. (1999) *In the Name of Liberalism: Illiberal Social Policy in the United States and Britain*. Oxford: Oxford University Press.

King, Desmond S. (2000) *Making Americans: Immigration, Race and the Origins of the Diverse Democracy*. Cambridge, MA: Harvard University Press.

King, Desmond S. (2005) *The Liberty of Strangers: Making the American Nation*. Oxford: Oxford University Press.

Kitschelt, Herbert, with Anthony J. McGann (1995) *The Radical Right in Western Europe: A Comparative Analysis*. Ann Arbor: University of Michigan Press.

Klausen, Jytte (2009) *The Cartoons that Shook the World*. New Haven, CT: Yale University Press.

Koehler, Jobst (2011) 'What Government Networks Do in the Field of Migration: An Analysis of Selected Regional Consultative Processes', in Randall Hansen, Jobst Koehler and Jeanette Money (eds), *Migration, Nation States, and International Cooperation*. London: Routledge, pp. 100–26.

Koopmans, Ruud, Paul Statham, Marco Giugni, and Florence Passy (2005) *Contested Citizenship: Immigration and Cultural Diversity in Europe*. Minneapolis: Minnesota University Press.

Koslowski, Rey (2011a) *The Evolution of Border Controls as a Mechanism to Prevent Illegal Immigration*. Washington, DC: Migration Policy Institute and European University Institute.

Koslowski, Rey (ed.) (2011b) *Global Mobility Regimes*. New York: Palgrave.

Kraler, Albert (2010) *Civic Stratification, Gender and Family Migration Policies in Europe*. Vienna: ICMPD.

Kraler, Albert, and Eleonore Kofman (2009) *Family Migration in Europe: Policies vs. Reality*, IMISCOE Policy Brief no. 16, available at: http://research.icmpd.org/fileadmin/Research-Website/Project_material/NODE/IMISCOE_PB_Familymigration_in_EU.pdf.

Krasner, Stephen D. (1999) *Sovereignty: Organized Hypocrisy*. Princeton, NJ: Princeton University Press.

Kymlicka, Will (1995) *Multicultural Citizenship: A Liberal Theory of Minority Rights*. Oxford: Clarendon Press.

Lahav, Gallya (2005) *Immigration and Politics in the New Europe: Reinventing Borders*. Cambridge: Cambridge University Press.

Lahav, Gallya, and Virginie Guiraudon (2006) 'Actors and Venues in Immigration Control: Closing Gaps between Political Demands and Policy Outcomes', *West European Politics* 29:2, 201–23.

Laycock, David (2001) *The New Right and Democracy in Canada: Understanding Reform and the Canadian Alliance.* New York: Oxford University Press.

Leach, Michael, Geoffrey Stokes, and Ian Ward (eds) (2000) *The Rise and Fall of One Nation.* St Lucia: University of Queensland Press.

Locke, John (1988 [1689]) *Two Treatises of Government*, ed. Peter Laslett. Cambridge: Cambridge University Press.

Locke, John (2003 [1689]) *A Letter Concerning Toleration*, in *Two Treatises of Government and A Letter Concerning Toleration*, ed. Ian Shapiro. New Haven, CT: Yale University Press.

Lucassen, Leo (2006) *The Immigrant Threat: The Integration of Old and New Migrants in Western Europe since 1850.* Champaign: University of Illinois Press.

Luhmann, Niklas (1982) *The Differentiation of Society.* New York: Columbia University Press.

McLaren, Lauren M., and M. Johnson (2007) 'Resources, Group Conflict, and Symbols: Explaining Anti-Immigration Hostility in Britain', *Political Studies*, 55:4, 709–32.

McLean, Iain (2001) *Rational Choice and British Politics: An Analysis of Rhetoric and Manipulation from Peel to Blair.* Oxford: Oxford University Press.

Marks, Gary (1993) 'Structural Policy and Multilevel Governance in the EC', in Alan Cafruny and Glenda Rosenthal (eds), *The State of the European Community.* Boulder, CO: Lynne Rienner, pp. 391–411.

Marshall, T. H. (1950) *Citizenship and Social Class.* Cambridge: Cambridge University Press.

Martin, Philip L. (2004) 'The United States: The Continuing Immigration Debate', in Wayne A. Cornelius, Takeyuki Tsuda, Philip L. Martin and James F. Hollifield (eds), *Controlling Immigration: A Global Perspective.* 2nd edn, Stanford, CA: Stanford University Press.

Martin, Philip L. (2006) 'Managing the Flow of International Labor', Harvard International Review, 17 July, available at: http://hir.harvard.edu/the-economics-of-migration?page=0,1.

Martin, Susan (2011) 'International Cooperation and International Migration: An Overview', in Randall Hansen, Jobst Koehler and Jeanette Money (eds), *Migration, Nation States, and International Cooperation.* London: Routledge, pp. 128–47.

Maxwell, Rahsaan (2012) *Ethnic Minority Migrants in Britain and France: Integration Trade-Offs.* Cambridge: Cambridge University Press.

Menz, Georg (2009) *The Political Economy of Managed Migration: Nonstate Actors, Europeanization, and the Politics of Designing Migration Policies.* Oxford: Oxford University Press.

Messina, Anthony M. (1989) *Race and Party Competition in Britain.* Oxford: Clarendon Press.

Messina, Anthony M. (2007) *The Logics and Politics of Post-WWII Migration to Western Europe.* Cambridge: Cambridge University Press.

Mill, John Stuart (1974 [1859]) *On Liberty.* Harmondsworth: Penguin.

Miller, David (1997) *On Nationality.* Oxford: Clarendon Press.

Money, Jeannette (1999) *Fences and Neighbors: The Political Geography of Immigration Control*. Ithaca, NY: Cornell University Press.

Morris, Lydia (2002) *Managing Migration: Civic Stratification and Migrants' Rights*. London: Routledge.

Mudde, Cas (1999) 'The Single-Issue Party Thesis: Extreme Right Parties and the Immigration Issue', *West European Politics* 22:3, 182–97.

Mudde, Cas (2007) *Populist Radical Right Parties in Europe*. Cambridge: Cambridge University Press.

Mudde, Cas (2012) *The Relationship between Immigration and Nativism in Europe and North America*. Washington, DC: Migration Policy Institute.

Münz, Rainer (2008) *Migration, Labour Markets, and Integration of Migrants: An Overview for Europe*, SP Discussion Paper No. 0807. Washington, DC: World Bank.

Neumayer, Eric (2005) 'Asylum Recognition Rates in Western Europe: Their Determinants, Variation and Lack of Convergence', *Journal of Conflict Resolution* 49:1, 43–66.

Norris, Pippa (2005) *Radical Right: Voters and Parties in the Electoral Market*. Cambridge: Cambridge University Press.

OECD (2004) *Migration for Employment: Bilateral Agreements at a Crossroads*. Paris: OECD.

OECD (2007) *International Migration Outlook – SOPEMI 2007*. Paris: OECD.

OECD (2008) *International Migration Outlook – SOPEMI 2008*. Paris: OECD.

OECD (2009) *The Global Competition for Talent*, Policy Brief, February, available at: www.oecd.org/dataoecd/58/50/42259140.pdf.

OECD (2010) *International Migration Outlook – SOPEMI 2010*. Paris: OECD.

OECD (2011) *International Migration Outlook – SOPEMI 2011*. Paris: OECD.

OECD (2012a) *International Migration Outlook – SOPEMI 2012*. Paris: OECD.

OECD (2012b) *Settling In: OECD Indicators of Immigrant Integration*. Paris: OECD.

Ohmae, Kenichi (1991) *The Borderless World: Power and Strategy in the Interlinked Economy*. London: Collins.

Olson, Mancur (1965) *The Logic of Collective Action: Public Goods and the Theory of Groups*. Cambridge, MA: Harvard University Press.

Palfreeman, A.C. (1967) *The Administration of the White Australia Policy*. Melbourne: Melbourne University Press.

Paoletti, Emanuela (2011) 'Power Relations and International Migration: The Case of Italy and Libya', *Political Studies* 59:2, 269–89.

Parsons, Talcott (1937) *The Structure of Social Action*. New York: McGraw-Hill.

Passel, Jeffrey S., and D'Vera Cohn (2011) *Unauthorized Immigrant Population: National and State Trends 2010*. Washington, DC: Pew Hispanic Center.

Pew Hispanic Centre (2006) *Modes of Entry for the Unauthorized Migrant Population: Fact Sheet*, available at: http://pewhispanic.org/files/factsheets/19.pdf.

Pew Research Center (2006) *America's Immigration Quandary: No Consensus on Immigration Problem or Proposed Fixes*, available at: http://people-press.org/reports/display.php3?ReportID=274.

Pew Research Center (2011) *Common Concerns about Islamic Extremism: Muslim–Western Tensions Persist*, Pew Research Global Attitudes Project, available at: www.pew-global.org/2011/07/21/muslim-western-tensions-persist/.

Phillips, Leigh (2010) 'A Far-Right for the Facebook Generation: The Rise and Rise of Jobbik', *euobserver.com*, 19 April, available at: http://euobserver.com/political/29866.

Phillips, Melanie (2006) *Londonistan: How Britain is Creating a Terror State Within.* London: Gibson Square Books.

Piore, Michael J. (1979) *Birds of Passage: Migrant Labour and Industrial Societies.* Cambridge: Cambridge University Press.

Putnam, Robert D. (2007) '*E pluribus unum*: Diversity and Community in the Twenty-First Century', *Scandinavian Political Studies* 30:2, 137–74.

Rawls, John (1993) *Political Liberalism.* New York: Columbia University Press.

Rawls, John (2001) *Justice as Fairness: A Restatement.* Cambridge, MA: Belknap Press.

Rawls, John (2007) *Lectures on the History of Political Philosophy.* Cambridge, MA: Belknap Press.

Reitz, Jeffrey (2004) 'Canada: Immigration and Nation-Building in the Transition to a Knowledge Economy', in Wayne A. Cornelius, Takeyuki Tsuda, Philip L. Martin and James F. Hollifield (eds) (2004) *Controlling Immigration: A Global Perspective.* 2nd edn, Stanford, CA: Stanford University Press, pp. 97–133.

Rooduijn, Matthijs, Sarah L. de Lange, and Wouter van der Brug (2012) 'A Populist Zeitgeist? Programmatic Contagion by Populist Parties in Western Europe', *Party Politics*, published online 20 April.

Rubio-Marin, Ruth (2000) *Immigration as a Democratic Challenge.* Cambridge: Cambridge University Press.

Rudolph, Christopher (2006) *National Security and Immigration: Policy Development in the United States and Western Europe since 1945.* Stanford, CA: Stanford University Press.

Rydgren, Jens (ed.) (2005) *Movements of Exclusion: Radical Right-Wing Populism in the Western World.* New York: Nova Science.

Saggar, Shamit (2003) 'Immigration and the Politics of Public Opinion', in Sarah Spencer (ed.), *The Politics of Migration: Managing Opportunity, Conflict and Change.* Oxford: Blackwell.

Saggar, Shamit, and Will Somerville (2011) *UK Immigrant Integration Policy: Cause and Effect.* Washington, DC: Migration Policy Institute.

Samers, Michael (2004) 'An emerging geopolitics of "illegal" immigration in the European Union', *European Journal of Migration and Law* 6:1, 23–41.

Sarrazin, Thilo (2010) *Deutschland schafft sich ab: Wie wir unser Land aufs Spiel setzen.* Munich: DVA.

Sartori, Giovanni (1970) 'Concept Misinformation in Comparative Politics', *American Political Science Review* 64, 1033–53.

Sassen, Saskia (1996) *Losing Control? Sovereignty in an Age of Globalization.* New York: Columbia University Press.

Savage, Charlie, and Carl Hulse (2010) 'Bill Targets Citizenship of Terrorists' Allies', *New York Times*, 6 May, available at: www.nytimes.com/2010/05/07/world/07rights.html?_r=1&hpw.

Schain, Martin (2006) 'The Extreme-Right and Immigration Policy-Making: Measuring Direct and Indirect Effects', *West European Politics* 29:2, 270–89.

Schain, Martin, Aristide Zolberg, and Patrick Hossay (eds) (2002) *Shadows over Europe: The Development and Impact of the Extreme Right in Western Europe.* Basingstoke: Palgrave Macmillan.

Scholten, Peter, Han Entzinger, Eleonore Kofman, Christina Hollomey, and Claudia Lechner (2012) *Integration from Abroad? Perception and Impacts of Pre-entry Tests for Third Country Nationals*, Final Report, PROSINT WP 4, available at: http://research.icmpd.org/fileadmin/Research-Website/Project_material/PROSINT/Reports/WP4_CompRep_Final_submitted.pdf.

Shachar, Ayelet (2009) *The Birthright Lottery: Citizenship and Global Inequality*. Cambridge, MA: Harvard University Press.

Sides, John, and Jack Citrin (2007) 'European Opinion about Immigration: The Role of Identities, Interests and Information', *British Journal of Political Science* 37, 477–504.

Silverman, Stephanie J. (2011) *Immigration Detention in the UK*. Oxford: Migration Observatory, available at: http://migrationobservatory.ox.ac.uk/sites/files/migobs/Immigration%20Detention%20Briefing.pdf

Simon, Rita J., and James P. Lynch (1999) 'A Comparative Assessment of Public Opinion toward Immigrants and Immigration Policies', *International Migration Review* 33:2, 455–67.

Smith, Rogers M. (2003) *Stories of Peoplehood: The Politics and Morals of Political Membership*. Cambridge: Cambridge University Press.

Sniderman, P.M., L. Hagendoorn, and M. Prior (2004) 'Predisposing Factors and Situational Triggers: Exclusionary Reactions to Immigrant Minorities', *American Political Science Review* 98:1, 35–49.

Soysal, Yasemin Nuhoglu (1994) *The Limits of Citizenship: Migrants and Postnational Membership in Europe*. Chicago: University of Chicago Press.

Spencer, Ian R. G. (1997) *British Immigration Policy since 1939: The Making of Multi-Racial Britain*. London: Routledge.

Statham, Paul, and Andrew Geddes (2006) 'Elites and the "Organised Public": Who Drives British Immigration Politics and in Which Direction?', *West European Politics* 29:2, 248–69.

Stevenson, Nick (2003) *Cultural Citizenship: Cosmopolitan Questions*. Milton Keynes: Open University Press.

Tamir, Yael (1993) *Liberal Nationalism*. Princeton, NJ: Princeton University Press.

Thouez, Colleen, and Frédérique Channac (2006) 'Shaping International Migration Policy: The Role of Regional Consultative Processes', *West European Politics* 29:2, 370–87.

Tichenor, Daniel J. (2002) *Dividing Lines: The Politics of Immigration Control in America*. Princeton, NJ: Princeton University Press.

Tichenor, Daniel J. (2004) 'Commentary', in Wayne A. Cornelius, Takeyuki Tsuda, Philip L. Martin and James F. Hollifield (eds), *Controlling Immigration: A Global Perspective*. 2nd edn, Stanford, CA: Stanford University Press, pp. 91–4.

Tirman, John (ed.) (2004) *The Maze of Fear: Security and Migration after 9/11*. New York: New Press.

Torpey, John (2000) *The Invention of the Passport: Surveillance, Citizenship and the State*. Cambridge: Cambridge University Press.

Transatlantic Trends (2010) *Transatlantic Trends: Immigration*, German Marshall Fund of the United States, available at: http://trends.gmfus.org/archives/immigration-archive/.

UNHCR (2011) *Global Trends 2011*. Geneva: United Nations High Commissioner for Refugees.

UNHCR (2012) *A Year of Crises: UNHCR Global Trends 2011*. Geneva: United Nations High Commissioner for Refugees.

UNPD (United Nations Population Division) (2001) *Replacement Migration: Is it a Solution to Declining and Ageing Populations?* New York: United Nations.

UNPD (United Nations Population Division) (2011) *World Fertility Report 2009*. New York: United Nations.

Van der Brug, Wouter, Meindert Fennema, and Jean Tillie (2005) 'Why Some Anti-Immigrant Parties Fail and Others Succeed: A Two-Step Model of Electoral Support', *Comparative Political Studies* 38:5, 537–73.

Van der Leun, Joanne (2003) *Looking for Loopholes: Processes of Incorporation of Illegal Immigrants in the Netherlands*. Amsterdam: Amsterdam University Press.

Van der Leun, Joanne (2006) 'Excluding Illegal Migrants in the Netherlands: Between National Policies and Local Implementation', *West European Politics* 29:2, 310–26.

Vargas-Silva, Carlos (2011) '*Migration Flows of A8 and other EU Migrants to and from the UK*', Oxford: Migration Observatory Briefing, available at: http://migrationobservatory.ox.ac.uk/briefings/migration-flows-a8-and-other-eu-migrants-and-uk.

Vink, Maarten, and Frits Meijerink (2003) 'Asylum Applications and Recognition Rates in EU Member States 1982–2001: A Quantitative Analysis', *Journal of Refugee Studies* 16:3, 297–315.

Vogel, Dita (2009) *Size and Development of Irregular Migration to the EU*, Comparative Policy Brief, Clandestino Research Project, available at: http://clandestino.eliamep.gr/wp-content/uploads/2009/12/clandestino_policy_brief_comparative_size-of-irregular-migration.pdf.

Weber, Max (1991 [1919]) 'Politics as a Vocation', in H. H. Gerth and C. Wright Mills (eds), *From Max Weber: Essays in Sociology*. London: Routledge, pp. 77–128.

Ye'Or, Bat (2005) *Eurabia: The Euro-Arab Axis*. Madison, NJ: Fairleigh Dickinson University Press.

Zaiotti, Ruben (2011) *Cultures of Border Control: Schengen and the Evolution of European Frontiers*. Chicago: University of Chicago Press.

Zolberg, Aristide R. (1994) 'Changing Sovereignty Games and International Migration', *Indiana Journal of Global Legal Studies* 2:1, 153–70.

Zolberg, Aristide R. (2000) 'Matters of State: Theorizing Immigration Policy', in Charles Hirschman, Philip Kasnitz and Josh DeWind (eds), *The Handbook of International Migration: The American Experience*. New York: Russell Sage Foundation.

Zolberg, Aristide R. (2003) 'The Archaeology of "Remote Control"', in Andreas Fahrmeir, Olivier Faron and Patrick Weil (eds), *Migration Control in the North Atlantic World: The Evolution of State Practices in Europe and the United States from the French Revolution to the Inter-War Period*. Oxford: Berghahn.

Zolberg, Aristide R. (2006) *A Nation by Design: Immigration Policy in the Fashioning of America*. Cambridge, MA: Harvard University Press.

Index